Radcliffe
Biography Series

❖ ❖ ❖ ❖

Alva Myrdal

Radcliffe
Biography Series

❖ ❖ ❖ ❖

Radcliffe
Biography Series

❖ ❖ ❖ ❖

Radcliffe
Biography Series

❖ ❖ ❖ ❖

Alva Myrdal

A Daughter's Memoir

SISSELA BOK

A MERLOYD LAWRENCE BOOK

Addison-Wesley Publishing Company, Inc.

Reading, Massachusetts   Menlo Park, California   New York
Don Mills, Ontario   Wokingham, England   Amsterdam
Bonn   Sydney   Singapore   Tokyo   Madrid   San Juan
Paris   Seoul   Milan   Mexico City   Taipei

Many of the designations used by manufacturers and sellers to
distinguish their products are claimed as trademarks. Where those
designations appear in this book and Addison-Wesley was aware of
a trademark claim, the designations have been printed in initial
capital letters (e.g., Monopoly).

Library of Congress Cataloging-in-Publication Data

Bok, Sissela.
    Alva Myrdal : a daughter's memoir / Sissela Bok.
       p.   cm.—(Radcliffe biography series)
    "A Merloyd Lawrence book."
    Includes index.
    ISBN 0-201-57086-6
    1. Myrdal, Alva Reimer, 1902–1986. 2. Feminists—Sweden—
Biography. 3. Social reformers—Sweden—Biography. I. Title.
II. Series.
HQ1687.B65 1991
305.42'092—dc20
[B]   90-26144
                                        CIP

Jacket and text design by Janis Owens
Set in 11-point Sabon by DEKR Corporation, Woburn, MA

2 3 4 5 6 7 8 9-MW-9594939291
Second printing, October 1991

Peer Gynt: Who are You?
The Voice: My Self. Can you say as much?

Henrik Ibsen, *Peer Gynt*

Radcliffe Biography Series

❖ ❖ ❖ ❖

On behalf of Radcliffe College, I am pleased to present this volume in the Radcliffe Biography Series.

The series is an expression of the value we see in documenting and understanding the varied lives of women. Exploring the choices and circumstances of these extraordinary women—both famous and unsung—is not merely of interest to the historian, but is central to anyone grappling with what it means to be a woman. The biographies of these women teach us not only about their lives and their worlds, but about ours as well. When women strive to forge their identities, as they do at many points throughout the lifespan, it is crucial to have models to look toward. These women provide such models. We are inspired through their example and are taught by their words.

Radcliffe College's sponsorship of the Radcliffe Biography Series was sparked by the publication in 1971 of *Notable American Women,* a scholarly encyclopedia sponsored by Radcliffe's Schlesinger Library. We became convinced of the importance of expanding the public's awareness of the many significant contributions made by women to America, continuing the commitment to educating people about the lives and work of women that is reflected in much of Radcliffe's work. In addition to commissioning new biographies, we decided to add reprints of distinguished books already published, with introductions written for this series.

It is with great pride and excitement that I present this latest volume.

Linda S. Wilson, President
Radcliffe College
Cambridge, Massachusetts

Contents

◆ ◆ ◆ ◆

❖ Contents ❖

Radcliffe
Biography Series

❖ ❖ ❖

Alva Myrdal

Alva Myrdal

1

Words

♦ ♦ ♦ ♦

"*What happens if I can no longer explain anything?*"
This was the first complete sentence I heard my mother speak that day in late June 1984. She suffered from aphasia that had come and gone for years. A brain tumor pressed against her language centers and grew slowly. Sometimes during the last years she had been mute for hours or days of intense, anguished headache; in between she had been able to talk with her customary subtlety and clarity. But now at last the aphasia had taken the upper hand almost completely.

I can't forget her eyes as she spoke. To the end they wanted to reach me, share from within herself. Her glance was clear, appealing, direct. I felt the immense effort with which she sought the right word, and her disappointment each time all was blocked and she remained mute.

All her life, Alva Myrdal had taken for granted that it was possible to explain oneself and to explain human problems in such a way as to offer new scope for imaginative responses. If she could only make some difficulty dramatically clear and suggest practical steps for resolving it, then how could people refuse to take action?

The impact of her first book, written with my father, Gunnar Myrdal, and published in Sweden in 1934, could only have encouraged this faith in the power of explanation. Entitled *Kris i befolkningsfrågan* (*Crisis in the Population Question*), the book created a scandal by linking a discussion of sexuality and family planning to proposals for social reforms. Many thought it offensive for a woman even to sign her name to such views. Overnight my parents became the notorious "Myrdal couple." Meanwhile the book went into one edition after another. Its radical proposals regarding housing, education, medical care, and the rights of women and children were debated across the country, and its vivid portrayal of the abject living conditions of many Swedish families led the government to set up commissions to consider the reforms the two young authors had proposed. Over the next decade most of these reforms were implemented, providing the foundation for Sweden's welfare state.

Alva played the same role of explaining and challenging when it came to the issues of child rearing, school reform, and postwar reconstruction in Europe, the battle against illiteracy and hunger, and the risk of nuclear war. To the end of her life, she kept her faith in the power of words to galvanize debate and bring about change. Even for the problems she found most intractable, those of human aggression and the mounting danger of mutual annihilation, she continued to advocate practical steps—not only in order to get changes under way but to combat the tendency to give up in despair that she saw as the greatest threat to survival. In her book *The Game of Disarmament,* published in 1976, she acknowledged that she herself had come close to despair over the inability of humanity to respond to the collective danger it faces. Still she insisted that there is always something, however modest, that each person can do: "Otherwise there would be nothing left but to give up. And it is not worthy of human beings to give up."

For Alva to be threatened with losing all recourse to words was therefore to become imprisoned in a silence that she had never chosen. Not to be able to speak out, to take a stand, to suggest changes, or even to explain if she were cold or in pain— this would force her to become alone with everything, perhaps tempt her after all to give up. Though she never feared death, the prospect of such isolation had caused her anguish from the time she first felt aphasia take hold.

I was struck with panic when her words were blocked. I shared her anguish, but was also afraid of not being able to keep up the contact that she already mourned as lost. For it had been words that had shaped our closest contacts and given us an intense shared joy from early on. As a mother Alva had experienced— and described in a diary begun when my older brother, Jan, was born—amazement at the miracle that children learn to speak at all and delight as she followed the conquest of every new word. For each child she described this development, not only in her diary but in notes about our expressions, dialogues, poems that she wanted to be able to show us as grown-ups. "I love words, I love words, I love words," I chanted as a three-year-old, according to Alva—perhaps not surprisingly, with such encouragement.

"Tell us a story!" was our constant plea. And Alva told us— about past exploits of Jan and my younger sister, Kaj, and myself, about events she remembered from her own childhood, and about how she had first met my father. Though she was tone deaf, she sang to us at bedtime—when she was home. Later came all the word games we shared, all the books: fairy tales, adventures, myths, explorers' accounts. The hope was that it would always be possible to overcome the empty spaces between us by means of words, to recreate and shape anew our contact, however thin it might have grown. Throughout her life, Alva knew how to dramatize her experiences by means of masterful storytelling—a talent honed for generations in the cottages and woods of rural Sweden. And her desire to explain had guided our talks even during those last few years when she shared her thoughts with me, her ever more insistent efforts to become clear about the shape her own life had taken.

Alva had never wanted to write her memoirs as long as she had the strength to work for other goals. Nor had she chosen my father's approach of including lengthy autobiographical segments in his books. She had long seen her life as self-evident and there-fore self-explanatory. When criticism late in life led her to feel the need for personal explanations, it was already more difficult for her to write. With groping words, she sought more and more urgently to explain, interpret, decipher her own life and to reply both to uncritical admiration and to attacks she thought too harsh.

In one of her last letters, she told me of questions she had come to puzzle over more and more:

> How is one an individual and how is one's fate shaped in interplay with other persons? How does one in turn contribute to forming those persons? How close can one really BE to other people? How *is* an individual vis-à-vis another individual? How do I become myself? How have I really been with you? How have I come to displace my own self in order to fit in with other selves? Where does one self merge with another?

Now that she had lived so long, Alva wrote, she could see, as in a fifty- or sixty-year-old rearview mirror, "the completely preposterous displacements that have taken place between what I have become and what I should have been able to, perhaps ought to, have planned." Metaphors having to do with displacement (the Swedish word *förskjutning* also has overtones of dislocation, setting aside, casting off, and shifting, as when cargo shifts on a ship) were to recur increasingly throughout her letters and conversations. She had not explained nearly enough.

Outwardly Alva had had a public life that many found great, exemplary, complete. In 1982, her eightieth birthday brought tributes and admiring profiles in the media. The same year she received the Nobel Peace Prize. Many saw her as a model of the woman who "has it all"—family, challenging work, and a close, long-lasting marriage. Gunnar had himself received a Nobel Prize in economics some years earlier; now the two of them were the only man and wife who had ever received the prize in entirely different fields.

Time after time, Alva was named Sweden's most admired woman in national polls. But she herself did not find her existence exemplary, blameless, least of all complete. She saw much that did not correspond with the public image, and she refused to regard her life as fully realized. There had to be room to breathe. There had to be a chance to create anew. "How do I become myself?" was a question that concerned the present as much as the past.

I received no further mail from Alva after the aphasia had taken hold. In vain she tried to form the simplest words: her letters crept out onto the paper like indecipherable squiggles. Illness had vanquished her written language as much as her speech. The brain surgery she finally underwent did not help. When she spoke I could barely understand a few isolated words; no one could decipher her sentences. It was too late for explanations, too late for questions. "Forgive me," she said over and over. My rush of panic came once again in response. How could I show her that it was not a matter of forgiveness? Was it not I, after all, who should have found words for two?

During the two years that remained of her life, I could still sense in her insistent efforts to reach through the wall of her aphasia that same Alva Myrdal who had once spoken out so vividly on so many subjects. But in her beating against that wall I had intimations, too, of the younger, equally determined but more hamstrung Alva Reimer whom I had never known. This was the girl living on a farm near the provincial Swedish town of Eskilstuna who ached to study and read and travel but who found all avenues blocked. The town gymnasium, or high school, was only for boys. She had no money to buy books. Even library books were out of bounds: her mother, the talented, artistic, but domineering Lowa Reimer, who had lost her only two siblings to tuberculosis and lived in fear of death, forbade her children to bring such books into the house on the ground that they might carry germs.

In witnessing Alva's refusal, even during her last illness, to give up trying to explain, trying to reach out by means of words, I came increasingly to wonder about that young girl in Eskilstuna. What had she been like? What had it taken for her, in her teens, to begin to break out of what she saw as the stifling family prohibitions and the small-town existence where the bounds of her life were so narrowly drawn?

And then one evening in October 1986, eight months after Alva's death, I heard that girl's voice. Sitting by candlelight after a day of teaching, I felt all grow still around me as I opened a package that had arrived that day from Sweden and saw the letters it contained. Alva had begun to write them at the age of fourteen, just when her schooling had come to a stop. They were addressed to a former teacher who later became the leader of Sweden's Quakers. Some years before she died she had written to ask me if I wanted to see these letters to "the very handsome Per Sundberg whom I had idolized at a distance"; but by the time there was a chance for me to do so, she could no longer tell me where to look for them.

Now I had them in my hand. An archivist helping my father sort through his papers had found them in a plastic bag behind a closet door and sent copies to me, knowing of my search for them. I began to read and did not finish until late at night. The girl who wrote them was as near as if she sat across the table from me and young enough to be my daughter. In her letters I heard an alternately urgent and hesitant voice. She was writing to the one adult she thought might take her aspirations seriously, a man who represented to her the larger world of the mind and of spiritual growth; yet she had to tread warily lest she presume too much.

The first letter, dated August 5, 1916, begins conventionally. Somewhat stilted, written with impeccable penmanship, it conveys her apologies for not writing sooner. Then she launches into what is uppermost in her mind: "I have now finished going to school after having completed all the [seven] grades." She speaks of her teachers and expresses the hope that she'll be able to begin going to some other school in the fall. But then she comes to the books that she has been reading, and out tumble names that were obviously talismans—Zola, Schopenhauer, Strindberg and his Swedish archenemy Ellen Key, the exuberant promoter of free love, family planning, and voluntary motherhood. The owner of a used book store, Alva explains, allows her to read to her heart's content. The letters that follow speak of her religious struggles, of a tedious year in a commercial school, of friendship and love and hate, but most of all of her continued reading: Voltaire, Auguste Comte, Jack London, John Stuart Mill, Maeterlinck, Scheele, Renan.

She also attempts to describe the traits her friends find most striking in her: honesty, self-control, and powerful enthusiasms and antipathies that lead her to be ready to do anything for those she admires but to be quite mean to others, especially her mother. What pleases her most is that her friends think that she is, above all else, utterly herself: "Ever since I read *Peer Gynt,* I have wondered whether I was myself." She is not of a directly envious nature, her friends have told her, and does not begrudge anyone anything, but she sees no reason why she should not have what others have. Finally, her friends find her less biased than most, something she has worked hard to achieve, and possessed of a strong will which she claims to have lacked altogether earlier. "Then I used to be stubborn but not strong-willed. Stubborn I still am, but not quite as much."

"No, this sounds quite unpleasant," the letter continues. And I put it down and wonder: Why should she think of this cluster of traits as so unpleasant? On reflection, I don't think she herself did; but at a time when girls were taught to be meek, humble, effusive, and long-suffering, she may have hesitated to reveal a different portrait—of someone with a will of her own who stood up to her mother, unable to see why she should not have the education and the potential for an adventurous life that others enjoyed. Perhaps she also thought that it might appear presumptuous, even unseemly, for a girl to reveal that she wanted most of all to be herself, and that she wondered, like Peer Gynt, what that might entail. In Ibsen's play, after all, it was Peer who asked such questions, and Solveig who sat meekly and lovingly and patiently at home, waiting for him to return from roaming the world in search of an answer.

In her letter, Alva immediately changes the subject: "I would rather talk about my plans for the future." But just as suddenly it is clear that she cannot go on. At that point this girl, so willing to reveal her innermost problems and her troubling view of herself to her correspondent, makes an about-turn. She withdraws into ambiguous silence. "But actually I have no plans for the future: they are too fantastic."

No more explaining. Her plans *were* too fantastic. They would sound naive or presumptuous if she so much as dared to set them down on paper. Here she was, a small-town girl with no money, no chance of going to high school, much less to the university. Yet somehow, she longed to have a creative, adventurous life that would lead out into the world and make possible great contributions—and to do so without sacrificing the traditional feminine role of being, as Peer Gynt said, "somebody waiting at home." She wanted to live both Peer's and Solveig's lives.

For such a life she had no models. It was not just that she saw most women as being restricted to domestic roles; the few well-known women she admired for having broken out of that mold led lives that seemed to her too austere, too one-sided. The great women authors and scholars, like those women who had fought for equality and liberty, had almost all been childless and usually also unmarried. For centuries many women scientists, educators, mystics, and poets had either chosen, or been forced to accept, celibacy. In her own time employed women were still routinely fired if they so much as married, let alone became pregnant.

Alva realized that she had to begin early to lay the foundations for a life that combined the two roles. Fifteen years old, with no further schooling in sight, she took a job in the town offices, helping out with tax returns and other official business. She split her earnings among book purchases, contributions to the family income, and a savings account for possible education in the future. With her parents, she kept up near-constant, often dramatic discussions of her predicament. At last, after two years and with her savings in hand, she prevailed. Her father agreed to try to persuade the town school board to offer, for a hefty fee, the same gymnasium-level courses to a group of girls that the boys received for free. And he succeeded. To be sure, the girls could not attend classes in the school buildings. The stigma rankled. But at seventeen, she was finally on her way.

And now the weaving together of the two roles could begin in all seriousness, for that same summer she met Gunnar, then a lanky university student of twenty. He enchanted her more than she had thought possible. Here she had an ally who wanted to get out into the larger world as eagerly as she. From then on she would improvise as best she could to make her "fantastic" plans come true. With Gunnar she sought to be both fellow student and loving companion. After they had children she worked to shed light on the condition of families. While she studied abroad she brought home ideas about kindergartens and teacher training. When she worked with refugees during World War II, she invited refugee children to live at home with us. And when she fought against the obstacles that stood in her way as a woman, she advocated the right of all women to combine work and family if they so desired.

That the two roles would at times clash was something the young Alva Reimer could not fully discern as she started out on the life that would take her so far from Eskilstuna. She would come to know every twist and turn of the struggle to unite them, yet she would also experience the joy and the creative force that come with trying to live both roles in as humane a way as possible. The essential task remained the same: to keep looking for practical ways out of each new impasse and to keep asking the interlocking questions that no amount of explaining would ever fully answer: "How is one an individual and how is one's fate shaped in inter-play with other persons?" "How does one in turn contribute to forming those individuals?" and "How do I become myself?"

In writing about my mother, I have had to try to reach the young Alva in a partially vanished culture, in an age I never knew. At times I have been able to compare what she and others said about her childhood and to ask how she herself looked back at that period on different occasions. In this way I have seen how she sometimes changed her view and in the end saw her life in subtly shifting nuances. Similarly, I have found layers and variations in my own memories and in my diaries concerning the complicated woman whose depth and many-sidedness I only gradually came to understand. I perceived only certain sides of her when I was a child and even fewer as an uncertain teenager with a life of my own that seemed to me so hard to fathom. It is easy, especially when one is young, to put on blinkers in coming to terms with someone who seems so forceful and so glowingly unambiguous.

During the years when I was growing up, I gradually became aware of the heated national debates my mother engendered about such issues as child care, schooling, working conditions, and housing policy—the more so since some of the debates seemed to turn on how she and my father were bringing up their own three children. Their words and our lives seemed to intersect from the outset. I came increasingly to perceive her and my father and certain other relatives and friends in part through their writings. What I now know about all of them has been filtered through their published words. In this way, I have come to understand them better and yet to sense them at times the more as strangers. I have realized that their words were not meant only to explain and describe; they created, also, opacities and phantoms, public selves that stood as shadows between them and me. At the same time I have found levels and depths in their works that I could not otherwise have fathomed.

Four of Alva's earlier books interest me especially from this point of view: *Crisis in the Population Question* and *Contact with America,* both of which she wrote with Gunnar, and *Nation and Family* and *Women's Two Roles.* Now that I read them over they speak to me in an entirely new way: about her frequently defiant way of illuminating crises, families, and the condition of women, and about triumphs and defeats and unavoidable tensions in her own life.

In the margins of her copies of these books Alva has written her own afterthoughts. As I come across them I can see how she must have smiled or shaken her head at times. "Autobiographical . . ."; "GM swinging high"; "Strange impression"; "Much is different now." And here and there I find signals in my own direction: traces, broken threads, messages I never received at the time but that she may have hoped would reach me in the end. Thus a yellowed note lies in her copy of *Contact with America.* It refers to the chapter comparing American and Swedish schools: "Show the cultural analysis to Sissela. Says much even about us personally, for instance *myself* as parent." This note takes me back once more to the text. And I see it as personal in a new way—grand, hopeful, naive at times, at times so questionable that I, too, have to shake my head.

I also have articles, studies, letters from my childhood on, and diary excerpts and notes that Alva left in my charge. She asked me to be a "depository" for such personal documents, just as she hoped that my sister Kaj would take care of her large collection of photos. Often when Alva visited me we would sit down in a corner and she would tell me about her childhood. I wrote down what I could and asked when I did not understand. Afterward, however, when it had become too late to continue to ask, these notes have seemed to me unutterably meager.

It is different when I read her letters. Not that they can answer the questions I shall never be able to put to her. But they make me see her and hear her voice as if she were quite near. Alva's letters are alive as few others, often intimate. They shaped, I believe, the long friendship that succeeded our mother-daughter relationship when I married at twenty and left Europe for America. Since we so frequently lived far from one another, our contact often depended entirely on letters and, during the last years, on telephone conversations.

However far apart we moved, it mattered that I could take this link for granted. Through letters we could prolong our intimacy, even express much that was hard to say face to face. They gave us the feeling that it was possible to explain what might never quite have been said otherwise. In July 1965, for example, Alva wrote after I had returned home from one of my visits to her in Sweden:

Darling Siss,

It is only a few hours since we waved you off at Arlanda Airport. Now we have settled down again—and as I predicted the *emptiness* is so hard to take. As I said—and as we then scarcely understood.

Of course it is not so simple as that one feels the loss only *afterward*. The explanation is, naturally, that we conventionalize our time together—as one does and must do with all grown-ups—and that all the rest goes unspoken.

. . . What I really wanted to say is that family intimacy on the one hand is something one never *wants* to give up but *must*, on the other hand that the respect for individual freedom is now so strong that one must try to find a personal response beyond that which is given by nature. Now I must say that I think I have an excellent relationship with the three of you. This is natural, if one thinks of one another as individuals— respect and interest are equally natural. But it is still, so to speak, hard won, if one thinks that it is what begins as intense familiarity that has been made to change thus.

Isn't this what makes early family photos at once so heart-rending and so alien?

. . . Now I would not want to speak of some hour-by-hour control . . . as against what we have achieved of pleasure, intimacy, and respect despite the distance. Perhaps one might even be tempted to believe that it is the geographical distance that rescues us from such oppression. But my experiences with my siblings, especially my "best friend" Rut, tells me that there is a middle way, and that the distance makes things unnecessarily hard.

As Alva's children, we knew that we called forth a conflict between nearness and distance in her. She wanted to be both bound and free. When she left on a journey she gloried in her freedom and in every new experience, but she longed at the same time for the closeness that she lost thereby—a closeness that was itself not complete, could never be complete, however near one another we lived. Like others who had taken part in the child study movement of the 1930s, she had high hopes for the creativity, the community spirit, and the sheer happiness that new approaches could bring to family life. Yet she was never without guilt; her letters to us as children profess a closeness that she seems to have found problematic from the outset.

When we ourselves went away, it was her respect for *our* freedom that clashed with her desire to have us nearby in a more intimate and constant symbiosis. Still—did not letters always offer the chance to overcome distances in time and in space? To weave together independence and closeness, perhaps even to start afresh? I believe that she thought so for a long time. But during a bitter period late in life she came to doubt it: the intermediate state between respect for individual liberty and the oppression she had witnessed in the intimacy of many families then seemed to her illusory. "Imagine if we could all live in different communities," she then wrote. "Preferably in different times. I don't believe much in the blessings of family ties."

My book resembles the letter Alva wrote after my visit. What I write about her and what I quote from her letters and notes constitutes yet another effort to overcome distances in time and in space. As I call her forth as a child and as a woman—in Eskilstuna, Stockholm, Geneva, New York, Paris, and New Delhi—I am also seeking an answer to her question that day in June about what happens when one can no longer explain anything. Do most past explanations simply ebb away? If some live on, how are they stored, held back, pushed aside, made to flow into one another? And how might they be sorted out when it comes to a life at once so public and so enigmatic?

Throughout her life, Alva pressed for explanations about what it means to be a woman. With no models and little support, she broke out of the stereotypes for femininity that surrounded her when she was young. She wanted to make room in her life for both love and work, as Freud put it, but aimed for a quality and an intensity with respect to each that few dare to seek even now. She came up against nearly every obstacle that can confront one who sets herself such goals. Each time she overcame one of these obstacles her world expanded; yet each time the difficulty of making everything fit took on new dimensions. Husband, family, work, larger causes—how does one reconcile obligations and challenges that seem to pull in so many different directions? And in this very attempt to seek a harmonious balance, does one risk pushing aside, "displacing" other individuals or certain aspects of one's self? These are questions with which most of us still struggle today.

Just as my mother wrote no memoirs, however, so I cannot

claim to have portrayed her life in full. Instead of writing a definitive biography, I tell of her life as I have witnessed it and heard about it, in order to convey something of what that life has meant for me—as her daughter, as a woman and a mother myself, but most of all, for more than thirty years, as her friend.

2

Childhood

❖ ❖ ❖

"*Dear God, please let Mother get a job!*" This is what Alva and her younger sister Rut used to pray for, only half in jest, before going to sleep in the bed they shared as children.

> We were friends throughout life, with that intimacy but also—
> as children—the squabbling that resulted from our sharing a
> bed for many years: our parents' discarded double bed, after
> they had become so modern as to acquire separate English
> iron beds. We usually made a "frontier" with sheet folds
> carefully separating our domains. 1918 saw the end of this
> intimacy that only existed in wintertime; during the summers
> we were gloriously free in the attic where we could make
> separate nests.

While the two sisters lay there longing for their mother to go to work, they dreamed of freedom and breathing space. Lowa Reimer, their mother, "poked her nose everywhere, decided about everything." She was "little and pretty and coquettish," excelled at music and storytelling, and was sharp-witted and skillful at all she undertook. Though she disliked many household tasks, she carried them out to perfection. "Her two passions were cooking and clothes. We children understood very early that this had replaced her lost dream of a career."

Lowa had been apprenticed to the finest seamstress in the town of Eskilstuna and could, according to Alva, have become an excellent hat designer. Instead all her energies were focused on her home. She planned and sewed the children's clothes, had strict notions about hygiene and fresh air, and regulated what they read. But her control over children and household was not sufficiently challenging to this capable and dominant woman. Like so many other women at the turn of the century, she thought of herself as "delicate." From time to time she would leave for a rest home to cope with ailments that were hard to diagnose but all too real to her.

Lowa, born in 1877, was the oldest of three. She had grown up in a moderately comfortable farming family near the town of Eskilstuna, located in the fertile, lake-strewn province of Södermanland about 110 kilometers southwest of Stockholm. In the late 1880s, most Swedes still lived in the countryside. The migration to the city, in which Lowa, too, would take part, increased sharply after the turn of the century. Among those who lived on the land, a crucial dividing line separated the "self-owning"— those who owned their land, however small the plot—from the many who possessed no land. Her father, Lars Erik Jonsson, was secure in his ownership of a farm that had long been in his family. He was skilled at his work, a solid force in the community, and known for his kindly, cheerful disposition. He sang and laughed with his children and was very close to his wife, Anna Sofia. When she died in childbirth the day she turned thirty-one, he mourned his "lily of the valley."

From then on Anna Sofia was known in the family as "the lily of the valley." The photo of her calmly gazing, profound, and generous face gave Alva and her brothers and sisters the sense of peace that their own mother never conveyed. It stood on Alva's bedside table in her last sickroom. On the back she had written: "AM's grandmother. Portrait that has followed me through the years—have felt *affinity*."

At the turn of the century, Lowa married Albert Jansson (later Reimer), a year older than she. He, too, came from an old peasant family, but landless, unlike hers, and often poor. His mother, also named Anna Sofia, had been born as a "love child" to a farmer's daughter and an eighteen-year-old farmhand who could not marry her until he came of age three years later. At twenty, this Anna Sofia married Fredrik Theodor Jansson, a skilled blacksmith. In the village many thought him a troublemaker: he had radical ideas about the conditions in which workers lived and took part in the Social Democratic labor movement that was forming in Sweden, as elsewhere in Europe, during the last decades of the nineteenth century.

Albert, born in 1876, came to share his father's political views. He always remembered his first impressions of politics and class differences during the election campaign of 1892, when a battle arose between his father—too poor to have the right to vote under Sweden's laws of the period—and the ultraconservative pastor J. E. Ekblom. As soon as his father set up campaign posters, the pastor painstakingly tore each one down, even "the one that had been put on the door to the store in our own house. . . . It is understandable that blessings were not exactly what my father called down upon the pastor."

At times Albert's father drank heavily. Once he beat his wife so hard that she took him to court—a highly unusual action at the time—and saw him sentenced to a month in jail for wife abuse. When he returned home he was milder in spirit. But his drinking and the cold, drafty smithy had already broken his health, and he died at the age of forty-six, when Albert was sixteen years old. Anna Sofia made her three children promise never to touch liquor. Albert remained a teetotaler all his life.

When he was twelve he had had to leave school to tend the cows of the nearby farms, where his mother also worked. He longed for more schooling but did not know where to turn. He admired, most of all, his grandfather, who was superintendent on a large farm that he loved to visit. Albert often thought, he wrote in the memoirs he began toward the end of his life, "that the highest and best I could wish for in life would be to own land and to be able to bring forth food for humanity. But how would that come to be, for one as little and poor as I felt myself to be?"

After scraping together money for a year's commercial schooling, Albert found work in a grocery store, where he was soon set to keeping the books. When he met Lowa, at twenty-

three, he had found work as an accountant in an office in Eskilstuna. In appearance he was something of a dandy, with deep-set
eyes, a mustache, and hair cut to stand up à la Strindberg, his
idol. Yet his shy, inward-looking expression could not have been
more different from Strindberg's stormy, expressive, at times almost demonic features, which often looked out from the scandal
sheets of the period.

Albert was of an austerely moralistic bent: when his widowed
mother fell in love with a policeman she dared not move in with
him or marry him for fear of what Albert and his siblings Theodor
and Mimmi might say. Talented, eager to learn but entirely self-
taught, he combed the local libraries and saved any money he
could in order to buy books. He became active early on in the
temperance movement that had been spreading in Sweden since
the 1850s. This crusade had originated, both in religious and
secular circles, as a passionate groundswell of protest against a
social system that oppressed the poor in part through drink and
victimized their families in turn. It was common for farm workers
to receive potatoes and aquavit in lieu of salaries; protesting
against such practices was part of a growing insistence on personal
dignity. At the meetings of his youth group Albert would hear the
familiar refrain: "Aquavit is the opium of the people!" Instead of
tolerating the helplessness induced by liquor, temperance advocates fought for self-empowerment through education and political action.

By the turn of the century, two other reformist crusades were
gaining strength: the labor movement and the cooperative movement. Albert was a member of all three. Having long been active
in the temperance youth group in his hometown, he joined the
labor party and founded one of the first consumers' cooperatives
in Sweden, linking it with the fledgling national cooperative society that had been formed in 1899. Self-help was essential to all
three movements. Members met all over Sweden in reading and
discussion groups to supplement their often meager schooling and
lay the foundations for more informed and spirited political advocacy. But, like Albert, they also sought to deepen friendships

and to give structure and meaning to their lives. They regarded being able to participate in their nation's cultural life as crucial to their struggle for equality, even though they often had to go to evening meetings after grueling twelve-hour workdays. Their struggle for an eight-hour workday, achieved only in 1920, aimed in part simply to provide time and strength for cultural as well as political activities.

During Albert's lifetime these "people's movements" (*folk-rörelser*) helped transform the nation. When he was a child Sweden had been a poor, backward, at times famine-ridden country that sent wave upon wave of emigrants to America—as many as 325,000 just in the 1880s. By the time he died, in 1943, Sweden had long since wrenched itself out of that condition and become a prosperous, self-confident nation, imaginative in its approach to human needs and capable of supporting all its citizens. To be sure, old problems remained and unexpected ones had already arisen. But the grinding poverty was gone. And at the forefront of the battle to ensure many of the new reforms was his daughter, Alva. To the day he died, he carried a press notice of one of her campaign speeches in his wallet. She in turn, calling herself "a child of the people's movements," knew that the foundation for her work had been laid by the extraordinary bootstrap efforts at social and personal improvement by so many in her father's generation.

From the beginning Albert showed signs of becoming what Alva called "a theoretical and practical idealist." His ideals were many but consistent. He had firm views, nurtured by his reading, about how one should live. He loved the soil and all that grew and dreamed about farming as the only truly natural and nourishing way to live. His feeling for animals led him to abhor hunting and to be a vegetarian off and on. Fascinated by new inventions, he launched a local club to study and further the uses of electricity. And egalitarian to the core, he remained active in the cooperative movement and the Social Democratic party to the end of his life— regretting only that he could not join a union once he had become an employer. In theory, he harbored even more radical ideas for

change. Having read the works of Kropotkin, the Russian an-
archist and libertarian, he claimed to be, at heart, a "barricade
socialist." And he drew on Rousseau (or "Jean-Jacques" as he
was familiarly known in the Eskilstuna study groups and family
gatherings and in their counterparts across the world) for his
gospel about human potential, freedom, and education.

All Albert's ideals—whether about ways of life, equality, freedom, progress of every kind, or morality and truth—were linked
in his belief that they furthered what he called "the good." And
to serve the good was for him far more important than all other
purposes. It was this aim that he hoped to be able to pass on to
others. When he began to write down his experiences late in life,
the reason he gave for doing so was the hope that his children
and grandchildren might perhaps "have something to learn from
my often vain attempts to make some contribution to the development of the good, which in spite of everything I have always
believed will win out in the end."

Albert was also a lifelong atheist, ever since his fifteenth
summer when, as was customary in Lutheran Sweden, he had
prepared for his confirmation:

> Even then I had my doubts about the "eternal truths," but the
> young minister who taught us was a good person and his
> teaching consisted in large part of talk about ethics and mo-
> rality, of course filled out with psalm verses and the com-
> mandments. I absorbed what I thought was right and truthful,
> the rest I tried to put out of my thoughts. . . . At the confession
> of faith I avoided answering, and I took "the wine and the
> bread" without believing in the minister's claims about its
> significance.
>
> All this I did because that was "how it should be," but after
> I came home I felt deeply unhappy about having taken part
> in something I did not believe in—yes, even in old age I
> remember that day as the unhappiest one in my life.

It was perhaps inevitable that there would be tensions between Albert and his wife Lowa. Whereas Albert was a socialist,

Lowa sided with the liberals, to the left of the conservatives, but to the right of the socialists. From the beginning she asserted her right to have political views of her own, even though two decades would pass before women had the vote. In this Albert fully supported her despite their differences in other matters. The couple went so far as to subscribe to two different newspapers, something that showed Alva from early on that there could be more than one opinion about most issues.

Lowa was drawn to art and to music and excelled in embroidery and weaving. When she felt inspired she could bubble over with humor and the joy of storytelling. She loved the theater, and when she came home from a performance she could replay the whole piece for everyone at home. Albert, on the contrary, was serious, matter-of fact, and entirely unmusical. Whereas he remained an atheist throughout his life, Lowa made gestures toward Christianity whenever it suited her purposes. If she bought a new hat, she had to wear it for the first time in church. When she felt in need of consolation she took out a little silver snuffbox where she kept a few religious verses clipped from newspapers and sat reading them in her beloved rocking chair.

> *Ask not, live and do your best,*
> *Till your life's goal has been reached.*
> *Help your neighbor when he's weak,*
> *Never ask for help yourself.*

Such fortitude was something that Lowa had needed already at her wedding. Her sister, Anna, had died of tuberculosis twelve days before, in May 1900. Her family was distraught, but it was too late to delay the ceremony. Lowa, dressed in black—for many their only formal clothes—looks disconsolate in the photo taken at the time. It may suddenly have seemed wrong, however inevitable, to be torn away from her home just at this time, to go moving from one place to another with a man whom the family thought something of an adventurer and whose ideals she did not share.

The middle-class life-style that they soon attained was, according to Alva, "hard-won by my mother, negated by my father." To be sure, the two shared an interest in all that could be called new; but Lowa sought out what was modern because it seemed more elegant, whereas Albert cared about the power of new technology to increase agricultural and industrial productivity. Faithful to his egalitarian beliefs, he worked to increase the standard of living more generally and hesitated to earn more than he thought the family needed.

By the time Alva was born, on January 31, 1902, her father had become an insurance agent in Uppsala. The month before, Lowa's adored brother, Edward, had died during his military service, also of tuberculosis. Thereafter she never ceased fearing that she too would meet the same fate. "She spoke of having weak lungs and was always tired." Because of her worry that she might already be carrying the disease and thus able to give it to others, she never kissed either her children or her grandchildren.

Alva claimed to have been warmly welcomed as the first child, even though her mother's diary expressed hopes about a boy—"our little Tage." Her name was newly minted from the first two letters of Albert's name and the last two of Lowa's into "Alwa," then almost immediately modernized to "Alva." Within a few years the same desire for innovation led Albert and Lowa to change their last name from Jansson to Reimer. Alva did not doubt that she was loved, even though her mother's love never took the form of caresses or other signs of tenderness. It was Albert who tucked her in at night. Not only did her mother worry about giving her children the tuberculosis from which her own siblings had died; she was also afraid of spoiling the children through too much tenderness. "Mother's conventions included the newfangled notion that one should not pick up babies when they cried. I was perhaps one of the first who was not tightly swaddled but on the other hand only fed at regular hours." The result was malnutrition and stomach cramps, until the doctor prescribed additional food when Alva was six months old. She remembers that her mother also insisted on the cold rubdowns every morning that were modern at the time, along with oatmeal porridge and cod-liver oil.

This for good health. For morality it was instantaneous obedience: "Pick up the thimble I dropped"—not a minute to finish playing, to put the top piece on the tower.

Alva's favorite sister, Rut, was born two years later. In her, Alva found an intimate friend for life with whom she could share all things. Rut was warmly extroverted, practical, and so helpful at home that she escaped her mother's nervous pestering. She was of such a sunny disposition that she made life easier both for Alva and for their mother, still living in the shadow of the deaths of her brother and sister. And Rut had a generous understanding of human beings that allowed her to come very close to her shy, distant, inwardly burning sister—and make her laugh as no one else could.

When Alva was four years old and Rut two, Folke was born, and effusively welcomed by the parents as their first son. Alva saw that they thought it entirely different and in every way better that he was a boy. Afterward she wondered whether her feelings stemmed more from outright jealousy or from her awareness of the inequality so typical of the period. In any event both she and Rut thought that this baby, whom they nicknamed "the gold dumpling," received altogether too much attention. When his head was sculpted in clay a few years later by a local artist, the girls discussed in secret how they might "accidentally" cause the sculpture to crash.

It was during these early years, Alva remembered, that she began to distance herself from her family. She spoke of having first experienced "the painful consciousness of the individual's irremediable isolation" in the summer of 1906, when the family rented a summer cottage by Lake Mälaren:

> I sat on a tree stump and *knew* suddenly that I was alone with myself. Folke, the son, the "golden boy," lay in the cradle. Rut was noisily cheerful. Mother said to Aunt Alicia "but then Alva, she is always so sulky." Since that time I probably never had an open, confident relationship with the family.

From their mother the girls learned to sew, weave, and embroider. They had both inherited Lowa's talents and produced with her help tablecloths and napkins and clothes, even underwear embroidered with the finest hemstitching. Lowa insisted that they must always be clean and neat inside and out: one never knew when trouble would strike and require one to go to the hospital. They remembered her joy when she talked about being "so fancy you could blow away." She took for granted that the girls would enjoy beautiful, stylish clothes; and so they did. Twice Lowa inherited 600 crowns from relatives' estates; each time she bought beautiful new dresses for her daughters and other luxury items that Albert would never have agreed to buy.

Around the time of Rut's birth, Albert was invited to work with his uncle and namesake, the builder Albert Jansson, who asked his nephew to be in charge of laying foundations for his buildings. Before long the younger Albert had gone on to construct houses of his own, calling himself a building contractor. Though he had no formal training beyond elementary school, many turned to him for new construction jobs. But he could never be certain of a steady income, especially since he often worked for free for persons he thought less well off than himself. Lowa complained bitterly—"Albert takes every unpaid job!" His affairs kept going up and down. Sometimes he was near bankruptcy, the specter that haunted families with finances as uncertain as theirs; at other times the family lived in apartments elegant enough to satisfy even Lowa. Alva remembered especially how the family moved, when she was six years old, to a large, luxurious modern apartment in south Stockholm with "dining room, electric lights, and garishly green wallpaper in the study." She did not dare invite school friends home—the home was too "fancy."

Each apartment had to be kept spotlessly clean—all dirt, all dust, all messy toys were banished. Alva recalled her parents' anger when she imitated a young naval cadet who had visited them. Fired with admiration for him, she had rushed around the apartment so that she fell and got "a scar on the forehead out of pure love." When King Oscar II of Sweden died in December 1907, the cadet had to stand in a funeral parade for long hours

wearing thin white gloves in spite of the cold. He did not complain, even as his fingers became numb and frostbitten. The next
time he visited the family his fingertips were black. His suffering,
his courage, his uniform all induced boundless admiration in Alva.
She dipped her own fingers in black ink and rushed around the
apartment once again, this time dripping. When she was spanked
she grew wild with hatred and wished she could die—it would
serve her parents right!

In 1909, Lowa gave birth to little Maj, who would die young
after a lifetime of illness. Everyone loved her; she was her mother's
favorite child. At seven, she came close to dying from a bone
disease; from then on she walked with a severe limp. No one at
home was allowed to mention the word "lame": Maj had to be
protected from the slightest reminder of her handicap. Once while
visiting one of her father's construction projects she fell two stories
and could not go to school for a year and a half. Tender, retiring,
beautiful, and artistic, she was kept from all arduous work by her
mother and encouraged to paint porcelain and play the spinet.

When Lowa became pregnant once again, two years after
Maj was born, Alva was almost ten years old. This time she and
Rut became anxious. They thought they understood how this must
have occurred and found it indecent—perhaps in part because
their mother, feeling her health increasingly delicate, complained
so pointedly about this unwanted pregnancy. When their brother
Stig was finally born in 1912, Alva kept silent about the event in
school. Questioned by her friends, she refused to acknowledge it.
There was no new baby at home, she insisted. To keep up the
false front, she embroiled herself in more and more intricate lies.
Once she had begun to deny her newborn brother's existence she
could not stop and was rescued only because her family moved
to another school district. But she feared that her new teachers
had learned of her deceitfulness and were sending reports back to
her parents and to each new school she attended. To make matters
worse, the school's religious instruction had come as a shock to
her since her own home excluded all Christian dogma. Now she
began to think that she had perhaps sinned against the Holy Ghost
and that she might never be forgiven.

After Stig's birth Lowa withdrew more than ever from the household. For the next thirty years she spent more than half of every day in bed. It was up to Alva and Rut to take care of the baby, and they found him very tender and amusing. Toward him they felt no jealousy, perhaps because they shared their mother's role in caring for him. He became, instead, their special favorite. To mark his graduation day in first grade, the girls sewed a sturdy new outfit for him—Alva the jacket, Rut the pants—and walked proudly with him to school.

The year Stig was born the family moved to Älvsjö, one of Stockholm's suburbs, where Albert built a cooperative store with a family apartment on top so up-to-date that it had electricity and a modern bathroom. Alva recalled how the cooperative's board members met at home while she sat under the dining table listening to their deliberations and reading forbidden books smuggled out of the book cabinet that her father kept locked in the parlor. She heard talk about social democracy, campaigns for the voting rights still denied to most Swedes, and other matters still new at the time. It was while she sat there so silently that she remembered first beginning to take politics and popular movements seriously and to learn respect for such procedures as keeping minutes and proposing motions. It was under that table, the writer Anna-Lisa Bäckman wrote after Alva's death, that she received the guiding insight of her life: that Father plans the world, not Mother; and that a world planned by only one half could never serve humanity well.

The outbreak of war in 1914 caused a severe recession in Sweden, even though as a neutral nation it was spared warfare on its own soil. When Lowa's father was widowed for the second time, Albert decided to take over Slagsta, the farm that had been Lowa's childhood home. At last he would be a landowner and fulfill his dream about producing food for humankind. Lowa was not pleased to be moving back to the farm she had left to get married, but Albert carried out his wish, convinced that farm life was the only right choice for them all. He had captivated the children with his Rousseauesque dream about life close to nature;

they would all, he hoped, help with the farm work and preferably become farmers themselves.

For Alva the reality turned out to be utterly different. She told how she and Folke had been sent ahead and how, when they arrived all dressed up by their mother for such a momentous move, their grandfather set them to pick stones out of a pea field. It was then that the dream burst—the dream of the paradise that their father had conjured up and that they had described to their school friends. "We were so disappointed and it was so bestial." The first Sunday the two children ran away, their large knapsack filled with food that they finished on their way to nearby Torshälla, where they were finally picked up, quite crestfallen, and taken home by horse and carriage.

Lowa and Rut were equally reluctant. Later Rut wrote about their return to the family farm:

> Poor little mother was not so pleased. She knew all too well how it would be with all the discomfort—so cold and cumbersome, and with more people to feed and endless work. . . . She was so utterly different from genuine, strong farmers' wives, and we were anything but genuine, strong farm girls.
>
> But father . . . had wild ideas about our learning all the tasks of farming, so that we should grow to love it as he did. For this reason we were sent out to weed turnips in fields that were burning hot and that seemed to us endless though I realize now that they must have been rather modest. We were to learn to tie the wheat, and I shall never forget how the thistle thorns scratched our arms. . . . In addition, we were to learn how to milk the cows. (I believe that Alva refused to do so.) . . . But one terrible thing remained and that was the hay. It had to be brought in and everyone had to help. I understand now that my heart probably was not too strong even then, because I didn't have the *strength,* the armloads were so large.

"Cheerful grandfather" Lars Erik lived on in his cottage on the farm, and on the other side of the road Albert built yet another house for the family. Like his earlier ones it was equipped with every modern improvement, but this house also had verandas, a flagpole, and a roof that sloped in different directions. With the children he planted a birch and pine grove in what had been an arid, stone-studded field. And above his desk he had, as always, a copy of Carl Larsson's drawing of Strindberg.

Albert went on to build several cooperative houses for families to share. As a socialist he insisted on selling them as cheap as possible, declaring that large gains at the expense of others were immoral. In his spare time he took care of the lands belonging to an old-age home and became a city councillor as well as a member of the communal boards for food and for the poor.

From her birth to this last change twelve years later, Alva had moved with her family as often as twice a year, in part so that the family could live in the apartments Albert had built until the moisture went out of the walls. The constant moves made it hard for her to make friends with other children at school. She never felt anchored in a community or securely linked to people around her.

> "Home" was not a place, not an order of things and furnishings. I have still never quite known in the mornings in which bed I had slept. I have adjusted very well to hotel life, learning in an evening where to find the lamp switch, but the fetuslike security in a bed of my own I have rarely experienced. New rooms, new streets, new schools, new friends—the catalogue of our moves is too long to write down.

In whatever school Alva attended, her work went well. But she was never first in her class. She thought later that this may have been almost deliberate: it would have seemed forward to try to outshine everyone else. Most of all she liked to play out of doors with boys, longing to be like them. At home she loved to read, especially since it was surrounded by prohibitions. Her mother thought reading more than was absolutely necessary was harmful to children's eyes, feared that library books might carry germs, and did not regard Albert's political and literary volumes as at all the right sort of reading for children. Every Sunday, however, Albert solemnly unlocked the glass doors of the parlor cabinet and allowed Alva to choose one book. The rest she had to read in secret and smuggle back without anybody noticing.

When the children were sick, Albert read aloud to them. Often the book turned out to be *Huckleberry Finn*, which he began all over again every time someone fell ill. They remembered how they used to enter into the adventures of this freedom-loving boy—adventures so much more desirable than their own routines and all the conventional rules that entangled them.

Alva herself wrote with gusto. A long poem from her twelfth year describes how a Viking allows himself to be baptized only to commit suicide—something far nobler and more manly according to Viking convictions than to die abjectly of illness or old age in one's own bed. Having thus returned to his old faith, he could look forward to entering Valhalla, the Viking heaven, and to taking his place among his ancestors.

> *As death approaches*
> *the old man aloud*
> *cries with voice*
> *hoarsened by age:*
> *Thor, take my treasure!*
> *Odin, take my body!*
> *Let me live*
> *in Valhall's chambers.*
> *White Christ, the warrior*
> *wants no repose!*
>
> *Now I long for*
> *Odin's groves,*
> *lay down my life*
> *therefore myself.*
> *Farewell my tribe,*
> *live well my son!*

To Asar's yard
my path now goes.
The dagger deep in
breast he drives.

Alva kept much of her writing and reading to herself, fearing
her parents' disapproval of her taking so much time away from
more useful tasks. She was often afraid of her parents and wondered, like many children, whether two people who seemed so
alien to her could really be her parents. Was she perhaps a change-
ling? Had her own parents gone away for some reason, and would
they not in that case come back to rescue her now that she needed
them so? She later told of how she finally packed a small suitcase
and walked down the garden path and through the gate. Then
she sat down by the roadside to wait, sure that they would come.
She waited all day in the drizzle, but no one appeared. Dragging
herself indoors, she could not share this fiasco with anyone, not
even with Rut, so fearful was she that her hopes about a new
family would crumble altogether.

Alva used to describe her childhood as "hellish." For a long
time I thought that all her siblings shared this view. But I could
never quite understand how she could simultaneously remember
so many amusing incidents and adventures within the family. Not
until I read her sister Rut's notes about the childhood years at
Slagsta did I realize that neither Rut nor the other siblings had
found their family life hellish. Quite the contrary, they seemed on
the whole to have enjoyed it. "We generally had a lot of fun in
our family," wrote Rut,

> because so many of the members of our family had a sense of
> humor. Elsa S. often talks about how glad she would be to be
> asked to Slagsta, sometimes ceremoniously invited by card.
> "You are hereby invited to taste our old rooster." Or perhaps
> she would be asked to come and have a bath! For we had a
> bathroom, a rather unknown luxury at the time in country
> houses.
>
> Elsa was an only child, who had a rather boring existence
> and thought it a joy to be with all of us noisy kids. We in turn

loved going to her home and enjoying the peace and being spoiled with all sorts of goodies. Just imagine that people could have such leisure that they could go into the parlor and sit down with a coffee tray in the middle of the week! In our home there was work with baking and slaughtering and the separation of milk and the churning of butter and a thousand and one tasks.

Of course Alva participated in it all. But she often felt like an outsider, quite unable to live as unreflectively as the others. She dreamed of being elsewhere, and was the only one who refused to milk the cows or bring in the hay. No one forced her to obey, but they clearly noticed her distance. Alva was sulky, said her mother; Rut wrote that she "only reads and reads and reads."

Reality must therefore have been bitterly double-layered for Alva. She experienced the fellowship yet also felt that it was superficial. It was as if her family were all strangers. She found Lowa's values hypocritical, but at the same time compelling—a fact that created tensions throughout her life.

We had to be "fancy" [*fina*]. Deep down I still judge it a *plus* that she made fine clothes and kept house in style, but it became a cross when one realized that this was her *only* value. She adopted different tones of voice for simple everyday life and being with "fancy" people. All her evaluations seemed superficial to me and I hated them. At the same time I was of course glad that she was so dainty and pretty. She walked with such quick steps always—all other Swedish housewives were heavy-footed.

Alva came to share her mother's interests more than she could have foreseen as a child. Throughout life she retained the reverence for poetry and art and theater and storytelling of all kinds that Lowa had shown. She went to the theater, she used to say, as other people went to church. Just as Lowa had, she sewed many of our dresses when we were little. And she half relished, half felt ashamed of her intense interest in fashions.

For her father's seriousness and righteousness, on the other hand, Alva had admiration from the outset. She shared his "builder's spirit"—his desire to improve human conditions even with respect to the smallest details. And his ideals about equality and justice and progress, like his wanting always to be in the service of "the good," remained models for her throughout life. "He was wonderful in all important ways," she wrote. But at the same time she realized how difficult his principles could make life for others.

When the First World War broke out, these ideals brought her parents into bitter conflict. In the fall of 1916, hunger drove many thousands of people to leave the cities. They drifted about the countryside and gathered potatoes, beets, and whatever else they could find from the fields. In 1917 there were hunger riots in many parts of the country. Albert was a member of the food board of the town of Eskilstuna; his task was to see to it that wheat and potatoes were distributed as fairly as possible. He did not want to keep one more grain of wheat than the board had prescribed. The rest was to be distributed among others. But Lowa wanted more for her five children. She began to grind seed in secret with a little hand mill. When Albert discovered her secret supply there was a great family upheaval. Lowa wept: "How can you let the children go hungry?" Albert retorted by asking which was more important for the children in the long run: to have been hungry for a period of time or to have learned about justice toward others?

For Alva, who could see both sides of this dispute, the battle over the wheat made a lasting impression. She recoiled from this as from so many other family quarrels, exploring, in her mind, ways to keep them from breaking out. Later, as she looked back at the union of her idealistic, thrifty father and her socially striving mother, she saw it as a truly Strindbergian family inferno:

> It centered around two things: One was sexuality versus the fear of children and the frigidity which it produced. Though we saw only glimpses of this conflict, we understood it as a masculine-feminine battle.

The second conflict, of which we saw so much more, had to do with money. The income was *never* secure. And since his social conscience limited my father's room for maneuvers, the discussion became even more complex. Otherwise it was a matter, in typically Victorian-Strindbergian fashion, of cash. Mother had to *ask* for every ten-crown bill for the household. We made long, strategic plans about what we would ask for and how we should justify our demands, and when it would be psychologically *wise* to bring up a request. I don't think we ever had regular pocket money; 5 öre for the Sunday movie had to be acquired through *begging*.

Against this background Alva's rebellious self-assertion grew. She came to understand the force of the Strindbergian anguish over sexuality and money. Her life, she resolved, would be different. She would earn her own money and never have to beg for it from a man; and "mother's complaints about childbearing and glimpses of her frigidity made me feel superior and resentful toward women who play the martyr."

When Alva became conscious of what seemed irremediable conflicts between her parents and between her mother and herself, she gradually stopped dreaming of some storybook rescue by her "real" parents. She chose instead to take an active part in breaking loose. But the art lay in doing so without damage, without anger or sharp words. She could express silent defiance, as when she refused to milk the cows or disappeared with a book when household tasks awaited her, but she kept her sharpest criticisms to herself. She wanted to fashion a new existence by the side of the old one, to show through her own life how one could make everything different. Whether it had to do with studies, love, interior design, money, family, work, or politics, she would never be in favor of revolution; instead she worked for a kind of fully lived reform that began, in Gandhian fashion, from within.

It took rare boldness to stake so much on freedom and a creative way of life that she hoped would prevent the most degrading conflicts between human beings from arising. But the price would turn out to be high. The problems of sexuality and power and money could not be uprooted as easily as she had thought. What did one do, in that case, if the same conflicts returned in the new, self-chosen life? The temptation was then to gloss them over in the hope that they would vanish—especially for one who wanted to demonstrate to the world through her own example that reform and creating anew can succeed.

In the long run this glossing over would come to imprison Alva in a public posture not far from the middle-class hypocrisy she had sought so passionately to escape. But such dangers never crossed her mind when she looked, as a young girl, for a way out of the narrow path she saw traced out for her by society and family. It was then that her method succeeded most dramatically.

3

School

❖ ❖ ❖ ❖

*N*o *one had ever thought* that Alva would continue her studies after elementary school. To be sure, the town of Eskilstuna had a public gymnasium, or high school, but it was only for boys. (Most such schools would not become coeducational until 1928.) That this course of study was closed to her just because she was a girl she felt as a piercing injustice. But even if the gymnasium had been a possibility, her parents would have resisted the idea. Lowa had achieved a level of culture that belied her six years of schooling and saw no reason why Alva should complain, least of all since the town's elementary school now had an optional seventh year of high quality that Alva had been able to take.

Albert likewise thought that seven years of schooling were more than sufficient for Alva. His hope was that his five children would grow up to be farmers and perform the task that he admired above all others: "bringing forth food for humanity." He revered learning, but faithful to Rousseau, he had nothing but suspicion for the ways it was mutilated in schools and universities. And because the high schools, which still educated less than 5 percent of the population, served primarily the middle and upper classes, Albert feared that exposure to their habits and outlook on life might alienate Alva from her own background. As for paying the expenses of private schooling for Alva when his own finances were so often shaky and when there was so much else worth supporting in the world, this seemed to Albert almost sinful.

Fourteen years old and with an incurable desire to learn, Alva was in despair at such an end to her schooling. The gymnasium was blocked to her, the university an impossible dream. She had neither the heart for farming nor the money to spend on travel or projects or books. And Lowa, still haunted by her fear of tuberculosis and other diseases, remained firmly opposed to her children's using the town library.

At this time, in the summer of 1916, Alva claimed to have been "the most naive idealist imaginable." Were she only that, however, she might have shut herself off in a dream world to offset the confinement of her daily life. But even then she groped for practical ways out. She took orders for embroidery and sewing in order to earn pocket money. She learned Esperanto, something that her puritanically idealistic father could accept, and studied astronomy by correspondence. And in August she did something daring: she began to correspond with Per Sundberg, a teacher she had admired in Älvsjö three years earlier. Only twenty years old at the time, he had been unconventional enough to discuss religion and politics with his third-graders and encouraged Alva to write to him when she moved away.

Alva wrote to him about a religious youth circle to which she planned to apply, about her teachers during the past year, and about her longing to start attending some other school in the fall. This correspondence lasted three years and turned out to be of exceptional importance in her life. It allowed her to explore her thoughts about her life, her interests, literature, and religion with a subtlety and sometimes a fervor she could not easily express in ordinary conversation.

Fall came, and the only possibility for continued schooling was to take courses at the town's commercial institute. At first Alva was happy to have a chance to study the English language and Swedish literature while also learning bookkeeping, shorthand, and typing. She did well but became increasingly bored by the routines and was greatly relieved when the courses came to an end. "At last the hateful commercial course is over," she wrote to Sundberg, "and I have my liberty once again." And yet "I would have gone to just about any school so long as there had been one." Now she could guide her own studies, which she claimed included logic and pedagogy, in addition to her continued literary readings. "I can hardly—in fact not at all—keep from reading."

After her commercial training, Alva found work in the tax office of the town of Eskilstuna. She was little more than fifteen when she first sat down in front of the town's shiny new calculating machine and began to add long columns faster than anyone could understand. People came in to stare at "the little girl with the big machine" as she sat so solemnly keeping the books. She took part in auditing and in tax surveys and became a skillful secretary, carrying out every task with nearly playful ease.

Best of all, she now earned an income of her own: 160 crowns a month. After giving her family 25 crowns "as a dispensation in return for food and lodging," she spent a goodly amount on books and lunchtime snacks. From that period she saved, among other things, a carefully wrapped, crumbling edition of Rousseau's early essays. When I read its introduction, I thought of Alva and her father reading about this man—more widely known all over Europe, even in remote villages, than any other thinker—who moved them both so deeply: "Jean-Jacques Rousseau, one of humanity's greatest spirits, philosopher and poet alike, saw the light of day in the little Swiss town Genève, by the lake of the same name." And I remembered going on outings as a child with Alva near Geneva after we had moved there in 1947, intrigued to see how much it meant to her to look for the specific walks he had written about, and for the particular parks and benches and houses that he had known.

Another book she bought at that time was the novel *Stella,* written by Camille Flammarion, a nineteenth-century French scientist and novelist. I remember how she gave me this blazingly romantic book to read when I, too, was fifteen and how I marveled at it. The novel concerns a young woman who falls in love with an unworldly astronomer, learns to see the skies with his eyes and through his instruments, and lives, with him, a short life of superhuman happiness: "their souls found their fill in science; their hearts beat to the same rhythm; their lives were a song of love." At last the two are overcome by electricity and magnetic radiation on a mountaintop in Switzerland where they camp one night to observe a comet. Tiny flames dance on their bodies but they feel no pain. They die blissful in one another's arms under a sky that the comet seems to have set aflame. In rereading the novel, I try to imagine Alva, after her office work was over for the day, settling down to her correspondence course in astronomy with *Stella* in her thoughts. Did she dream, then, of finding a man with whom she could experience a similar sharing of work and life? One with whom she could even imagine dying a glorious death—no longer alone like the self-immolating Viking in the poem she wrote at twelve?

Yet Alva's salary did not nearly suffice for all the books she wanted to read. And inwardly she grew increasingly rebellious against her mother's ban on library books. If she could not borrow them openly, she would do so in secret. She carried home volume after volume under the wide skirts worn at the time and buried them in the sawdust in the attic. Whenever she had time to spare she could climb up the stairs and sit there in the dust reading in peace and quiet. She also discovered that a family on a neighboring farm used discarded schoolbooks with translations of Shakespeare's plays as toilet paper in their outhouse; she would sneak away a play or two at a time to read in the attic, careful to put the ones she hadn't read deep down under old newspapers and other scraps but always worried that she would not have time to read them all before they disappeared.

During these years Alva found a close friend in Märta Fredriksson, another gifted, imaginative, book-loving girl. A photo from 1917 shows Märta tousled and beautiful, with clear, roguish eyes, obviously conscious of her powers and aims. A few years later she is sitting in a photographer's studio with her hair beautifully brushed, wearing a black silk dress and high heeled shoes; but the deliberate, clear gaze is the same. About this friendship Alva wrote to Per Sundberg when she was fifteen:

We two have our questions in common like everything else. It is hard to think of anything that we do not share: food, clothes, amusements, work—everything. The same friends, the same enemies are ours.

Yes, Märta is closer to me even than my own siblings. That is, I feel this in the sense that I prefer her happiness to theirs. You may find that it is wrong of me to think so, but then you do not know Märta nor the great difference between her and my siblings. But I feel, also, the responsibility that comes with having a friend, and such a friend.

Alva and Märta shared a quicksilver temperament that they did not always dare to show to others. They could be childishly giggly one moment and convey the awe of their vast plans for the future the next. Each knew just how to follow the other's shifts of mood. To seal their friendship, they had chosen a rock by the side of the road between their homes under which to leave secret messages for one another. Stealing away unsuspected in the dusk from all the noise and bustle of her family to look under the rock became a ritual for Alva. "Do you remember the notes under the rock?" one of them would always ask whenever they met later in life. And all the memories from those years would come rushing back, and again they would relish following one another's shifts and twists—from gossip about all the friends and foes who had once figured in their secret messages to political issues and readings and back again—with the same lightning-quick responses as ever.

In Alva's letters to her former teacher, one sees her striving for what she must have thought would be a more consistently adult tone. After concentrating at first on her schooling and on the religious and literary interests she shared with him, she gradually moved on, in later letters, to more personal topics. As she reflected on her relationship with her parents, she came increasingly to see her father as someone whose strength her mother had undercut. Her feelings for him had grown deeper, she wrote, while at the same time she grieved over his fate. She thought of all he could have done if he had not been dragged down by Lowa, with her growing heaviness of spirit and her insistence on so many matters that Alva found trivial. In one of her letters, Alva wrote:

I love in him first of all my father, no, the father in the second place, first a great soul, a poet's soul. If father had not been married to mother, I know that his strength of spirit would have been something extraordinary. But he is married, and held down with indissoluble bonds. To say it all: I cannot see that it is my duty in any way to love a mother who is no mother. I place spiritual relations much higher than earthly ones, and all the duties I should have had toward a mother devolve manifold upon my father instead. For father and I are both spiritually and physically related.

It was not until later that Alva could acknowledge that perhaps Lowa, too, could have had a different life—that she had perhaps been equally weighed down by duty and convention. In a letter in 1983 Alva wrote that it had been very difficult for her to forgive the near-hatred that she had felt from her mother "until I began to understand her life's crisis—that her entire middle age was marked by the fear of having more children." Lowa's discouragement at the endless household tasks that had multiplied so when the family moved to the country must have contributed to the antipathy and the sense of dissatisfaction that Alva found so oppressive.

Alva always remembered her adolescent years as ones of awakening and of wholeheartedly joining with Märta in "the book discoveries, the religious speculations, the defiance of petty conventions, the longing for a great and noble life." Together they went to lectures on psychology and filled the question box in the local religious youth organization to overflowing with inquiries and suggestions. Most of all they relished having found a second home in the town's used book store—almost living there, Alva remembered later, in spite of having to be on guard against its lecherous owner.

Her reading sparked Alva's newly discovered religious feeling. Nothing had prepared her for this. Her father, as a thoroughgoing atheist, had excluded religious writings from his collection of books. She found her mother's sporadic piety sentimental and artificial; and in school the harsh Lutheran messages had merely given her a sense of guilt over sin and hatred and her own revolt. Now her world seemed to expand, and she entered wholeheartedly into her new feelings for the supernatural and the holy.

During the summer months the girls bicycled each Sunday to different churches and took part in religious youth meetings around the countryside. A very fuzzy photograph, evidently saved for personal rather than aesthetic reasons, shows a corner of a churchyard at night. On the back Alva has written: "There *were* ghosts. At least in the summer of 1917."

Alva and Märta decided to be confirmed together that summer. But by Christmastime, shortly before she turned sixteen, one of Alva's letters to Per Sundberg already expressed stormy religious doubts. She declared herself to be a freethinker: "I have fought a long time, but I could not resist—the Truth. I do not believe that there is no god. No, a creative world spirit, a force, the first molecule, God—all this is one and the same." Only persons, she continued, who could bring all contradictory views, including those of Christianity, into a harmonious whole could dare claim knowledge of the truth. And no one could have full knowledge of this kind since each person knows only one side of the infinitely many-sided truth, which is nevertheless always one and the same.

In later letters she wrote of her profound longing for inner peace and for the ability to believe in God without posing any questions. She felt thrown between despair and ecstasy and sometimes asked her correspondent's forgiveness for all the "crazy things" she wrote, including thoughts of finding and making use of her father's revolver. Sundberg replied with delicacy and insight, explaining to her the ways in which he had come to find meaning in even the minutest aspects of life in spite of not having answers to the largest questions. When Alva reread her letters in her eighties, she found them imbued with false pathos: "One exaggerates, intimates that crises are worse than they really were—or rather, one creates more literature or drama from what were less articulate spiritual upheavals." And yet I wonder: Might not any strong character dramatize her life thus if she felt forced to act out her destiny on too constricted a stage?

Increasingly, Alva's religious doubts took the upper hand. Once again, books speeded up this development. Alva began to read critical studies of the Bible—among them Ernest Renan's *The Life of Christ,* Herbert Spencer's works, and the Swedish poet Viktor Rydberg on biblical doctrines. John Stuart Mill, she wrote to Sundberg, was the thinker whose clarity and good sense made him, to her mind, most irrefutable, while Auguste Comte was the one who appealed to her least. Comte, whose influence around the turn of the century is now difficult to understand, divided history into three periods: an age of theology, an age of metaphysics, and then the coming positivistic era when science, sociology, and ethics would take over and a new, humanistic religion would conquer folly and superstition. Though his optimism was hard to maintain later in our century, it persuaded many before then. Through examining such theories Alva strove to nourish what she always saw as her underlying rationalistic perspective, hoping to conquer in herself what she increasingly perceived as a tendency to wallow in emotional thinking and to indulge a romantic interest in the supernatural.

In the fall of 1918 she had an intellectual showdown with Märta that marked the final stage of her religious life. But her feelings concerning what she found holy did not die away. When her doubts about the supernatural won out, these feelings found two other expressions: in a deepening respect for poetry and art and theater and all that had to do with the experience of beauty that her mother so valued; and in the ethical attitude that she had found both in religion and among atheists such as her father. And just as her father had brought his ideals about equality, integrity, justice, and progress within the framework of "the good" that he wanted to serve, so Alva added beauty—something she regarded not as a luxury but as indispensable for what she saw as the life most worthy of human beings.

Gradually, this view of the good crystallized into what she called "an almost Zoroastrian way of thinking," according to which the powers of evil battle against those of goodness and all human beings must choose sides. This view seemed to her to answer the problem that had tormented so many believers and that she, too, had earlier struggled to answer: how could a God who was good have created a world so filled with suffering and evil? The answer was quite simply that there were two powers, and that the God of goodness could never have created evil; rather, he battled against it with all his force.

This dualism, so typical of the efforts in adolescence to distinguish good from evil and to sort out what belongs to one's own personality as opposed to what comes from outside, gave Alva, at sixteen, the means to counteract the Lutheran guilt feelings that school and society had evoked in her. It also allowed her to temper the fear of not being sufficiently "fine" or fancy to satisfy her mother, or idealistic and upright enough to suit her father.

Alva was to retain this conviction about the battle between good and evil all her life. In an interview in 1971, she said that she always tried to do what was right even if she had to overcome opposition or practical obstacles. "I think that if I don't do so, then I don't increase the proportion of goodness in the world. For me, this supplants religion." As late as in her Nobel acceptance speech, in 1982, she spoke of a personal confession she wanted to make:

> I have always looked at the world's development as a battle between the forces of good and those of evil. Not, therefore, simply expressed as a battle between Jesus and Satan, since I don't see the development as limited to our own cultural sphere. Rather perhaps the metaphor about Ormuzd—the good and Ahriman—the evil. My personal philosophy of life is that of *ethics*.
>
> Now it seems to me as if the powers of evil were gathering ever more numerous means of power in their hands. Shall we dare to believe that the leaders of the great nations of the world will wake up, see the abyss before them, and *change course?*

Alva's dualistic perspective made it easy for her to seek to identify herself with the good powers and to see all conflicts as coming from outside. Seeing oneself in the service of what is good gives force and conviction, but it can also become a way to avoid the self-questioning, the hesitation, and the explaining that might otherwise seem necessary. One can then quite simply take for granted that one serves what is rational and humane without puzzling over one's motives or possible misunderstandings. And if one stands for such self-evident ideals as those of justice, equality, and peace, persons who express other points of view can easily seem irrational or blinded by prejudice or even in league with the powers of evil.

This sense that it is self-evident which ideals are the right ones permeates books such as *Crisis in the Population Question*. It lay behind the forcefulness and the clarity that so many saw in Alva. Not until the end of her life did she begin to question this attitude. Can one always be certain which power is good or evil? Is it possible that the confident invoking of goodness, justice, and equality can contribute to what she came to call the "displacements" between what she had become and what she "could, perhaps even should, have become?"

During this period of reading and thinking in her teens, Alva also wrote feverishly. She mimeographed a small newspaper at home, submitted articles to the local press, and produced poetry, diaries, adventure stories, even short historical novels. At the same time, she became active in the Social Democratic youth movement and took part in many debates and excursions—jolly and somewhat flirtatious occasions, judging from the photos she saved from that time.

But the dream of continuing her studies only grew, the more so as she recognized the limits to her efforts to study everything on her own: "What an idea of mine to try to learn Greek!" she wrote to Sundberg. "How could I not realize that it would be impossible, so long as I had no real teacher? Yet I have to have more insight into this subject in order to be able fully to understand books such as those by Flammarion [on astronomy]." Up to then, she said, she had always hoped to become a schoolteacher, and her parents had said that she might consider taking the courses then needed for a teacher's certificate.

But—I don't want to. I cannot become a teacher, that is not meant to be. "But what *is* meant to be, in that case?" you and many others ask. That I don't know, but something is meant for me and in due course of time I am sure I'll find out.

She saved money from her salary and began to send away for brochures from several boarding schools. At sixteen she picked out one such school, was elated to be admitted, and managed to persuade a friend of the family's to underwrite a loan to help her pay the tuition. But the hardest task remained: how was she going to persuade her parents to allow her to go?

It turned out to be more painful than even she had expected. Her father, to be sure, was neutral; though he would never take the initiative for such studies, he was unwilling to go against her free choice. Her mother, on the other hand, was dead set against the plan. She forbade Alva to go to any school away from home. Perhaps she feared that Alva might "go astray," even become pregnant if she left home at such a young age. Small quarrels grew into intense confrontations. Alva wept and begged and said that she would die if she had to continue at the town office. Finally, Lowa took Alva's application—which needed only her parents' signatures—and tore it in two. Alva felt wildly powerless. It was as if her future had been torn up—her future in the real world, the world where she knew she could feel at home, beyond the prison of her family's stifling half-life.

Later, when she thought back on this great quarrel, she perceived her mother as herself imprisoned in her role and threatened by this daughter who wanted to break loose as she had never been able to do. Lowa was now forty years old, afraid of yet another pregnancy, and spending large parts of each day in bed. She must have seen Alva as a repudiation of her sacrifices. Here stood this daughter, whose need for food, clothing, care, and upbringing had long constituted part of her own maternal burden. And now that same girl wanted to live in freedom! Now she wanted to create another type of woman's life, throw off and thereby reject her mother's shackles!

As an aside, I must acknowledge here that I believed for years that it was Alva's father who had torn up her application. Not until I reread my notes about her youth did I see what I must have pushed aside—that it was her mother. Somehow that did not fit with my ideas about dominating parents or with the situation in my own family, where it was Gunnar who hectored us (though never about schooling) and Alva who stood silently—too silently—by and suffered from family arguments.

I had to ask Alva one more time what had happened that day, and she explained it to me all over again. And I realized that my mistake had partly stemmed from not having had a mother such as hers: that Alva, by reshaping her own life, did not have the same need to channel mine, to live through me. Of course she bore traces of the conflict with her mother, especially evident in her avoidance of family conflicts in her later life; and of course I could feel bewildered, even isolated, because she never forced her views on me. But by freeing herself from her mother's heavy-handed control, she also helped free me and in the long run my own children.

When Alva's father understood that her desire to study was incurable, he changed his position. Perhaps his conscience was also troubled by the view of her impotent bitterness. As a follower of Rousseau and a lover of Strindberg he valued liberty, after all, however suspicious he was of schooling. He worked out a shrewd compromise. Together with the parents of a few other girls, he urged the town school board to establish a "private gymnasium" for girls in Eskilstuna. After much stubborn advocacy, they finally succeeded. The school board agreed to allow the high school's teachers and a few others recruited for the purpose to meet with a group of girls privately.

This is where Alva at last began her studies, at seventeen, along with ten other girls. It was expensive—900 crowns a year for the courses that boys received for 80 crowns. And since the newly instituted classes could not be held with those for the boys in the high school building, the girls had to shuttle back and forth across town from one makeshift classroom to the next during the course of each day. To the end of her life, Alva could remember the resentment with which she regarded this arrangement. But the most important thing for her was, nevertheless, that she could study, and for her mother that she could remain at home.

During the first term the girls had to prove themselves. This was a challenge for Alva, who had never studied either French or German, unlike most of the others in the beginning class. For her first writing assignment she chose, with some trepidation, to discuss the plans for the League of Nations that President Woodrow Wilson had recently proposed. At seventeen, in neutral Sweden, she was as skeptical about its chances as the most war-weary European. She contrasted the peace imposed by violence by conquerors like Alexander the Great and Napoleon to efforts to build peace through alliances, leagues, and utopian schemes, and she doubted that the time had yet come for a solution "to the enigma of a world organization."

Money was a source of constant worry. During the summer months she could not study much since she had to keep up her work at the town office to help pay her father back. The constant scrimping and saving marked her for life. Not that she found it difficult to spend the money that eventually came her way—on trips, beautiful living quarters, clothes, presents, and every form of philanthropy. But it was as if she could never be quite sure how long the money would last, just as she never quite knew each morning in which bed she lay, having moved about so much as a child.

For a long time I found it hard to understand this split in her attitude toward money. How could someone be so generous so often—as when she gave away nearly all her Nobel Prize award for peace research—and at the same time so punctilious about expenses and at times so parsimonious? All through her life Alva meticulously entered large and small expenses in little black notebooks that she never threw away. When my siblings and I needed money for studies or lodging, she counted such expenditures as loans just as her father had, and finally as advances on any inheritance in her and my father's will. And whenever she asked me to send her something from abroad, she insisted on calling my expenditure a loan that she should repay. Not until I saw her own father's equally meticulous accounts and his way of giving his

children loans that were later counted against their inheritance
did I understand how entirely Alva entered into his spirit when it
came to financial responsibility and accountability—and how, for
both of them, such accounts constituted *one* type of explanation
for how one led one's life.

It did not take long for Alva to catch up with her classmates;
and during the second year she was nearly bored. In order to
speed the process and save her family money she decided to
compress the courses of the last two years into one. Her final
exams went well, and in June 1922 Alva Reimer received her
degree in Stockholm, with highest honors, after a set of official
oral exams that could not be conducted in her hometown. At
twenty she had attained what at fourteen she had thought impossible—"studentexamen," her matriculation.

During the previous years she had also experienced an intense
friendship and then a love that came to stamp her entire life. The
friendship developed, again, through letters. As part of the activities of a youth organization, Alva and Rut had begun corresponding with two young Norwegians: Rut with Johannes Smemo, who
later became a bishop, and Alva with Andreas Arnesen, more
interested in literature and psychology. Next to her father and
"the idol of her conscience," Per Sundberg, and later Gunnar, no
one had greater influence over Alva than Andreas. He broadened
her perspective and gave her personal contact for the first time
with the world outside Sweden. They wrote one another several
times a week, sometimes letters of thirty to forty pages, baring
their most intimate feelings. They shared views about poetry,
religion, history, and about the Great War. And when they came
to discuss Norway's political crisis and newly won independence
from Sweden, they discovered that they had been given wholly
different accounts in school, even in the history textbooks that
they traded for comparison.

Alva looked back at that correspondence as a great experience, perhaps too exalted, perhaps too exuberant, but still a
chance for a shared spiritual life that she had not known before.
It was friendship on the verge of love, and it could have been
more had Gunnar not come into the picture. Andreas was plan-

ning to bicycle to Sweden to meet Alva the summer of 1919. She wondered what someone who had received her letters brimming with ideas and feelings and who had answered just as intensely would turn out to be like in person. But shortly before he was to arrive she met Gunnar and all was changed. She realized that she had to write a letter to ward off Andreas; but when this did not succeed, she had, at last, to tell him about Gunnar. "Then the letters ended."

Gunnar was the great love affair. Before meeting him, Alva had often felt drawn to boys and men—the naval cadet with his black frostbitten fingers when she was five, or Ivar, who held her in a way she thought felt delicious when they shared a sled down a snowy hill a few years later. But those who sought her out always seemed to her too narrowly cut, too finished as persons, "without adventurous possibilities for development." Rut teased her for being so choosy—she herself had kissed twenty-two boys and Alva had not kissed one! And Alva remembered worrying about this:

> I was so conscious of this fastidious approach with its resultant withdrawal, always in good time, that I was ashamed inwardly for being so "calculating." But then it was not money or titles or elegance that I sought. I wanted above everything to be myself—never be tied to a housewifely existence that would center on a man.

4

Gunnar

❖ ❖ ❖

*T*he story of how Gunnar arrived has become a family myth. Alva was seventeen that summer of 1919, he twenty, and they lived happily from then on, we heard tell over and over as children; and how it happened had overtones of fairy tale. Not until much later were we able even to begin sorting out what was myth and what was reality in that story.

About the beginning everyone agrees; and it *was* like a fairy tale. Alva and Rut were woken up one June morning by their father, who shouted upstairs, asking them to make coffee for three tramps who had slept in the hayloft. The girls rolled over and went back to sleep. Then their grandfather gaily called out that three university students had spent the night in the loft. Couldn't the girls carry over a coffee tray? Instantly the two sisters jumped out of bed, pulled on clothes as fast as they could, brushed their hair, and bustled about preparing coffee and rolls. Since their mother was at a rest home just then, it was they who took care of the household. They could serve exactly what they wanted and carry out a beautifully set tray to the three students about whom they were so curious.

One of the three was Gunnar. Alva was deeply struck. With gleaming blue eyes and a lanky figure, he attracted her from the start. And when they began to talk with one another, it seemed to her that she had encountered an entirely new sort of person—superior, broad-gauged, with a playful genius that made whatever others said seem heavy and muddled. His laughter, his freedom,

the depth she sensed in his thoughts, all drew her to him. To top
it off he sang student songs and exuberant lyrics by the eighteenth-
century troubadour Carl Michael Bellmann with exceptional feeling and a clear, warm voice. He in his turn seems to have been
equally struck—and for life—by this beautiful, merry, profound
young girl. Now he had to rethink the entire bicycle trip; after
such a meeting he could hardly just continue on his way as if
nothing had happened.

There is a photo of Alva, Rut, Gunnar, and his friends Gösta
Lundborg and Sven Tisell taken that first June morning as they
sit in the sun on a wooden gate. Rut, the little sister, a Pippi
Longstocking of those days with a striped blouse and straggling
blond hair under a sun hat, is clearly proud to be included in the
picture. Gunnar, turning to Alva, sucks on his pipe and looks as
if he is pondering various ingenious remarks. Dark blond locks
fall over his high brow and the bicycle clips are still on his pant
legs. Alva looks glowingly happy, in a white blouse with a black
bow, a long, dark, full skirt, and a black ribbon around her
forehead. Her smile, with her face in full sun, warms them all;
her hand almost touches Gunnar's.

Since Alva was working at her office job in Eskilstuna that
summer, they decided to meet at a pastry shop there for lunch.
The boys paid; Alva remembered being so happy that she de-
voured eleven pastries. Afterward, instead of returning home, she
followed Gunnar and his friends to the neighboring town of
Torshälla having called Rut to ask her to tell their father she had
gone to visit a friend. Alva may never have acted so impulsively.
It was as if she knew that this chance would not come again.

The next morning she bicycled home, still giddy from this
adventure. But Gunnar could not let matters end in that way. He
wrote her a letter that he always later thought was a desperate
attempt and asked what he knew was unthinkable—that she come
with Gösta and him on their tour. (Their friend Sven had returned
home by that time.) Could she take a train north with her bicycle
to the station of Floda in the province of Dalecarlia? If so, they
would meet her there. He could not dare hope that she would
come—but she did! Nor did he dare ask her how she had managed

to get her parents' permission for the trip. It was fortunate, Alva thought, that her mother was still in the rest home. Circumventing her father was altogether easier, and the office gave her the two weeks of vacation that she requested with no questions asked.

The three lived a vagrant life, bicycling and talking their way along the roads and in the woods of Dalecarlia. All that Alva had thought about and written in her diaries she could now share with Gunnar. She asked whether he had read Strindberg, Pascal, Rousseau, Maeterlinck, even Ernst Haeckel, the German evolutionist, on "World Riddles." Yes, every one of them, he answered. But she wondered about that, since he had so little to say about these thinkers. He soon confessed that he had been so afraid of disappointing her that he had not dared to admit his ignorance. She told him of her veneration for the Indian poet and philosopher Rabindranath Tagore, many of whose works had been translated into Swedish after he won the Nobel Prize for literature in 1913. This prompted Gunnar to seek out the volume entitled *Gitanjali, A Song-Offering* by Tagore and to inscribe it as his first gift to Alva; she, in turn, reciprocated with the play *Chitra*.

Without knowing it, Alva was shaking Gunnar's condescending view of women to the core. He prided himself immensely on his already considerable erudition, yet he had met his match in her—an unschooled country girl to boot. Right away, he knew her as an equal. "Intellectually, we were of an age—Alva, to be sure, three years younger but more mature." He would never again subscribe to the prevailing stereotypes about women as suggestible creatures not meant to overtax their minds. The previous year he had given a high-flown, sophomoric talk advocating the formation of a party of the educated (*intelligensens parti*) to guide the unthinking masses now that the Swedish Parliament had granted the right to vote to all adult men and women. Alas, he said, women only added to the problem. They were likely to undermine the rationality of the masses even further, "to the extent possible." Alva caused him to abandon for good his condescension in thinking that women would automatically fall into the category of the masses and have such a debilitating effect on them; and she challenged his elitist attitude toward those masses as unthinking in its own right. The universal and equal suffrage that was finally the law of the land was, after all, what her grandfather and father had fought to bring about; without it, she doubted that genuine social reform would be possible.

Sophomoric or not, most of Gunnar's views nevertheless seemed to Alva of breathtaking scope. Whether he spoke of the changes that the Great War had wrought around the world, of religious objections to Darwinism, or of the role of Gustavus Vasa and other fellow Dalecarlians in preserving Sweden's freedom from foreign domination, he had a way of juxtaposing seemingly incompatible ideas and of conveying unexpected conclusions with a brash self-confidence that she found exhilarating. Wherever they traveled from then on, she could see how he strained to understand how people lived, what problems they struggled with, and how they envisaged the future. He used to say that he had been born "quite abnormally curious." As a child, one of his first memories had been of walking in a city and of itching to know about all the people living behind the many thousands of windows:

> Men and women and children who work, eat and sleep, argue and laugh, talk over the telephone and read the newspapers: Where does their money come from? How do they get food? Why do people turn out to be what they are? Why do they marry precisely those they marry and have the children they have? Why do they act as they do, anyway? Why not otherwise? What would happen if they did? How does it all mesh?

Gunnar was impatient with many efforts to answer such questions, then as later. He would come to see most studies attempting to do so as either naively anecdotal or narrow and unperceptive. On this first trip he confided in Alva that he hoped to gain a more solid understanding of how society worked by studying law, but already he doubted that such studies would provide an adequate methodology for satisfying his urge to know. Alva reveled in these talks as in no others. They would never peter out, of that she felt sure.

The three came to the small town of Skattungbyn and looked up the very modest cottage where Gunnar had been born in December 1898. Sofie and Carl Adolf Pettersson, his parents, had arrived in the town some weeks before his birth. Carl Adolf was proud, at the age of twenty-two, to have been offered his first construction job: to build a small train station for the new railroad link between Solvarbo and the city of Falun. Sofie and he rented a room in the cottage for the duration. When the birth pangs began, Sofie, twenty years old and very shy, agonized about staining their borrowed bedding. She sent her husband to the stable for a load of hay, on which Gunnar was safely born. A few months later, the train station completed, his parents brought him back to Gustafs, their home parish, on a flatcar used by railroad workers going up and down the new line. This time it was loaded with rocks, leaving barely enough room for Sofie and Carl Adolf to sit with Gunnar in a basket between them.

Alva and the two boys followed the river Dalälven upstream and slept in haylofts and summer cottages. At the campfires each evening, Alva cooked what she later thought must have been extremely uninspired food. Gunnar recalled that he had been surprised that she did not even seem to know how to heat up canned fish patties. But at the time they were not choosy. After some days, Gunnar had the idea that they should travel back south to Solvarbo, the beautiful village in Dalecarlia where he had relatives on every farm and where his parents were spending the summer. They forwarded their bicycles by train and built a raft from three logs. In the center they hammered together three sugar boxes for kitchen things and as a "throne" for Alva: there she was to sit while the boys guided the raft with poles.

In this way they drifted down the river, sometimes very slowly, sometimes frighteningly fast, always in just that adventurous and unplanned manner in which she had dreamed of traveling. Gunnar later thought that they got the idea from Mark Twain. Perhaps it was Alva who told them about *Huckleberry Finn,* which her father had read aloud so many times when she or Rut had been ill. Now it was she who lived on the river. At night they slept by the shore and scraped together what they could find in the way of food. And when the raft sometimes got caught in the mass of timber that floated down the river from forests upstream, one of the boys had to jump into the water to work it loose.

Finally they arrived in the village of Solvarbo, with its cottages painted red and its narrow gorges carved out by streams flowing toward the river. They walked to the old family mill where one of Gunnar's uncles lived. Alone with Gunnar (Gösta having bicycled back to their last overnight location to find something he had left behind) Alva then had what she called an "explanation" with him. Seated on rocks by the millstream in the white northern midsummer night, they talked until morning, but still dared not come physically close to one another.

Gunnar remembered a sense of almost dizzying depth as they talked through the night. He shared with Alva his ideas about how he wanted to live, based, first and foremost, on a thoroughgoing belief in the value of rationality. If only human beings could reason more clearly and scientifically, they would be able to guide their lives quite differently. He had received a superb education in the natural sciences and in the social sciences in the Stockholm gymnasium where his parents had enrolled him. His history teacher there, John Lindquist, had led him to study the English, Scottish, and French Enlightenment thinkers and to choose them as guides. Thomas Jefferson, he later recalled, had exercised especially great influence on him as one who drew on these thinkers both as a philosopher and as a man of action, and who strove for clarity about the moral conflicts and compromises in life.

The Enlightenment thesis that Gunnar adopted most unreservedly was the faith that human conditions would improve as soon as reason triumphed over misunderstanding, bias, and superstition. Alva was less certain on this score, and Gunnar's own optimism would be sorely tested as he lived through the decades to come. But at twenty his faith seemed as self-evident to him as Alva's reverence for all that she gathered within the confines of the concept of "the good" was to her, and as little in need of analysis or questioning. He admired Alva for her ideals, but without rationality they would not go far, he believed, and on that score he succeeded in persuading her.

In Solvarbo they stayed with Gunnar's family, who were spending the summer in a cottage not far from the mill. There, according to Gunnar, began, in all secrecy, "a devoted love life." Perhaps his parents wondered a little about this shy young girl— clearly no adventuress—who came traveling with their son. But customs in rural Sweden were relaxed when it came to relations between unmarried young people. Like many other couples, Sofie and Carl Adolf had married only when they were expecting their first child. They welcomed Alva warmly, not least because Gunnar had asked them to be especially nice to her "for I like her so very much!"

A portrait shows Gunnar's mother Sofie as a stately woman with dark blond, wavy hair that was softly pulled back and rather sad eyes. In another photo her husband Carl Adolf poses as a self-assured, well-to-do businessman. Shrewd, cautious eyes peer out of his heavy face. He was large and noisy and seemed to have opinions about everything. Shy as she was, Alva could hardly discuss his views with him, but it was clear to her that she had met a remarkably gifted man and one who seemed more openly, even vulnerably, human than most.

In this family Alva felt welcome and in many ways at home. Like her own father, Gunnar's father had made his way in the world by building and doing business. Both fathers had had poor rural childhoods in families without any land of their own, and both had had to be satisfied with a sixth grade primary school education.

At the age of twenty-two, newly married and having had only six weeks of carpentry training, Carl Adolf had begun building the small station for local trains in the town of Skattungbyn, where Gunnar had been born. As the network of railroads spread across Sweden, Carl Adolf was asked to erect other stations near his home village. From there he took on further construction projects, moving to the larger provincial city of Falun in 1900 and finally to Stockholm. Both Alva's and Gunnar's families lived at a time of rapid industrial growth in Sweden and of migration from the countryside to the cities. Industrialization opened doors for persons with energy and luck and ideas that they wanted to carry out. Albert and Carl Adolf took every chance they saw. Their families had to move time and again, and their children went to one new school after the other. But all still felt most at home in the countryside where their relatives lived. "I have always thought," Gunnar later wrote, "that my true identity lies in this proud, obstinate, individualistic, traditionally stable, and utterly democratic Dalecarlian countryside [Dalabygd]."

The two families were also alike in that they had changed names—another way to break away from tradition. A few years after Alva's parents had adopted the name Reimer, Gunnar's father decided to take the name Myrdal for his children; he himself retained the name Pettersson for business reasons. Both he and Gunnar's mother Sofie came from peasant families in and around Solvarbo. One was called the Myres family; they lived on the farm named Myres, near Myrdalen (the Myr valley) by the river known as Dalälven. It was from there that the name Myrdal was taken.

Gunnar's home, however, was at the same time quite different from Alva's. The fundamental Swedish egalitarianism in both homes drew on different traditions: hers was imbued with Albert's internationalist and Social Democratic ideals, whereas Gunnar's family stressed patriotic and communal pride and a conservative stance that grew more pronounced as his father made his way up in the world. Whereas all religious and other dogmas were freely questioned in Alva's family, Gunnar's parents observed traditional Lutheran practices. Most apparent of all was the difference that alcohol played in the two families. Alva's father had remained a teetotaler all his life, true to the promise he made to his mother after his father's early death. But Carl Adolf, who had sworn as a young man that not a drop of alcohol would ever cross his lips, had taken to drinking increasingly after he came to Stockholm. Alva could see, too, that in spite of the fact that Carl Adolf had become a forceful figure in the business world and was as interested as her own father in new kinds of enterprises and in modern farming methods, he lacked the latter's social conscience and was more given to speculation.

Sofie, Gunnar's mother, was kind and quiet and almost completely focused on creating a warm, stable home for her four children: Gunnar, who was the oldest, the daughters Elsa and Mela, and the youngest son, Robert. She lacked Lowa's interest in theater and style and fashionable clothes, preferring, rather, an orderly and traditional life-style. She expected her children—and later us grandchildren—to obey, to eat all the food that was put before them, and to behave. About their conduct Sofie could remain firm; but she felt rebuffed and oppressed by her husband. She was extremely fond of her various relatives in and around her home parish of Gustafs and did not appreciate the upward social mobility that drove her husband; in that way too she was entirely unlike Alva's mother.

Gradually, Alva came to understand how much Sofie suffered from her husband's drinking and his affairs with other women. She had married at the age of twenty as a submissive young girl, inexperienced outside the home though, as the eldest of nine siblings, already a capable housekeeper. She felt that Carl Adolf had gone astray by wining and dining with his business friends. Perhaps he had begun by taking an extra glass or two to alleviate any sense of insecurity, as a peasant boy among his new city associates, only to grow used to their ways. All the while she sat alone at home with the children and brooded about why things should have turned out so badly. During Alva's visit Sofie cornered her in the wash room and talked for hours about her unhappy life. To this quiet, clear-eyed, somewhat astonished girl she felt she could open her heart. Each time they met after that she returned to the same complaints.

Now Alva gained insight into a feminine fate she decided to avoid as categorically as that of her own mother. But she could also relate more warmly to Sofie than to Lowa, whose resentment and disapproval she felt so keenly. Alva's many letters to Sofie during the next few years express affectionate thanks for one holiday visit after another, and sadness, often, at having to return home, so far from Gunnar and his family. In one letter, after a long Christmas visit in 1921, she writes Sofie that she can't help longing to be back: "Now everything is so rushed and yet so monotonous and outdoors the wind blows constantly. The memories are almost the only thing that warm and give life."

Even during her first stay with Gunnar's family, she could not help noticing how his role within the family differed from her own. He had always considered himself, and been considered by his parents, as the one among the children who was most important in every way. He was the firstborn son as his father had been, and Carl Adolf hoped that Gunnar would go far in life. As for Sofie, she may have hoped that her son would compensate, through his achievements, for her own sense of inadequacy. Gunnar was the first among his relatives to have received a gymnasium education. In his family this accomplishment was seen as a great triumph, worth every sacrifice, whereas Alva had had to beg for the opportunity to study and always had to be careful not to seem proud to be in any way different.

That Gunnar felt himself to be remarkable was easy for Alva to understand: she thought, as did most others, that he *was* remarkable. Many who knew him in his youth have described his wealth of ideas and leaps of thought—how talking with him made one feel, as one friend commented, as if one had been invited to a feast of imagination, intellect, and playfulness. That is exactly how she herself felt. Did not such a person have the right to be proud? Eight years later she could still write with admiration in her diary that he was the most self-glorifying man in the world.

Around Solvarbo, Alva met many others, almost all related to Gunnar. When she and Gunnar later searched the church registers kept since the seventeenth century in each Swedish community, they found that three-quarters of his relatives had lived in that one village, the rest in neighboring villages. Thanks to a strong taboo against marriage between cousins, there had been little inbreeding. Each villager knew the ancestry, achievements, and foibles of every other in intimate detail and kept careful track, over innumerable cups of coffee in one another's cottages, of those who had moved away—not least those who, like Gunnar's uncle Albert, had emigrated to America.

As her visit wore on, Alva forgot time and duty altogether,

forgot that the vacation weeks she had asked for at the office had ended July 1, forgot that her parents would begin to wonder over her long absence. When the office manager called her father to ask if she was ill, Rut was finally forced to reveal the secret. A great family crisis ensued. Her mother returned from the rest home and her father sent a telegram to Gunnar: "Do you know where Alva is? She must come home immediately."

Alva traveled home by train. Somberly the father went to meet her; silently they walked home along the country road. Both realized what a crisis Alva's escapade represented for Lowa, always worried about what the prying Aunt Mimmi and other relatives and neighbors would find to gossip about. Albert himself was too shy to ask what had taken place. And Alva, protecting her joy and her great tenderness, could not speak about it, least of all to her parents. Since she knew that her mother would read Gunnar's letters, she had asked him to write an "innocent page" that she left about on purpose. Then they could continue to make plans for the future.

Alva's admiration for Gunnar was so limitless, and she had such a clear sense from the moment she met him of the new, more intellectual life that had begun for her, that she decided to take an irreversible step: she would burn her poems, her adventure stories and novels, even all her diaries. Everything that had been emotional and exalted now had to be over and done with. She would never reject her love for literature and art; but when it came to her own writing she wanted to retain only what could be elucidated and worked out scientifically and rationally—all that she could share openly with Gunnar.

In him she had found someone who not only loved her but who took her seriously in the way that mattered most to her: as a thinking person. The two would live, she hoped, as if in their own Enlightenment period. As soon as she could pass her gymnasium examinations and move to Stockholm, where Gunnar was already a student at Stockholm's Högskola (now the University of Stockholm), the new life would begin— and it was going to be quite indescribably self-created and creative all at once.

So the story began. That "once upon a time" it was thus I can well believe. But that they lived happily from then on, as Gunnar long insisted—such was not the case. And one of the reasons that life diverged from the story was precisely that Alva could never quite follow through on the self-denial that she had initiated by burning her writings. She was not purely the rationalist she often claimed to be. She should never have tried to sacrifice the other sides of herself; it was like throwing her heart into the fire.

"How have I come to displace my own self in order to fit in with other selves? Where does one self merge with the other?"

The transition began, I believe, during those first weeks with Gunnar. And I understand her so well. Did not *Stella* and other novels exalt just such a merging of selves? And was there not infinitely much to be learned, in this union, from Gunnar—older, more self-assured in his knowledge of the world, and with exuberant ambitions for them both? At the same hesitant, uncertain, identity-seeking age I, too, had been tempted to sacrifice part of myself, though, to be sure, the opposite part—all that had to do with rationality—as a reaction against Alva and Gunnar, but most of all to identify more completely with Michel, a young poet in Geneva. But I also felt the danger of doing so; I wrote in my diary that slowly but surely I was losing my personality and gliding over in his: "In everything I want to be like him, I have noticed it myself. I must begin to see him from the outside . . . otherwise I am going to bleed to death within *his* personality."

Alva's willingness to sacrifice herself was far greater than mine. Her magnificent but self-limiting gesture of burning her writings helped conceal her need for explanations, the need to ask questions about her own past and how it had contributed to the present, the need to look for displacements and half-buried experiences, possibilities that had been put aside, thoughts that had been written down only to be burned. For if one really comes to believe that all is entirely open and clear and rational, nothing more seems to be needed to understand a life than simply looking

back to see how it has turned out. One can then more easily fall
victim to myths.

The difficulty in living a myth is that one cannot fully acknowledge shadows and inconsistencies when one begins to sense
them. For Alva, with her idealism and her spirit of sacrifice, the
meeting with Gunnar seemed too astoundingly fortunate not to
signal the beginning of just the kind of adventurous and fulfilled
life she had always hoped for—the opportunity to escape and to
grow into her true self, as a whole individual, not just as a butterfly
caught, like her mother, in the sticky web of a conventional
woman's role.

But there is in fairy tales and myths another story, one that
runs parallel in Alva's life with that of the blissful couple. It is
that of a young person—almost always a boy—who, like Ibsen's
Peer Gynt, goes out into the world to seek his fortune. That dream
was hers long before Gunnar came into her life, and the more it
was fulfilled the happier she felt. From Eskilstuna she came out
into the wide world as few others had done; and like the young
men in the heroic tales she had to use all her ingenuity, overcome
many obstacles, and carry out many tasks in order to make her
way. That the two roles—as eternally happy companion and as
active seeker in the world—did not always fit and at times conflicted she did not discern when she moved to Stockholm at
twenty. On the contrary: she would show, with Gunnar's help,
how they could be united.

5

Marriage

❖ ❖ ❖ ❖

On a luminously sunny October day in 1979, Alva and I
drove to the Copper Tents in Haga Park near Stockholm. The
majestic Roman tents, built by King Gustavus III in the late
eighteenth century, had recently been restored and gleamed
against the trees in the park. In one we drank cocoa with whipped
cream, just as Alva and Gunnar had done fifty-five years earlier
after their marriage on the eighth of October 1924. Alva was
twenty-two years old at the time, Gunnar twenty-five. They had
wanted to marry sooner, in 1923, when Gunnar received his law
degree and could support himself; but Albert, who had under-
written a loan that Alva had taken out in order to study, convinced
them that she should finish her degree first—the "Filosofie Kan-
didat," which was approximately equivalent to a B.A.

The only guests at the wedding were their two closest
friends—Märta Fredriksson and Alf Johansson, one of Gunnar's
fellow economics students. In order not to upset Gunnar's mother
they had asked a minister to wed them. But they had invited
neither her nor any other family member to be present.

This was not just an expression of a desire to be different, to
start completely from scratch. For Alva and Gunnar, their parents
represented responsibilities rather than shared intimacy. Alva
longed to escape her own family home, though with some twinges
of guilt at the thought of Rut, who now had to take over almost
all the housework on account of their mother's invalidism. And
Gunnar was increasingly anxious about his father's heavy drink-

ing. In 1918 Sweden had introduced strict rationing of alcoholic beverages to cut back on the widespread alcoholism that was the scourge of families and communities alike; but Carl Adolf got around this by insisting that Gunnar, along with all others on whom he could prevail, use their rationing books as supplements to his own in buying liquor for him. Not knowing how to refuse these requests, and torn by feelings of love and dismay, respect and shame, Gunnar did as he was told. For years he had also tried to sort out his father's debts, carefully concealed from the outside world, in order to help avert an open scandal.

On that fall day fifty-five years later Alva thought that there had been no need to hurt their parents' feelings by shutting them out of the wedding—the first one in each family, to boot. But she and Gunnar had had little interest in shared rituals. For them, getting married had merely formalized bonds far deeper and more unique than any document could ordain or ceremony reflect.

Alva had simply not understood that anyone would feel bitter at having been left out. She had no one to confide in about such questions, no one to go to for advice. When she was young, she had known no wise older woman to turn to for advice or as a role model. Of her inspiring maternal grandmother—the "lily of the valley" who had died before she was born—she had only a photograph; her "charming and misunderstood" paternal grand-mother, Anna Sofia Jansdotter, in whose cottage she had spent many vacations and from whom she had heard so much about the "frequently rotten family life of the old peasant households," had died in 1921.

When Alva described this lack, which she had only gradually come to notice, I thought how different everything had been for me precisely because of her. Of course I wanted to lead my own life just as much as she had, and we often had different views about what I should do. But I could count on her as someone who would give me advice without trying to steer me or exert power over me, and without feeling hurt if I went my own way. Through her I also met other women with energy, courage, and creativity and, more often than not, with broad-gauged humor aimed as much at themselves as at the peculiarities of the world around them: women whose lives I could compare and try out in my imagination, like the Swedish writer Amélie Posse, Margaret Mead, Eleanor Roosevelt, and Elsa Brändström, known as the Angel of Siberia during World War I and its aftermath.

But at her wedding Alva felt no need for models. On the contrary! The world was hers and Gunnar's; life lay before them, and it was going to be a life entirely independent of old, ingrained traditions and disputes. Models were precisely what they believed they could do without.

Alva whisked off a letter thanking Gunnar's parents for the flowers and the telegram that arrived in time for the wedding. Perhaps they might pay a visit soon to the small apartment that she was struggling to put in order? Already it was looking quite beautiful, she added. And she had made an apple pudding good for at least a week's desserts—Gunnar had complained the first few days about there being too little to eat, but no one need fear for his life any longer.

And why should they not succeed on their own in this new life? Their first two years in Stockholm, before the marriage, had already seemed to combine all that they wanted to do together. Gunnar studied law and did research. Alva took courses in subjects that had long appealed to her—the history of religion, the history of literature, and Nordic languages—"with intense interest and excellent results." During the first term she attended lectures on Rousseau and the following spring she signed up to study Strindberg's novels and short stories.

At first Alva had hoped to become a *själasörjare*—a spiritual guide for souls in distress—by studying psychiatry. But she had to give up such plans once she realized that no outside agency would pay for many long years of medical school for a girl who "was only going to get married"; and she knew that she could not ask her parents to help her carry such a burden after the expenses they had had to incur since her gymnasium years. Still, the essential thing for her, after all, had been to come to the university, and in this she had succeeded. If someone asked her how she was going to use her studies, she would answer that she hoped to be able to work as a librarian. But inwardly she was still unsure about what direction her working life would take.

Meanwhile, she found life with Gunnar as stimulating as she could ever have imagined when they first met. In the summer of 1921, before she had moved to Stockholm, the two hiked in the provinces of Värmland and Dalecarlia. Once again they built a raft on which they traveled down the Västerdalälven (West Valley River) just as they had followed the Österdalälven (East Valley River) two years earlier. The following summer they bicycled around the Gustafs region in Dalecarlia, searching the meticulously maintained church registers in the various villages for records of Gunnar's father's ancestors. After tracing these men and women—mostly peasants—back to the early seventeenth century, Alva and Gunnar prepared a volume containing the records for Carl Adolf's fiftieth birthday some years later. Was there a contradiction between their strong interest in family history and their desire to lead their own lives, untrammeled by convention and by the shackles of the past? I think not. Rather, their sense of rootedness in the history and the fundamental values of rural Sweden seems to have given them the security they needed, and in turn the freedom, to shape their own lives as they thought best, with little concern for fashions and conventions.

During their first journeys in Sweden and later while they were studying in Stockholm, they carried on discussions about every conceivable topic in an ongoing dialogue that Alva described as "reaching almost psychoanalytical depths." They found the shared processes of learning, debating, and trying out new ideas so all-absorbing that they took, as yet, little active part in public affairs. One indication of this absorption can be found in the bibliography listing Gunnar's many writings: after three articles published in May 1919, the month before he met Alva, there is no entry until his dissertation, *Price Formation and the Change Factor,* appeared in book form in 1927.

Since they were the only ones among their close friends who had married, they invited the others to their first small apartment once a week for free-ranging discussions that could go on all night. Märta Fredriksson, who was a teacher by then, would sometimes have to go straight from the apartment to her school. Gunnar was the star—original, sardonic, and far-reaching by turns. Alf Johansson, who would later be director of the Swedish Housing Board, was an inspiration, not only at these meetings but in all his contacts with the young economists then coming into their own in Sweden and later known as the Stockholm School. Johansson was like a learned and circumspect English don, guiding them all, never hurried, "his fountain of wisdom ever sprinkling to the delight and edification of those who were there." He in turn remembered Alva as rather quiet and shy at the evening debates, yet the one who somehow held them together and made them productive.

Their foreign trips during these early years, to Weimar Germany, England, the United States, and Geneva, were even more exhilarating than they could have hoped; Gunnar would often describe how they had relished sitting in libraries like the Deutsche Bücherei in Kiel or the British Museum reading room in London and how close they felt to thinkers like Hobbes, Mill, Ricardo, and Sidgwick. In the works of such thinkers they found the same excitement about ideas and the broad perspectives that they themselves experienced; they felt as if they had found true kindred spirits. They explored neo-Darwinists and utopian socialists, absorbed the Enlightenment philosophers' undogmatically critical attitude, and admired the collaboration in research and advocacy of Sidney and Beatrice Webb and like-minded couples. They believed wholeheartedly in the power of science to illuminate human problems so clearly that all would come to see the self-evidence of the reforms they regarded as necessary. Progress toward these reforms seemed within reach, to them as to so many others during what Gunnar called the "lucid interval" between the end of the Great War and the series of domestic and international crises initiated by the stock market crash in 1929.

In the spring of 1925 the two traveled for the first time to England, living carefully on modest stipends that they managed to stretch over six months. Alva, twenty-three and newly married, wrote home with delight as she discovered a culture that until then she had known only through books. But England also gave them their first experience of discrimination. In an interview held in New Delhi fifty years later, Alva spoke of their friendship with several Indian students in London: "All of us foreigners had to stick together because the British did not care much for us." One young man in particular, a nephew of the poet Rabindranath Tagore, took them to visit an Indian restaurant for the first time. He told them of the bitterness so many Indians felt at being looked down on by the British,

> and that was the first inkling I had of racial discrimination. In Sweden, I had never seen or heard or understood anything of it. So that was an eye-opener. If the British could look down upon a people that had brought forth a man like Tagore, I really could not take it.

For a change of scene, they wandered with knapsacks along rivers and in mountains in England. Alva's dialogue with Gunnar continued about everything they experienced. Later they were to describe this dialogue as "a natural form for us, after having, for several decades, worked out almost all our thoughts in joint discussions." For Alva, the dialogue fulfilled a need that no one else would ever be able to satisfy. She relished what she saw as Gunnar's capacity to grasp and explore in minutes what others would painstakingly plod through, his way of playing with ideas and juxtaposing them in novel ways, his soaring to unexpected generalizations and then lighting on particulars with luminous perception. Thirty years later she wrote to Gunnar from India that, however deeply she experienced its gripping culture and however happy she was with her work and her friends, she longed to have "you with your intellectually keen ear always here for the eternal commentaries."

They were intimate friends physically as well. Alva never hated men and was not afraid of sexuality. Apart from those women who were abandoned sexually, like Gunnar's mother, she had observed two ways of rejecting close relations with men: that of the married, frigid women who, like her own mother, feared endless pregnancies and the risk of dying in childbirth like "the lily of the valley"; and that of women who rejected all men, all traditional femininity. Alva wanted to live with a man and longed, if still only in a rather abstract manner, for children. Three children, she had concluded, seemed an ideal number. And by means of contraceptives, she would be free of her mother's fear of sexuality: she would bear children only when she and Gunnar were ready for them.

As a young girl, Alva had been taken with the views of the Swedish writer and social reformer Ellen Key and had come to see contraceptives—then still outlawed and regarded as indecent to the point of being unmentionable—as necessary for the liberation of women and children. As soon as she came to Stockholm she quietly looked up more works on the forbidden topic of family planning in the Royal Library. By such means she, along with increasing numbers of other women, hoped to avoid the slavery that came with ceaseless pregnancies and to ensure that children would be desired and warmly welcomed from the beginning.

In books that found a wide audience throughout Europe and in America, Ellen Key had spoken out for the rights of women, for a freer, fuller conception of spiritual and erotic love, and for making the option of divorce lawful in marriages where such love was no longer possible. In a book entitled *The Century of the Child,* published in 1900, she had set forth a philosophy of practical education that drew on Rousseau and Comte and taken a strong stance against the common forms of brutality toward children that many still thought "character-building."

But Key was also at odds with many feminists of the period about the direction women should take once they had won the freedoms that she advocated. Echoing prevailing stereotypes about masculinity and femininity, she insisted that women's only true fulfillment lay in motherhood. To be sure, she saw women as strong rather than as the weak, sentimental souls idealized at the time, but they were nevertheless utterly different from men. Women, she repeatedly argued, should not try to imitate men in occupations for which they were not suited by nature, nor should they shortchange their children by working outside the home.

Social reforms would make it possible for even the poorest women to devote themselves to their children instead of having to toil in factories or other people's homes. And those women who, like Key herself, were childless should exert their maternal instincts and their feminine talents in behalf of oppressed and needy persons and of peace among nations. Only at the end of her life, during World War I, did the fierce aggressiveness of women in the warring nations shake Key's faith in women's special talent for peacemaking, and this realization in turn brought her around to the view that women should be free in their choice of occupation.

Although Alva would increasingly question the conventional view of masculinity and femininity underlying Key's earlier prescriptions for women, she had not yet thought this issue through early in her marriage. She took for granted that home life and household belonged to the realm of femininity, along with the love for art, theater, beauty, stylish clothes, good food—all that she had seen in her own family as her mother's domain. Even as she went on to work out in her own life a far less stereotyped view of how both men and women might combine freedom with intimacy, she would hold fast to those elements of traditional femininity that she had been taught to value as a child. She would always love beautiful clothes, elegantly tailored and combining striking colors—an inclination that she would later call, only half in jest, her "original sin." And she relished designing everything from her own hats to interiors and garden plots.

Alva wanted to build her marriage on a "foundation of friendship," as she later wrote. The marriages made at the turn of the century—the generation of her and Gunnar's parents— seemed to her especially hypocritical and riven by conflict. The traditional farming life, which had once given women a central role to play, was on the way out, and the new marriages, in which man and wife shared all as friends, were still rare.

But though it seemed possible to combine two such intense and wide-ranging lives as hers and Gunnar's before their marriage and during the first years thereafter, there were even then the beginnings of genuine problems—problems that Alva sought to trace back to their student years as we sat with our cups of cocoa in the Copper Tent. Why, to begin with, had she been so subservient with Gunnar? Why did it seem natural, she later asked in a letter, to give up so much that was her own? Especially with Gunnar,

> toward whom I now see how ludicrously obedient I was. Franciscus [the nickname for Gunnar's close friend, Fritz Thorén, later a novelist] did not like to see girls wearing their student caps; therefore I did not put mine on, even though it was in reality for me such a proud triumph to have conquered it—with my own power.

And before their marriage, when Gunnar wanted to invite his student friends to his rented rooms for the evening, he asked Alva to come over to prepare the food. Since Franciscus insisted that only men should be present at such gatherings, grumbling that this had always been the case in the past, Gunnar took for granted that she would remain in the kitchen or leave when the men began to eat. Once again, she later asked herself: Why had she gone along with it all so humbly? She had been willing to make any sacrifice, especially since she knew that Gunnar accepted her as an intellectual equal from the start. It hardly seemed to matter, at first, that neither he nor anyone else fully honored that equality in practice.

Even when Gunnar made no overt demands on her she was silent when it came to her own needs. In spite of their long talks there was much that she did not bring up with him, being too proud to admit a need or hurt that he did not himself perceive. If he did not see how things should be, she felt it was better to wait rather than to state an ultimatum or to insist on her rights. But her silence also resulted from her own belief that his needs, his career, his strong personality had to come first.

For of course *his* position had already been staked out in this uncertain balance that she hoped to maintain—the balance between adventure and domestic happiness, between freedom and chosen bonds. For him the choices were clear. Though his moods could swing from the grandest visions for his work to despair when he felt stymied, he never doubted its overriding importance in his life. He knew that Alva shared his dedication to achieving all that he hoped for, but the balancing he left entirely to her. As he saw it, he always came first. To be sure, he loved her, admired her immensely, and fully accepted her as his intellectual equal. Unlike the great majority of men at the time, he had every intention of encouraging her career. But he did not expect this to entail any sacrifices on his part. He took for granted her subservience and with it men's dominance in general. In his own family, his mother and sisters had had to make sacrifices to support his studies and had waited on him and cleaned his quarters as he sat studying in the family's best rooms; that Alva should continue to help him after their marriage and do all the housework seemed to him only natural. At times her letters to him, when he was away from home, express fatigue and impatience:

> And I *must* be right when I refuse to call homemaking my life's challenge! . . . I want to be something that only I can be, and not feel forced to compete with all who perform a job that I never thought to choose.

There is no hint in any of these letters, however, that Gunnar might share some of the burden. Alva appears to have accepted his attitude as typically masculine, seeing herself as more feminine and understanding. In her inexperience, she may have sought sanctuary in such thoughts about femininity to avoid admitting that the problems with Gunnar were deeper still: it was more than a matter of gender. For Gunnar not only accepted the advantages accorded to men; he saw himself as unique. He knew his extraordinary intellectual force and saw vast and challenging tasks before him; as a result, he demanded all the practical help he could get and felt mild contempt for the many who did not have his gifts.

Against Alva's egalitarian ideals, nourished by her father and by her readings and the debates in the youth groups to which she had belonged in her teens, stood Gunnar's Nietzschean faith in himself as different. He saw his talent as releasing him from ordinary norms of responsibility toward others. "I am asocial," he used to proclaim with satisfaction. And his eyes glittered teasingly whenever he explained that he, unlike Alva, was not a good person: his work would be his greatness; he did not need, as a result, to probe his conscience when it came to humane concern or goodwill.

Some ten years later their friend, the poet Gunhild Tegen gave them a poem she had written about this polarity between the two of them. Its portrayal of their relationship was as frightening as it was sentimental. And even though Alva came to realize the dangers in such an attitude toward the world, Gunnar held fast to it: he proudly sent me a copy of the poem as late as 1962. At the time I replied that I thought the poem inspired more laughter than solemnity; but now, whenever I look at it, the laughter sticks in my throat.

> *As a wild young lion*
> *I went out into my morning*
> *to play and strike.*
> *Nothing was holy or great to me*
> *for I felt my strength*
> *greater than that of others.*
> *As the lion despises the antelopes,*
> *the timid gazelles,*
> *the striped little zebras,*
> *which with rapid hooves speed away from his roaring—*
> *so I saw human beings*
> *little*
> *frightened*
> *inferior—*
> *and my pride was immense.*
>
> *Then I met you.*
> *Clear, wise, strong, and still.*
> *All that I lacked you possessed.*
> *Had I lacked anything?*
> *The depth of uncertainty under my proud roaring*
> *opened up*

like a chasm in the mountains
but there you stood
and gave me your hand
and your belief in me
threw a bridge over the depth.
. . . .
He whom a god loves
or a woman like you
he is invincible. . . .

The difficulties for a woman who believes herself chosen to accompany and assist such an "invincible" man to carry out his work in life are staggering—especially when one remembers that Alva herself had high hopes for what she wanted to experience and achieve. The desire to achieve great things in the world was risky enough for a woman who did not want to give up all chances to have a family. But to be married, in addition, to a brilliant, ambitious man can create the allure of another ideal—the model of the calmly self-sacrificing and angelic being who sees to it that everyday details do not burden such a man. Among professors' wives of that period, Alva met many who had chosen or been pressed to accept that role and almost no one who shared her thirst for simultaneous independence.

During the first years, she barely discerned these conflicts with Gunnar, but of course they did not disappear after the wedding. Her subservience and silence concerning her own needs continued, in spite of all her radical discussions with him about everything else, all the joy over shared discoveries, all the travels, all the plans. So struck was she by the richness of his intellect and his sweeping worldview that she accepted and even nourished his urge—increasingly insatiable with the passage of time—to be the center of attention. She was convinced that he was a genius. For herself she had no such pretensions. Just as she was always second best in school, so she took second place within the marriage. If she could help such a man, be his "muse" as she often said, it seemed to her a duty, especially as he had such great need of guidance, practical help, and inspiration.

It was Alva who had given Gunnar hope when, in 1923, he

encountered the first great crisis in his career: receiving his degree
in law and feeling, as he later put it, "intellectually crushed and
deeply depressed." His earlier notion that studying law would
give him a grasp of how society functioned now seemed preposterous: he cringed at the thought of a lifetime of lawyering
founded on such a misperception. It was Alva who then surprised
him by suggesting that he make an about-turn and study economics—a subject that might enable him to observe the workings of
society in a more rigorous, perhaps even scientific way.

Gunnar would always remember how she had struggled home
one day with heavy tomes by the brilliant, world-renowned Swedish economist Gustav Cassel. From then on there was no stopping
him. His earliest works, prepared during the seven years that
followed, brought him into the first rank of world economists; as
the economic historian Mark Blaug wrote, their caliber was such
as to merit the Nobel Prize in economics even if he had done
nothing more. His intelligence was like a powerful as well as
sensitive instrument that could be turned in different directions.
But I believe that it was Alva's concern for practical social issues
and for the unjust conditions under which so many people lived
that reinforced his scientific acumen and gave him material for
much of his research.

For Gunnar, these years brought what he later called "just
the right combination of the hardest toil and pure creative joy."
It was as natural for him to ask Alva to help him in every way
she could as for her to accede. Whenever they traveled, she assisted
him with languages and library work; when they returned home,
he needed her help in sorting out all the material he had brought
back. She spent most of the year 1926 typing and going over his
doctoral dissertation so that it could be ready the following spring.
She knew how much he needed her help in order to maintain his
momentum and no doubt also realized that she was sharpening
her own analytical and creative skills in the process.

Inwardly, however, Alva felt increasingly miserable and torn.
Gunnar grew so absorbed in his work that it was only by sharing
in it that she could be close to him. Thirty years later, when he
came across one of her diaries from that period, he wrote to her

how he understood, for the first time, her sense of emptiness and solitude—"when I did the thesis and you were so unhappy." Belatedly, he wrote, he recognized how his intense drive to forge ahead had intensified his selfishness even as it generated extraordinary creative energy. In turn, he had tried to encourage both drive and self-assertion in her to compensate for all that he could not give her of himself.

Alva still had no comparable focus for her own interests with which to counterbalance Gunnar's energy and intense concentration. Sometimes she felt as if she lived with distracting chores hanging over her day in and day out. And it was difficult to make their meager income suffice. They could splurge, at times, on books and pastries and small presents; but her little black notebooks from the early years often mention loans and pawn tickets. "Got the watch back from the pawnbroker's: 26 crowns," reads an entry in March 1923. The same watch seems to have made the trip to and from the pawnbroker's with some regularity that year. As late as May 1927 an entry reads "Broke—sandwich dinner."

Both she and Gunnar were marked for life by having to scrimp and carry debts in their youth and by their problems in helping Gunnar's father avoid open bankruptcy. Alva warned me, shortly after my own marriage, not to let life be destroyed by such anxieties. Nothing could be more dangerous in life, she wrote, than always to have a guilty conscience:

> It reminds me of a situation from our youth. We struggled and typed and cleaned house—and lived with the old family furniture. Didn't want to use up more than we earned (I a small stipend, Gunnar 500 a month from a Rockefeller fund). But a few months before the public defense of his doctoral dissertation, Erik Lindahl came and *forced* upon us 300 crowns as a debt to the future, claiming that it was *now* that Gunnar needed a new bed. So we bought a comfortable couch—that we could not at all "afford." Now, on the other hand, when the money is there, a new bed can hardly perform such miracles!

Alva's earliest hopes of becoming pregnant had been broken in April 1926 by a miscarriage. It had been a grueling experience. Like so many other women, she experienced first the dizzying fear of losing the baby, then each ominous sign of danger, and in the end a desolate certainty that all was lost, an emptiness without bounds, and doubts that she would ever be able to bring a child into the world. And when Alva and Gunnar sought help from a doctor because of her great loss of blood, he threw them out, certain that she was suffering the aftereffects of an abortion.

The following year, when Alva at last succeeded in carrying a pregnancy to term, she kept her condition a secret from the family as long as she could. Of course her mother, her colleagues and the more sharp-eyed among her friends noticed that she was pregnant, and Alva shared all secrets with Rut throughout her life. But no other relatives were let in on this great new reality in her life. If Gunnar's sisters stopped by to visit, she went to bed and claimed to be ill.

About this time in her life, I now wish that I could ask Alva more, request further explanations. To be sure, women were much more discreet at that time when it came to pregnancy. But why did she conceal her condition from the family in particular? It is possible that the earlier miscarriage led her to wish to guard against all who would otherwise come running with good advice and warnings, perhaps begin to knit or sew for the baby in whose arrival she did not yet quite dare to believe. I remember how she wrote to me when I was expecting my own first child, also after a miscarriage suffered through in anguish, that it was not worth "awakening joy in advance in too many hearts." But when Jan was finally born, in July 1927, joy and tenderness won out as she lay in the hospital and saw him next to her. She then began a new diary as follows:

Darling Jan, beloved child, you wonderful little life, Gunnar's and mine, sacredly in common and yet a little self of your own, drawing your own dear, dear breaths—thank Goodness for you!

She was proud and happy but at the same time conscious of the great responsibility she had now assumed. And in spite of having helped her mother and Rut take care of Stig she felt uncertain and alone in this period, which is hard for most new mothers. Jan was a demanding, colicky baby who required less sleep than most. After five days in the hospital, she noted in her diary with mingled concern and pride: "Has kicked his heels bloody. A forceful little fellow."

A baby nurse, Frida, took care of Jan for a week after he and Alva came home from the hospital. "After that, dress rehearsal for Gunnar and me—we thought the kid would never survive it." A few days later they left with a sigh of relief for the farm where Gunnar's family stood ready to admire Jan and help take care of him. Carl Adolf did not disguise his delight that the firstborn child in this new family should have turned out to be a boy—occupying the place of honor that both he and Gunnar had enjoyed in their own families. And Sofie bustled about arranging for the baptism to be carried out in the parlor.

That fall Gunnar took over the teaching duties of Gustav Cassel at the University of Stockholm, having earned highest academic honors the previous spring with a dissertation on the theory of price formation that drew on Cassel's teachings and also broke new ground. Cassel had gone to Geneva to attend a world economic conference on the fate of the gold standard and was pleased to be able to further the career of a scholar for whom he had exceptionally high hopes. By then the two were also close friends. In Gunnar's mind, Cassel was a thoroughgoing and most admirable rationalist. Having started his scholarly career with radical views on economic and social issues, he had come to adopt mainstream, often conservative stances that Gunnar would increasingly challenge, but these differences never stood in the way of their mutual esteem.

For Gunnar, the brilliant, charismatic, warmhearted Cassel was both the older brother he had never had and a father figure whom he could truly honor and respect. Alva and Gunnar felt as welcome in the Cassel home as if they had grown up there. And the letters that Gunnar wrote to Cassel on his trips abroad speak

Lowa Reimer, Alva's mother   *Albert Reimer, Alva's father*

ABOVE CENTER: *Anna Sofia Jonsson,*
"the lily of the valley," Alva's
grandmother

Carl Adolf Pettersson, Gunnar's
father

Anna Sofia (Sofie) Pettersson, Gun-
nar's mother

Rut, Maj, Alva and Folke Reimer around 1910. The youngest child, Stig, was not yet born.

Alva with Rut and Folke, the "gold dumpling"

Alva with her mother and father

Alva at 15, in her confirmation dress.

*Alva, Gunnar, Gösta
Lundborg, and a goat
in June, 1919*

*Gunnar and Gösta on
their raft. Alva's
"throne" can be seen in
the middle.*

*Gunnar, Alva, Sven Tisell and Gösta
Lundborg*

Newly wed, 1924

Gunnar, around 1928

Alva, around 1928

Alva, 1932

Alva, 1935

Going to America, 1938 (photo: Dagens Nyheter, *Stockholm)*

far more freely and vividly about all that he was thinking and planning than any sent to his own relatives. Cassel, in turn, spoke of Gunnar as a spiritual son. After Cassel's death in 1945, his daughter Inga wrote to Gunnar that at times she felt Gunnar meant even more than a son to her father. She remembered Cassel's saying with humility that he had done the "static" part of the new economics; now it was up to Gunnar to "contribute the dynamic parts."

Gunnar could also rebel against Cassel as he never dared to against his own father. Cassel, along with Knut Wicksell, Eli Heckscher, and other Swedish economists, was by then renowned throughout the world. "It was a hard crust of ability and authority to break through," Gunnar later wrote, "both tempting and deterring to anybody trying to sprout into independent thinking." Gunnar and a younger group of scholars that included Erik Lindahl, Bertil Ohlin, and Dag Hammarskjöld would break through that crust decisively in the late twenties and thirties. Gunnar had a ready-made platform for doing so as soon as he took over Cassel's lecturing duties. Immediately he set about clearing away the "metaphysical cobwebs" from economics as it was then taught, criticizing the prevailing laissez-faire doctrine in economic theory as based on unexamined premises. In so doing, he clashed especially sharply with the conservative Eli Heckscher. He aimed to teach the history of economics in such a way as to show how the uncritical recourse to concepts such as "nature," "value," "utility," and "welfare" allowed economists to smuggle in their own unexamined biases and value judgments in the guise of scientific objectivity.

Alva, meanwhile, was at home with Jan, increasingly nervous and exhausted. She took poorly to his frequent wakefulness at night and to his crying, especially since this irritated Gunnar, making him feel protective toward Alva and even jealous. He wanted to be at the center of her world and found everyone else's demands on her time invasive. Looking back, she remembered feeling so locked in that she wanted to scratch the walls. While she continued to read for a higher degree in psychology and began to plan a dissertation, her time was no longer her own. Until then

she had always been able to come and go with a freedom from
guilt that she would not recapture for a long time. Now she felt
her ideals clash. She had hoped to be able to give herself wholeheartedly both to work and to family life. But at the level of
intensity and dedication that she wanted to devote to each, the
two roles seemed at odds—the more so because of Gunnar, in
whose eyes the baby threatened the all-absorbing fellowship in
love and work that he and Alva had shared up to then.

Alva responded in part by idealizing her future relationship
with Jan. She hoped that it would be one of true friendship
between equals that would allow them to avoid the conventional
parent-child roles founded on authority. And she could not help
wishing that Jan, unlike Gunnar, would fully share her interests
in art and poetry. Perhaps he might even someday play the violin?
When he was one and a half years old, she bought a book of
poetry by the young Swedish poet Arthur Lundquist for herself,
trying to imagine, as a syrupy inscription explains on the flyleaf,
what Jan would like to give her for Christmas. It conveys
her maternal pride in him and her overweening hopes for their
relationship:

> I know his goodwill, his good mind, and our good partnership,
> freed from all respect and obedience, from this false position
> of subservience. Just such a bright little son as mine would
> come upon the idea of giving his "Avva-mother" this book of
> poetry.

When Jan was almost two years old, a chance arose for both
Alva and Gunnar to spend a year in the United States as Rockefeller Fellows. They had applied successfully for funds for separate
projects. Though it was extremely rare that a husband and wife
were thus funded together, each had been promised $750 for the
academic year 1929–30. Alva's project focused on the methodology of social psychology in the United States; Gunnar's on
methodology in economics and the social sciences, again in the
United States.

The offer came as a momentous opportunity. Nearly every

Swedish family had relatives who, like Gunnar's uncle Albert, had emigrated to America when poverty at home became too pressing. All knew about the freedom and the opportunities that beckoned on the other side of the Atlantic, but also about the dangers of the ocean voyage, the hardships in finding a place to settle, and the adventures in building a new life that letters home recounted over the years in more and more broken Swedish. And now—that by contrast Alva and Gunnar should be offered free passage across the Atlantic and scholarships to study and travel and write in the United States—such a chance seemed to them nearly miraculous.

They never had a thought of refusing. But in deciding to go, they confronted their first truly rending conflict. What should they do with Jan? Their decision to leave him at home with Gunnar's parents was something Alva always regretted as a great mistake. She did not then know what psychologists have stressed since: the importance of the bond between parent and child in the sensitive two-year-old period when self-confidence and trust in the outside world are established. But she must surely have wondered whether going away for over a year might not injure their relationship with Jan. Meanwhile, both their families as well as Jan's pediatrician advised her to take advantage of the occasion to travel. All were sure that living in the countryside would be safer and healthier for Jan than knocking about in foreign lands. Alva could not help longing to be free once again to pursue her studies. And Gunnar pressed her more and more. He was eager to have her all to himself again and to revive the unchallenged intimacy of their student days.

Alva decided then, as she did so many times later in life, to go with Gunnar. They took Jan to live with Gunnar's parents on Gesta farm. Alva's parents lived not far away; in 1925 Albert had finally bought his own farm nearby in Kvicksta, and Jan was equally welcome there. Rut had married a farmer, Elon Westerberg, and their daughter, Jan's first cousin Ulla, was born the same year as Jan. Folke and Stig were by then twenty-three and seventeen years old, lighthearted uncles who enjoyed inviting Jan home to the farm that their father still hoped they would come to enjoy running. In farm families such as Alva's and Gunnar's, shared child care was common; everyone took for granted that children were better off in the country than in the city or traveling around.

Having arranged for Jan, Alva and Gunnar went first to London for three months to finish off existing writing projects and to prepare for their trip across the Atlantic. They left Sweden at the beginning of June, reaching London a week later. Alva's letters home describe their bliss in being able to sit undisturbed in the reading room of the British Museum and do research to their hearts' content, but they also convey her anxious balancing of the pros and cons of having left Jan behind. "We couldn't have offered him as happy an existence, even if we had stayed at home for his sake," she wrote in a letter to Gustav Cassel's wife, Johanna, at the end of July, describing Jan's joy in the wide-open spaces and the closeness to nature that he could never experience in the city. But in the same breath she acknowledged how deeply torn and worried she felt: even her listing of all the reasons why Jan was bound to thrive in the country sounds defensive.

To her friends Märta and Andreas, who had by then decided to marry, she wrote even more achingly at the end of August. She could not understand, she said, how she had had the courage to leave Jan. She consoled herself, she added, with the thought that Jan's happiness, so glowingly described in letters from Sofie, meant that the hardship fell solely on her. Crossed out, before she chose the word *hardship,* is another: *punishment.*

Lowa, meanwhile, told all who would listen that perhaps Alva and Gunnar ought never to have had a child, so much did their careers seem to matter to them. Alva compensated for her guilt and for her longing to be with Jan by sewing clothes to send home to him along with torrents of postcards, and by asking her mother-in-law to keep a diary about every detail of his development. Sofie, in response, wrote wonderfully warm, long letters, sometimes giving hour-by-hour accounts of Jan's doings and sayings. She was sorry for Alva and Gunnar, she wrote, that they could not see him grow and change: "But that's how life is—to get one thing, you have to forsake the other."

In London, Gunnar worked on turning his lectures on the

concepts of value and utility into a book. He had hoped to do so before leaving for the United States, but the work turned out to require more research and led to far profounder and more critical reflection on the history of economics than he had imagined at the outset. The book that resulted became a classic—*The Political Element in the Development of Economic Theory,* published in 1930. Alva, meanwhile, wrote an evaluative survey of the literature in her article "Emotional Factors in Education" and began revising the critical study of Freud's *Interpretation of Dreams* that she was planning to submit as a dissertation when she returned to Sweden.

Both she and Gunnar felt that, because of the greater availability of books at the British Museum, three months there allowed them to do as much work as they did in a year in Sweden. They hoped their productivity in London would give them greater leisure to allow their curiosity and sense of discovery free play once they reached the United States. And they delighted in being alone together, as they had been on so many earlier trips. This time there was no competition from Gunnar's absorption in his thesis or from Alva's sense of duty toward Jan. Even before they began concentrating on their projects in earnest they saw new ways in which they could work together. From England Alva wrote to Gunnar's sister Elsa:

> Gunnar's and my greatest joy is the new light that our interests shed on our plans for the future. For strangely enough our studies are coming closer and closer to one another's interests. And we have very amusing plans for joint work.

It was nevertheless with some trepidation that they thought about the various universities they had been invited to visit in the course of their stay in America. About the country itself they felt they knew a great deal from novels, travel accounts, and social and economic history. But they did not know how the education offered in American universities might differ from that in the rigidly formalized universities of Uppsala and Stockholm, where brilliant teaching and research in certain fields such as economics and Oriental studies contrasted with dull, dogmatic backwardness in too many others. They had come across an alarming prospect in reading Upton Sinclair's extended diatribe *The Goose-Step: A Study of American Education*. It expounded the view that Americans had died in vain in the Great War since the worst of German autocracy had been transplanted in American colleges and universities for the purpose of capitalistic exploitation:

> Suppose I were to tell you that this educational machine has been stolen? That a bandit crew have got hold of it and have set it to work, not for your benefit, nor the benefit of your sons and daughters, but for ends very far from these? That our six hundred thousand young people are being taught, deliberately and of set purpose, not wisdom but folly, not justice but greed, not freedom but slavery, not love but hate?
>
> . . . see if I am not right in my contention that what we did, when we thought we were banishing the Goose-step from the world, was to bring it to our own land, and put ourselves under its sway—our thinking, and, more dreadful yet, the teaching of our younger generation.

Sinclair was no Rousseau when it came to writing about the evils of formal education; his indictments were so self-indulgent and exaggerated that they put readers on guard from the outset. Even Alva and Gunnar, though they knew little about American universities, decided that they had to take the book's claims with a grain of salt until they could judge for themselves. Their greatest personal worry was that Sinclair seemed to indicate that students and professors who spoke out too freely could be dismissed or "let out," as he put it. In Sweden it had never even occurred to Gunnar that the political views he expressed could have the slightest influence on his career. Alva could not help wondering how he would take to an oppressive intellectual climate given his habits of free-wheeling debate and mercilessly irreverent joking.

6

America

❖ ❖ ❖ ❖

*A*lva *and Gunnar arrived in New York* in mid-October
1929, only weeks before the stock market crash. They were welcomed at Columbia University with nearly overwhelming cor-
diality. Far from having to be cautious about expressing their own
views, as they had feared after reading Sinclair's *The Goose-Step,*
they found a more open and exhilarating intellectual climate than
they had ever known. In his first letter to Gustav Cassel, Gunnar
wrote that people were spoiling them both: there seemed to be
no limits to the kindness and encouragement they encountered.

Alva's host was the sociologist Robert Lynd, author, with his
wife Helen, of *Middletown,* the celebrated study of a midwestern
American community. He began by providing her with an office
at the Social Science Research Council, where he and a number
of colleagues were also located. Having set out with the aim of
studying the methods in American social psychology research, she
had already concluded that the most abundant research at the
time was in child psychology. She therefore decided to focus on
recent work in child development and in social work with children. Lynd encouraged her in this effort and helped her to work
out plans for her year of study, setting up trips for her to universities, nursery schools, and child development institutes across the
country.

Up to then, no academic adviser had ever conveyed to Alva
anything like Lynd's confidence that what she was planning to
study was worthwhile. To Alva, he was "life-giving as a friend."

He encouraged her to press forward with her own writing while
pursuing her research, and his letters of introduction opened doors
for her wherever she went.

Gunnar was equally pleased with the arrangements made for
him. Professor Edwin Seligman, nearing seventy and a leader in
the field of public finance, took him under his wing. "Seligman is
delightful," Gunnar wrote to Cassel. "He sees to it that our
existence is ideal in every way." Seligman, whose writings had
formed the basis for America's income tax law of 1913, was as
interested as his colleagues in what this young emissary from
Sweden had to offer: "I am to meet everybody and everybody
wants to do things for me. Swedish scholarship must be respected
abroad; otherwise I don't understand why they should all be so
interested to hear whatever foolishness I have to convey about
this or that."

When the crash came, on October 29, 1929, Gunnar and
Alva were unprepared at first to understand its full import. Even
as the crisis deepened and the country's economy slid closer to
collapse, they puzzled, as newcomers, at the lack of forceful response. They saw banks fail one after another, unemployment
grow as millions lost all their savings, soup kitchens provide food
for long lines of hungry people, and investors and ruined family
providers commit suicide, yet Herbert Hoover's government
seemed powerless to reverse the process. Slogans took the place
of action. Gunnar wrote to Cassel about the campaign designed
to convince Americans of their economy's bright future:

> Prosperity, prosperity, prosperity—the word assaults us
> through loudspeakers and illuminated street signs. One cannot
> travel on the "elevated" without suddenly being confronted
> from the wall by some company chairman assuring one that
> the country's business life is "basically sound." That is the
> catchword.

Gunnar had to agree that the nation might do better if people
could be convinced that all was well. But that would hardly
suffice. In the Hoover government's lame responses to the crash

he saw yet further evidence of the immobilizing power of the doctrine that "a return to normalcy" was bound to come about. He had lectured on that very doctrine the previous spring at the University of Stockholm, criticizing the underlying metaphysical faith in the economic theory of laissez-faire. In so doing, he later wrote, his main concern had been negative: "the need to protest against the intellectual domination of the older generation" in Sweden, Gustav Cassel foremost among them. He had then enlarged the scope of his criticism to encompass much of economic history in *The Political Element in the Development of Economic Theory*. When the book finally appeared in Sweden in 1930, the Great Depression offered the clearest possible demonstration of the risks of government inaction. "*Laissez-faire* had lost because of events, not intellectual criticism."

Alva's and Gunnar's letters to friends often compare what they find optimistic, well intentioned, sometimes naive in American culture to their own more skeptical, tradition-bound European background. Alva was struck, too, by the contrast between the exuberant, liberating atmosphere in America and the pervasive frustration expressed by everyone she met in the face of the nation's crisis. She relished "all this frontier spirit, these marvelous people, the literary geniuses, the freedom of expression," yet wondered how it could be that there seemed to be no way for people to turn their ideas into legislation, "no way for them to stand for something *together*." This recognition made her see Sweden in a new light, feeling "glad we had public railroads and hospitals, which I'd never thought about until I saw the other option." She realized, she later said, that she could work in Sweden in a much more organized way to get reforms accomplished.

It was in the United States that Alva and Gunnar always felt that they had woken up politically. They had been profoundly shaken from the outset by the brutal contrast between millionaires and slum dwellers. Sweden was a poorer and more backward country, yet one in which there had long been greater equality and a sense of shared responsibility, in local communities as well as in the country as a whole, for supporting those in need. To see such great poverty and such injustice toward racial and religious minorities radicalized both of them. Earlier they had been more preoccupied with their research and their plans for the future and above all with one another than with practical efforts to change social conditions at home or abroad. Neither Sweden's widespread unemployment nor the other economic aftershocks following the Great War throughout Europe, nor even the battles for women's suffrage in Sweden and many other nations had engaged their political commitment as did the inequities they encountered in America.

Alva and Gunnar came increasingly to use the word *radical* to describe their desire for fundamental rather than superficial reforms. They resolved to work in the future for change from the ground up, though never by violent means. *Tradition* became a word of rebuke to their ears, representing all that was hidebound and backward-looking and resistant to progress: "the irrational tying down of our beliefs and opinions." They claimed to want to "free us from the power of the dead over our own lives" when it came to social questions, something that they saw as possible only if traditions could be "fixated intellectually, explained, and criticized." They both dated their adoption of this form of radicalism to their year in the United States. Seeing far-reaching practical intervention as necessary to a society's well-being, they rejected as superstitious any economic doctrines invoking some "unseen hand" or "natural harmony" that would set all to rights. For Gunnar, economics could never again be primarily theoretical.

It was a heady experience for them to be so far from their own country and from their families. They felt like newlyweds exploring the world. The distance between all that they were now experiencing and the lives of their families back home seemed immense. Their correspondence with both sets of parents was warm and respectful, but it was in letters to their friends and colleagues, and especially to the Cassels, that they felt freest to set forth their thoughts about all that they were going through. In turn, their own parents wrote them primarily about what was happening at home, knowing how hungry they were for such news, especially about Jan.

Albert alone wrote about world events as well, often asking

their opinion. In a letter of September 29 he recounted that Professor Cassel had spoken to the members of Eskilstuna's Technical Club, criticizing America's protectionism. Others spoke of the possibility of forming a United States of Europe, he added, wondering if they had in mind a customs war with America. He found much foolishness in it all but hoped that it might speed better conditions in the world. His closing words betray both pride in Alva and Gunnar and a wistful sense of the distance between their expanding opportunities and his own limits:

> I hope that you will have a continued happy trip with a good yield from all that you are learning and experiencing, so that you will then be able to help in leading the development. Many times, I am sad that my education is not sufficient for me to be part of the struggle.

During the year in America, Alva and Rut began a correspondence that was to continue most of their lives. Almost all of it has been lost or destroyed. The few letters from Rut that remain from this period give a sense of the familiarity, humor, and intimacy with which they confided in one another. To Rut, Alva's accounts of their journey, beginning with the luxury of their steamer trip to New York, sounded exactly like a novel. And she exclaimed over an entire trunkful of gifts, all wonderfully foreign in design—slippers, towels, napkins, stationery, wallets, stockings, even a necklace of artificial pearls and a small painting—that Alva had bought to send home to the family shortly after arriving in New York. She and Gunnar had to watch their expenses carefully to make their stipends last all year, but she knew how much it would mean to the family, already hard hit by the oncoming Depression, to receive such gifts from the New World.

While at Columbia, Gunnar put the finishing touches to his *Political Element* and tried to absorb as much as he could about American economic theory and research. His first letter to Cassel spoke of his wanting to get a grip on American economic theory and its underlying methods, especially those used by the younger scholars who were so critical of established theory. And Alva, he added, was happily settled in:

> There are two great Europeans here as visiting professors, and strangely enough precisely those with whom Alva most hoped to make contact: Adler from Vienna, the psychologist of individuality, a tremendously learned and amiable gentleman; as a psychologist he is frankly more of an enlightened spiritual guide than an analytic anatomist of souls . . . ; and then Charlotte Bühler, the famous child psychologist, also from Vienna.

The two made a powerful impression on Alva. Charlotte Bühler, whose book *The First Year of Life,* was about to appear in English, had been one of the first Rockefeller Fellows in 1923. Ten years older than Alva, Bühler was the first woman professor with whom Alva had ever studied. She admired Bühler's perceptive, down-to-earth detailing of children's early growth, based on the methods of careful observation of the daily life of children that she had helped to pioneer. Compared to Freud's accounts of psychosexual child development, Bühler's approach was less speculative, less concerned to fit the observations of children into a system; rather, she focused more fully on the practical reality of their lives in all its vivid concreteness.

Alfred Adler appealed to Alva's sense for drama. She knew of the battles between his adherents and those psychoanalysts who had remained loyal to Freud after the two men broke off their close collaboration in 1911. Adler had repudiated Freud's focus on biological and sexual factors in childhood as excessively narrow and instead stressed the role of social and interpersonal factors in the development of character and personal life-style. As a lecturer, his face alternately urbane and pugnacious, he dwelled on topics that seemed to symbolize the breach: sibling rivalry, the inferiority complex, compensatory dynamics, the hated child, masculine protest.

This last concept presented Alva with yet another interpretation of the role of gender. Neurotic individuals, Adler taught, feel to an exaggerated degree the conflict that everyone experiences between girlish passivity, sensitivity, and weakness, on the one hand, and boyish activity and striving for self-gratification on the other. The result is a "masculine protest"—an exaggerated desire for recognition and self-assertion that is especially noticeable in girls since society reinforces the felt inferiority of women. What method had pedagogy offered up to now, he had asked in a 1913 paper, "for reconciling one half of mankind with an unalterable condition which it dislikes?" The answer, he had suggested, was to convince women that they need not see the social disadvantages resulting from sexual differences as unconquerable, but rather as difficulties that other women have known how to battle against. Reform was possible; anatomy need not be destiny. As an outspoken socialist, moreover, Adler advocated putting his new psychological insights into practice more generally in guidance clinics, court rooms, and schools. By making the social milieu, beginning with the family, more responsive to human needs, individuals could be encouraged to overcome whatever handicaps they had started out with rather than react through aggression and maladaptation.

While in America, Alva also came into close contact with two spirited figures in the expanding field of child study: Dorothy Swaine Thomas and W. I. Thomas. Both became lifelong friends of Alva and Gunnar's, later visiting them in Sweden and joining them in demographic studies there. Dorothy Thomas, a year younger than Gunnar, had received her doctoral degree in economics at the London School of Economics and made a name for herself at twenty-six with the publication of *Social Aspects of the Business Cycle.* She had recently published *The Child in America: Behavior Problems and Programs* with W. I. Thomas. With her quick, intuitive grasp of ideas cutting across all disciplinary boundaries and her professionalism, she was an inspiration to Alva, who was more uncertain still of the direction in which to go.

W. I. Thomas, thirty-six years older than Dorothy, was one of the founders of American social science and the author of a monumental study of Polish peasants as well as of *Sex and Society* and *The Unadjusted Girl*. The Thomases, who would not marry until W. I. Thomas divorced his first wife in 1934, at age seventy-one, offered Alva and Gunnar a different model of a couple united in work as well as in everyday living—more cosmopolitan, more given to enjoying the finer things of life, and wittier than any they had known before. They invited Alva to observe the studies that they were conducting at Columbia Teachers College on the behavior of nursery school children.

Alva felt she could draw on all that she was learning, with no need to subordinate herself to any one doctrine or approach. Without responsibilities for Jan, she could also immerse herself in observing American life. She was fascinated to see just how many more women doctors, lawyers, and writers there were in the United States than in Sweden. Later she would recount her amazement, on returning in 1938, to find proportionately fewer American women in these occupations, and still fewer in 1949—the more so since she, inspired by what she had seen in America the first time she visited, had meanwhile been able to help Sweden move steadily in the direction of expanded opportunities for women.

Alva and Gunnar went from New York to Washington for a month and then spent six months traveling around the country to different universities, research institutes, and nursery schools. Their Rockefeller stipends permitted no extravagances; they tried to rent a cheap room and kitchenette wherever they went since it would have been prohibitively expensive to pay for hotel rooms week after week, and they ached at not having the money to buy and send home all the new books that they came across in their separate fields. In March, however, Gunnar was surprised to receive a scholarly prize from the Swedish Academy of Sciences. With the money he bought not only books but also something they had not even dared dream of: a shiny black Oldsmobile in which they traveled from then on, delighting in this unexpected change in their fortunes.

They were entertained almost to the point of exhaustion by colleagues they met wherever they went. After Robert Lynd showed Alva the community of Muncie, Indiana, which he had reported on in *Middletown,* she began to think about doing a study of her own of a provincial Swedish town. "If only I could do it as entertainingly and reliably as Lynd," she wrote in a letter to Gunnar's sister Elsa. The differences between American and European social science had been "magically fruitful" for her:

> I see problems wherever I turn. Have made a long list of future work projects, and have no less than fourteen research tasks waiting. . . . I am mad with the joy of discovery, even though so far it is only problems that I've discovered and not their solutions. But I have come to the point where I have that sense of seeing social science from within and then I know that I am able to continue.

Among Alva's papers I have found a list of such projects in a notebook filled with topics and sketches for future papers and books. The list conveys the high excitement of this twenty-seven-year-old faced with so many tempting paths for inquiry that she hardly knew where to begin. It reads in part:

Experiments with learning; Rorschach tests
Overview of the literature on the best ways to learn
Comparison between school reforms in European countries
Critical review of Rugg's and Piaget's classifications
Comparison of the contents of city and rural newspapers
The psychology of strikes
The magical representation of children
The small Swedish town (like Middletown)
Mental development in early childhood
Advances within social psychology
Industrialization in Sweden, 1860–1925:
    —one part demography, with Gunnar and Boris Tullander
    —one part Gunnar and Alva
The psychology of religion
New professions or schools for women
Social pathology
The politics of education

Alva added, "Later more literary and artistic studies, and especially the most psychological of all art forms: *the drama.*" For now, however, her central focus was on children. She took special interest in the pioneering nursery schools and kindergartens at Yale University and the University of Chicago and in Minnesota and elsewhere that had begun to put into practice the most recent findings in child psychology, as well as in the courses in parenting that were meant to complement the schools. Like Gunnar, she now understood that she no longer wanted to do purely theoretical research. And she saw more clearly that her own study of child development had a double purpose: not only to acquaint her with the most scientifically advanced application of psychological theory, but also, as she admitted in a letter to her friend Märta, to prepare for the difficulties she anticipated in restoring her severed relationship with Jan. She recognized how hard renewing their bond would be. "Perhaps there is no remedy: the boy now has two mothers." But studying child psychology might at least help her not to make needless mistakes in bringing about the transition, she added, as if to reassure herself.

For these studies Alva gathered all her courage to ask for and conduct interviews with Charlotte Bühler, Arnold Gesell, Florence Goodenough, Frances Ilg, Dorothy Thomas, and others who did observational studies of children. With Thomas and those she knew well, the encounters were pure pleasure; with the others, she admitted that she had to steel herself to achieve what she saw as a brash American knack for "making contacts." She was especially interested in learning about children's social roles and their development in freedom—what she called "the maximal development of the personality."

From the scholars with whom she talked she learned to focus in a new way on seeing each child as an individual within its own environment and as having what Adler called its own life-style and constellation of needs. She saw the dangers of raising babies and small children in as antiseptic and severe a manner as her mother had believed necessary, and of denying them tenderness out of fear of spoiling them:

This year of studies . . . led to my pioneering the pedagogy
that *liberated* the child from the pediatricians' straitjacket—
"feed them only after four hours," "let them cry," "never pick
them up"—into which [Swedish] pediatricians . . . had forced
mothers, including myself.

As the Norwegian ship *Nordstjernan* (North Star) brought
Alva and Gunnar back home from their year in America in the
company of emigrants returning to the "old country," Alva made
plans for publicizing these new ideas in Scandinavia. To be sure,
she would continue to urge regularity when it came to the sleep
and feeding of small children; otherwise, she was certain, the
conflicts over such matters would only make life more difficult
for the entire family. But she now saw clearly that the coercive
rules of pediatricians in Sweden went entirely against her own
battle for freedom as a young girl. It was no wonder that she
returned brimming with a desire for reform. It had become both
a social and a personal priority.

During her stay in America Alva also worked on the dissertation she had started at Uppsala University and revised while in
London: *Sketch of a Critique of Freud's Dream Theory*. (The
degree she was seeking was called "licentiat" and corresponds
approximately to an American doctorate.) Bertil Hammer, her
professor in Sweden, had encouraged her to work on this subject
before she left. During her absence she was saddened to hear that
Hammer had died suddenly. She wondered what would become
of her project without his support. As it turned out, she never
completed this work. In a note on the first page she has written:
"Impossible since Anderberg took over as professor in pedagogy."
Unlike his predecessor, Anderberg thought Freud unworthy of
scholarly attention, as did many in Sweden at the time. While
Alva was away a storm had been brewing over whether Freud
should be awarded a Nobel Prize. For every admirer of his work,
others dismissed it as sensationalistic, unscientific in its reliance
on untestable evidence, even fraudulent. For them, as for Anderberg, Freud was nothing but a charlatan and as such a menace.

Alva submitted another thesis proposal that was also rejected:

she had planned to construct a test scale for practical use with preschool children that would build on Florence Goodenough's tests of Swedish-born children in Minnesota. "But the whole thing was chopped off and I never became 'licentiat.' Professor Anderberg did not permit work with a test series that did not rely on his own scale for children in Southern Sweden aged seven and up."

Once again, therefore, Alva was shut out from continued studies. Once again she felt the rejection bitterly. And she could not help noticing the difference between the warm encouragement she had received in the United States and the narrow-minded repudiation of new ideas that confronted her as soon as she returned to Sweden. But she had no intention of giving up. Instead she decided to pursue her interests in childhood education in more practical ways. As a result, the dissertation about Freud did not matter as much to her as when she had planned it at twenty-six.

This unfinished work is nevertheless of great interest both in its own right and with regard to Alva's lifelong interest in "explanations." She had chosen to consider *The Interpretation of Dreams,* first published in 1900. Of all Freud's writings, it was the one he saw as setting forth and elaborating on the most valuable of all his discoveries: the idea that dreams represent the fulfillment of wishes, most often erotic ones. He had written in the preface to the 1911 edition that "insight such as this falls to one's lot but once in a lifetime."

Alva's critique shows her admiration for Freud's theory of dreams as a brilliant construction and for "its creator's magnificent imaginative force and his scientific exaltation." Even his exaggerations, she wrote, flowed from the same source of personal power. She saw much for psychologists to learn from him but warned at the same time that the "profoundly unscientific trends" among Freud's followers would lead to fanaticism and sterility rather than to greater insight if psychoanalysis did not meet standard scientific demands for coherence and empirical verification.

Alva's sense of all that is subtle, at times unfathomable, in dreams sharpened her critique of what she took to be Freud's often simplistic and unprovable interpretations. She found the method of association to be defective and thought that the doctrine of symbols stood on shaky ground when it came to evidence. Freud himself had expressed his disdain for the "dreambooks" popular in his time as during so many centuries before. He knew that he was risking "guilt by association" with charlatanism by indicating that certain symbols in dreams had widespread, possibly even universal interpretations. One can sense Alva's impatience with Freud's speculations about some of these interpretations—such as, for instance, "wood" as a dream symbol for "woman":

> Perhaps the most drastic example of this dilettantish comparative linguistics is provided by his etymological exploring of the symbol wood = woman. He claims that the German word *Holz* comes from a Greek word *hule,* which means materia (Latin). This word, in turn, is part of the name Madeira, for the Portuguese word madeira = wood. The Latin word *materia* is "naturally" derived from *mater*–mother–woman. Therefore: if we dream about wood, for instance a table or a table that has been set or even a tray that has been set, it is a symbol for "woman."

Through her criticism of this simplistic symbolism, Alva anticipated Freud's own move away from archetypes and symbols during the decade to come toward interpreting people's dreams as much more closely linked to their personal situations. But while she could look critically at Freud's teachings and never had the slightest temptation to subordinate herself to his or any other orthodoxy, she always retained her strong interest in psychoanalysis. In teaching child psychology later on, she frequently referred to his views of human development and child sexuality, seeing them as supportive of views set forth in the flourishing child study movement of the 1930s rather than as at war with those views.

The return to Sweden brought what Alva and Gunnar felt was a sunny and undisturbed reunion with Jan, who was astonishingly grown, in their eyes, since they had left him over a year earlier, then not quite two years old. The summer allowed them what they saw as a needed rest from the bombardment with new ideas, new friendships, new experiences abroad. Both sensed that they could not simply take up where they had left off. They needed time to think through all that they had learned and to chart a new course, incorporating the changes the year had brought for them both.

They were therefore delighted to accept an invitation to Gunnar to serve as assistant professor at the graduate Institute for International Studies of the University of Geneva. This time they planned to take Jan along, setting off in September 1931 in their beloved black Oldsmobile brought back from America; and they invited Gunnar's beautiful and kindly younger sister Mela to come to stay with them, in part because her health had suffered the previous winter in Sweden and in part so that she might help out with Jan and the household.

Alva was eager to study pedagogy at the Rousseau Institute with Jean Piaget, the young professor whose theories about the stages of child development she had come to admire. His first book on psychology, *The Language and Thought of the Child,* had attracted great attention both in Europe and in America when it appeared in 1923. She hoped to have the opportunity to interview him at length about how children think and understand the world around them; he seemed to her to have a uniquely imaginative and understanding yet also analytical way of observing children. But for the first time in her life, poor health would stand in the way of nearly all her efforts.

7

Illness

❖ ❖ ❖ ❖

*A*t first the move to Geneva seemed to augur a year as stimulating for both Alva and Gunnar as that in America, and far more comfortable economically. His new salary, combined with a government stipend to support his writing, allowed them to look for a small house to rent that would be more suited to their larger household than the two-room flats and hotel rooms they had lived in while traveling around America. In a letter to Gunnar's sister Elsa, Alva exulted at having found *Les Pluviers,* an idyllic villa complete with antique furniture, on the shores of Lake Geneva in the village of Versoix: "We imagine we are 'millionaires for a day' who have received a flowering house by the shores of the world's most romantic lake as a honeymoon present."

Soon after moving into the new house, however, she suffered another miscarriage, later in pregnancy than the first. She developed an infection, accompanied by a fever that would not go away, and later a large internal tumor. Egon Glesinger, an agricultural economist who was working on his doctoral dissertation at the Geneva Institute for International Studies at the time, describes hearing about Alva's illness when he first met Gunnar:

> I came to the Institute one afternoon in September to find both my teachers deeply upset and completely uninterested in my problem. They were talking about the sad fate of a young man, whose beautiful wife was fighting for her life after giving birth to a dead child. Before I had time to inquire who they

99

were talking about, a tall, blond, blue-eyed Swede stepped
into the room and looked so miserable that he was obviously
the answer to my question. It took weeks before Alva Myrdal
was out of danger, and although few of us had ever met her
or even Gunnar, his love and fear of losing her were so intense
that the whole Institute lived in an atmosphere of gloom. It
was in these weeks that I experienced for the first time the
strength of Gunnar's personality and his exceptional ability to
create happiness and sorrow around him, simply by the intensity of his own feelings.

Alva found this second miscarriage utterly dispiriting. She,
who so longed to add to her family, now had to postpone all
hopes of doing so indefinitely. She underwent a difficult operation,
which she later realized was mishandled by the Swiss physicians
she had consulted, and had to be confined to bed off and on
during much of their stay in Geneva. The operation, in late November, represented the only real threat to life that either she or
Gunnar had experienced up to then; they had always previously
taken their good luck for granted. Alva wrote to Gunnar's sister
Elsa that Gunnar had confessed to her that he had "almost postponed living" that winter; in letters to Gustav Cassel, Gunnar
reported that he had lost much of his interest in the outside world
and that his principal exercise came from carrying Alva from
room to room.

"For a long time, I could not even see a doctor in a film
without nearly losing consciousness," Alva wrote me much later
when I was in the hospital, feeling shaken in the aftermath of
childbirth. "It does pass, however, so be in good spirits. But it is
the valley of darkness."

She recovered slowly from her operation, only to be told that
she needed a second one in the spring. The doctors thought it
safest simply to remove her reproductive organs; the alternative
was a more dangerous and complicated operation, needless in
their view, since they had warned her against running the risk of
yet another pregnancy. But Alva refused point-blank any inter-

vention that would leave her unable to have children in the future, no matter how many difficulties were associated with the alternative operation or with any future pregnancies. Gunnar wrote to Cassel of his admiration for Alva, who could muster the strength to stress such a "relatively unimportant matter" after the horrors that she had been through, especially since her decision made the operation more dangerous. In reading his letter I cannot help seeing my own life, still to come—along with that of my sister Kaj—as hanging by a thread, while my mother-to-be, at twenty-nine, insisted on having her own way.

The year in Geneva did have intermittent periods of cheer—weeks when Alva seemed almost restored, so that they could walk in mist or sunshine by the lake or drive to their favorite village restaurants in the Jura Mountains nearby. At Easter they took Jan along on a trip to southern France, driving through Provence to Nice and Monte Carlo on the Riviera. Being away from Sweden had given them time, as Alva reported in a letter home, to "digest all the impressions from the New World" against the cosmopolitan background of the League of Nations and the other international organizations in Geneva. Because the year had also been so difficult personally, she felt that it had allowed them to mature and perhaps to deepen their understanding of what mattered most to them and to return to Sweden with a much clearer idea about where they stood intellectually and politically.

The weakness of the League of Nations in the face of mounting international tensions and the ceaseless intrigues among delegates made them long to grapple with their own country's problems, so much more manageable by comparison. As soon as they returned, they intended to join the Social Democratic party. For Alva, this step seemed especially natural after her years in the Social Democratic youth movement and as a reaffirmation of the ideals of her father (but not her mother) and her grandfather. She expressed the essence of being a Social Democrat as being opposed to all special privileges and supportive of all those groups in society that were held back or left out. It was equally natural for Gunnar to seek out the party committed to stronger and more innovative measures for the public good given his own long-standing opposition to the economic doctrine of laissez-faire, even though his family background was more conservative.

In Sweden, the dominant form of socialism had always been reformist rather than revolutionary. Wedded to democratic forms of change, it was also less doctrinaire than others about implementing the goal of public ownership of major means of production. This goal had, in effect, been continually set aside in favor of resolving the more pressing problems of unemployment, poverty, low productivity, and labor strife. Per Albin Hansson, who was to become Sweden's prime minister in 1932, owed his success, in part, to having launched a more down-to-earth goal of public well-being: *folkhemmet,* or the nation as a true home for all its people. Citizens ought to be able to feel at home in their society, he insisted; basic necessities were owed to all, no matter how old, or poor, or sick; society's benefits ought not to be reserved for only a few. He persuaded his party to stress such means as redistributive taxation and reforms of the health care system to ensure greater "equality, care, cooperation, and helpfulness."

Both Alva and Gunnar used the time abroad to write about population issues—a subject Gunnar had already treated in a chapter written for, and then taken out of *The Political Element in the Development of Economic Theory.* And as so often happened, they found encouragement and intense stimulation as they discussed issues from quite different perspectives—he from the point of view of economics, she with respect to human and social conditions. As Alva wrote to a friend, "An economist and a social psychologist, united in marriage and authorship, naturally combine to form a sociologist with the greatest of ease."

In this way, Alva came to study the decline in population that worried so many Europeans between the wars. She arrived at the dubious conclusion that it was the patriotic and human duty of women to have children, and that those who did not engaged in a practice she called "birth strike." This judgment became a central theme in everything she wrote about population problems. It helps to explain her own efforts to have more children, but her very longing for children and her sense of how empty life would be without them may perhaps also explain the uncritical manner in which she adopted this conclusion.

After Alva and Gunnar's return to Sweden in the summer of 1931, the doctors whom Alva consulted did not want to risk operating to remove the tumor so long as her fever lasted, and since penicillin was not yet available, there was little to do about the fever except wait for it to go away. Only after two years was she sufficiently recovered for the operation.

In spite of the fever, Alva found part-time employment at the clinic for law and psychiatry at the jail of Långholmen in Stockholm. With Gunnar, she turned more and more to concrete proposals for social reform. At the same time, her interest in women's questions caught fire. She sought out women's organizations and began to take part in the debates about women's and children's living conditions—and in turn to a focus on housing policy, working conditions, and the promotion of better circumstances for families. And she combined her concerns for child development and greater freedom for women by setting up a course in the training of parents: "what I think was the first course of that kind that existed" in Sweden.

This seminar, expressly open to both fathers and mothers, was advertised in the newpapers in the fall of 1931. It was intended for parents who cared about their children's "happy development under auspicious conditions" and focused on the psychological aspects of child care. I can imagine the skepticism Alva's mother must have felt when she read the advertisement. What in the world was this daughter up to now? First she, who in Lowa's opinion was not especially suited to have children, went off to America for over a year, leaving her only child behind; then her hopes for more children were crushed in Geneva; once returned, she neglected her health and her home by taking on far too many outside tasks; and now she ventured, not yet thirty years old, to lecture others about how to bring up their children—as if that were not something best done by love and sheer intuition!

Such comparisons between her ideas and her personal life were to pursue Alva from then on, precisely because the changes that she advocated were so often themselves of a personal nature. Her sense of privacy prevented her from replying to the most intrusive questions, but the last part of the charge—that love and intuition sufficed for child rearing—was one she disputed from the beginning. In her preface to an unfinished book on parenting she rejected as sentimental the refusal to allow new knowledge to enter the family's protected realm. Why, in fact, should love without information be preferred to love with information?

> Once upon a time, it seemed a self-evident rule that mothers know best when it comes to child care. That self-satisfied rule took the lives of thousands of infants every year. When physicians succeeded in gaining the ears of mothers for other, scientifically tested rules, infant mortality decreased sharply.

Just as medicine could save the lives of infants and children through up-to-date information about hygiene, nutrition, and illness, she argued, so psychological knowledge could now contribute to their well-being, sometimes even to their survival. Testing, for example, could tell us much more about what to expect of children at different ages and how to identify children in special need of help. Understanding the role of play and of the imagination could allow parents to support, rather than to crush, a child's creativity. Information about the sexual development of children could lessen the thoughtless instilling of debilitating fears or obsessions. Too many children grew up abused and neglected; it was worth doing all she could to help improve their chances by encouraging what she called a "culture of parenting" that would raise the quality of child care through information and advocacy.

The first series of talks went well, and others followed. It was in the course of her extensive lecturing on the problems of child care and of families more generally that Alva discovered how much she enjoyed public speaking, in spite of her shyness. She dared to talk personally and often dramatically about the subjects she took up. Each time she could feel the response from her listeners. In one of her first speeches, she called on her audience to look at current child-rearing practices as if they were from another planet. Much would then appear comical, much useless:

> A giant effort is needed in order to pull ourselves out of the indolence—yes, I don't hesitate to say the torpor—in which tradition maintains us when it comes to education. And this very effort to make ourselves over, that is the feat that requires such doggedly conscious and collected energy. It will not happen by itself and we receive precious little help from the outside.

To make themselves over would be possible for more parents if just such outside help were available, and Alva decided to work to make such a change possible. She began by sketching plans for a collective dwelling that would "free married women for outside work, free them from the slave role in housework."

> Their freedom and the children's right to the company of friends fitted together there, day care and play schools were for me a common solution to two problems that had become acute in modern society. The enthusiasm led a group of friends to gather to discuss plans for a collective house. . . . And we had an extraordinary ambition for the future. We met quite privately and made plans for a large collective building with a thousand apartments if I remember right.

In that building cooking and child care were to take place collectively and in a "rationalized" manner. Alva would smile, later, as she reminisced about this exuberantly utopian model for collective living, where infants would be cared for by skilled professionals in sunny, hygienic quarters away from their parents, children play together nearby with the most up-to-date educational equipment, all parents be free to work and pursue other interests, and an intricate system of dumb-waiters bring food to each apartment from a central kitchen. Collective reading rooms and sun-rooms, and athletic facilities in a park surrounding the building would facilitate every form of recreation. At the time, however, she was all enthusiasm. She wrote about the project to her friends in America, the young economists Eve and Arthur Burns:

> We have the idea to build a "Kollektivhus," an ideal family hotel with cooperative organization to take care of all your material needs and unload your responsibility also for your offspring! . . . The children will be in nurseries in another wing, tennis courts in the park . . . everything you can dream of . . . and for a rent which will save us about half of our costs for the household.

Since the building was only in the planning stage, Alva had to make different arrangements for herself in combining work and childcare. She compared the nursery schools already established in different apartment buildings in Stockholm and placed Jan in one such institution. "I had reasons of both principle and ideal to believe it would be good for him. But I admit that I was dissatisfied with the practical realization!" In particular, she found the personnel poorly trained. This problem led her to take on yet another task: to work out better training possibilities for child-care personnel.

How she was able to carry on all these activities in different locations while caring for a small child is hard to understand. She herself remembered those years as a period when, even though she had household help, she was often at home. Jan visited his grandparents and other relatives at times, and the play school took some of his time. But both he and Gunnar demanded attention and care. The dream about the collective house that would free women was, like so many other reforms of Alva's, personally motivated. "I remember that time as one of horribly exhausted nights. Jan craved company and often slept only between midnight and five in the morning."

Perhaps it was her constant fever that gave Alva a tired intensity that worried those who knew her. Lowa, herself always expressing fatigue and worrying about her health, said that Alva

squandered her strength. Professor Olof Kinberg, in whose clinic
at the Långholmen jail she worked, warned her to take more time
for herself, not to live so vehemently and risk burning herself out.
And sharp-eyed, generous Johanna Cassel, whose home had always been open to Alva and Gunnar, wrote to her daughter Inga
about Alva's health problems and pregnancies. Alva appears to
have both charmed and puzzled Johanna—a young woman, as
interested as she in children and homemaking, yet also "so modern," with "a certain tendency to become abstract and see everything collectively."

To what extent did Alva fully confront the contrast between
her theories about how to live and her own life? Between her
clearheaded, understanding view of parenting and human relations and the conflicts that she experienced in trying to make
everything fit? Between her rational, at times doctrinaire solutions
to family needs and the interwoven complexities of daily life? The
temptation must have been to push any awareness of that contrast
aside, to conceal it even from herself.

In photos from that period Alva often looks tired and sallow;
they are the only ones in which she does not glow with the energy
that is usually so striking. She was ill, worn down with miscarriages and the infection that caused such anxiety, and greatly in
need of rest. And she had begun to worry: Jan would soon turn
seven. Perhaps she would never manage to have the siblings for
him that she longed for, never be able to fulfill what she saw as
a woman's duty to give birth to more than one child. She was
even burdened by the belief voiced by Ellen Key and reinforced
by Alfred Adler that it was dangerous for families to have only
one child. For Adler, the only child was often spoiled in every
sense of that word. Alva, not to be outdone, wrote that children
without siblings in "miniature families" often carry with them
throughout life

> a burden of a shrunken and in different ways twisted emo-
> tional life that expresses itself particularly in an overwhelming
> egocentricity and a lack of social understanding.

Here it seems to me as if once again Alva's feelings of intense longing for children, and of anguish at the thought of failing, color her theories, so outwardly matter-of-fact. Her interest in issues of population must therefore also be seen as a very personal matter. When the articles she and Gunnar had written on that subject were refused by the Social Democratic journal *Tiden*, because they were too long, they decided to rework the material into a short book. By then the fever from which she suffered had finally abated and she had undergone the long-awaited operation. At last she was recovering her old energy. This book was the first effort on which she and Gunnar would collaborate outside their studies and their private life; now they had to try to blend the theoretical and the practical and to discuss the issues until they reached common conclusions.

They finished most of the book during a summer of walking in the Norwegian alps in 1934, housed in a small cabin overlooking mountains that looked like stage sets behind clouds and still more mountains. Once again Jan stayed with relatives. Alva was by then finally pregnant again—this time with me—and had regained her good health. Their enjoyment of debating, writing, and walking together was boundless—Alva described those weeks as a vertiginous combination of intellectual and human fellowship. This was the joining together in marriage that she had read about in the novel *Stella* where all was shared, all was worked out together. Alva saw herself as a "spray can" or fountain of ideas; then Gunnar and she developed the thoughts, fitted them together, turned them inside out if need be. For her this was an intensely fruitful companionship, intellectual as well as emotional, in the service of the population question, with a newly conceived baby as a sign of their personal engagement in the issue.

In ten years of marriage Alva had experienced more than even she could have hoped for as a girl. She had come out into the world, lived in a marriage she found intensely stimulating, albeit conflicted, with a husband who, unlike most, fully supported her efforts to study, write, and take part in public life. She had given birth to one child and looked forward to the arrival of a second one. She was active in women's groups, the Social Democratic party, and other movements, and had succeeded in finding unexplored issues that she enjoyed writing about and fighting for. But what was going to become of all this activity? Late in life she wrote that it gradually became clear to her that she did not have a well-defined emerging life path:

> And I, who was called an advocate of women's rights from early on, never insisted on a career of my own, going along quite naturally with being an appendix. Of course I could not avoid undertaking certain things, but it was Gunnar's path, his career, his interests that had to have first claim. . . .

Gunnar's career plowed straight ahead. In 1933, at the age of thirty-four, he had succeeded Gustav Cassel in the Lars Hierta Chair of Economics at the University of Stockholm. And as the world's economic crisis reached Sweden, his advice was increasingly sought by the Social Democratic government that had been voted into office in 1932. Alva as yet had no career. Instead she had done whatever she could wherever she had been, much like the pioneer women in the New World. Of course it would have been better if she had stood up for herself more from the outset. But to have planned her own life in detail would have required a degree of self-confidence that she never possessed. Even if she had tried to plan in that way, she could never have steered her life in the direction that turned out to be hers. She improvised and wove her life together, always making of it something greater and more alive than she or anyone else could have worked out in advance. But the whole time she continued to ask herself: How do I become myself? What should I do to guide my life better?

These were questions she could not answer for many years. But she became more and more aware of seeking answers, and her quest came to be linked with the searchings of other women throughout history. She began early to collect books by women writers such as George Sand, Virginia Woolf and Selma Lagerlöf, the Swedish novelist and teller of legends who had been the first woman to win the Nobel Prize for literature, in 1909. Late in her life, in her and Gunnar's last apartment she arranged shelves near her bed for books she wanted to have nearby to read at night, when she often lay awake. In the margins of these books she made notes that referred to her own experiences. She gathered books on those shelves about and by Mary Wollstonecraft, Sweden's Queen Christina, Madame de Staël, and Aleksandra Kollontai, thinking she might one day write about some of them; as well as by Margaret Mead and by Alva's British friend Marjorie Allen, whose *Memoirs of an Uneducated Lady* described a life she had seen at close hand and especially admired.

On those shelves, too, stood memoirs by two modern Swedish writers whom she thought especially incisive on women's issues, however strongly she occasionally disagreed with them: Ellen Key and Elin Wägner.

Several books by Simone de Beauvoir were also gathered there. In de Beauvoir's life, Alva at first thought she saw her own almost completely mirrored. She read about the young French girl's childhood and her battle to be able to lead her own life, about her intensely religious period, about her encounter with Jean-Paul Sartre, then a brilliant, forceful fellow student who became her companion for life, and about her efforts to think through the conditions of women's lives. Simone de Beauvoir even described the intimate, all-encompassing dialogue that went on continually with Sartre in a manner that astonished Alva, so much did it resemble her own dialogue with Gunnar.

After reading the first volume of de Beauvoir's *Memoirs of a Dutiful Daughter,* she wrote me a strange letter in August 1959. She had sent me the book, she wrote, after savoring it "to the last drop" on long journeys across India by plane and train. "And—as I said to Kaj—now that it exists I never have to think about writing my own memoirs." She found so much that corresponded to her own experiences, sometimes down to the smallest details. "At any rate, all you have to do if you wonder what I thought and what guided me when I was young, is just to open it up and read. Write what you think!"

It was natural that I should approach this book with special interest. And true enough, I could see many similarities. I wrote to thank Alva, agreeing with her on that score; but I added that, however much the book fascinated me from that point of view, I hoped she would nevertheless write a book about her own life. Why, I now ask myself, did I not urge her more strongly to do so at the time? She surely knew that her life was her own and that not even its outlines could be understood by reading the memoirs of another. Her wholehearted response to de Beauvoir's book may have come like the spontaneous identification with the experiences of another that most of us feel in reading certain personal accounts. But perhaps the thought that she had now been released from any need to write about her own life also reflected Alva's reluctance to put herself forward, a little like her drawing back from being first in her class in school or hesitating about being equal, or even entirely herself, within her marriage.

In 1961, while taking a week's rest with Gunnar by the seaside on Sweden's west coast, Alva had a chance to read the second volume of de Beauvoir's memoirs, just out: *The Prime of Life*. This volume took the author from 1929, when she wondered, at twenty, what form her new, liberated life would take, to the end of the war sixteen years later.

Alva was fascinated by the book's perspective on the world events that she, too, had lived through and on the life of a woman of letters that de Beauvoir had shaped for herself. But she was taken aback by de Beauvoir's unflinching account of abandoning personal freedom in order to "conform in every respect" to Sartre and to strive to see the world, other individuals, even his mistresses, with his eyes. The book conveyed a willed subjugation to another's mind that intrigued Alva from a psychological point of view but also made her recoil. She could no longer claim that Simone de Beauvoir's life mirrored her own.

Still later, reflecting on her own experiences in the light of these memoirs, Alva sent me a series of "autobiographical items" about the additional differences she had come to see. Simone de Beauvoir had had a more secure and comfortable childhood and had not moved about as much as Alva, and she had been satisfied with the conventional finishing school for girls she had attended whereas Alva had been in active revolt in order to be allowed to undertake serious study. Unlike de Beauvoir, Alva had never had the slightest inclination to conceal her intellectual life from those whom she saw as true friends. Most important, perhaps, de Beauvoir had chosen not to marry and had remained childless, whereas Alva had taken a more traditional path with marriage and family. But since de Beauvoir had focused so much of her life and her writings alike on Sartre, she seemed, paradoxically enough, as more of a dominated, sometimes resigned, wifely figure than Alva, who for long periods in the last half of her life lived and worked separately from Gunnar.

Simone de Beauvoir, like Margaret Mead and the other women whose memoirs interested Alva most, lived with all of our century's contradictions and possibilities for women. But Alva did not have their examples to look to when, as a young girl and later as a newly married student, she tried to think through how she should direct her life. At that time she had most often taken men as models; she had had little empathy for queens and female saints or conquerors. It was hard to find women who combined the roles she sought in life: the creative, adventurous role often regarded as masculine and the traditionally feminine roles of warmly supportive wife and protective mother. "Great" women like Joan of Arc, Queen Christina, the Brontë sisters, or Florence Nightingale were almost always childless and usually unmarried. So were Ellen Key and Selma Lagerlöf, however much they protested the conditions that forced them into such a state. For centuries, women of distinction in literature, philosophy, science, and other fields had had to make a choice between their calling on the one hand and marriage on the other, with its likelihood of having a large family and the ever-present risk of dying in childbirth.

With improved contraceptives (which, however, could not be advertised or openly sold in Sweden even in the thirties) women had the chance to aim high professionally without renouncing marriage and family. Those who chose to combine these roles were pioneers, and their own lives were seen as models or warnings depending on whether they succeeded or failed. Alva was one of these pioneers. But since she found no guidance either in books or from other women she knew, she was unprepared for the practical difficulties she encountered. In spite of the financial difficulties that had burdened both her own family and Gunnar's, she had not thought that lack of money could stand in the way of her doing research. She had not anticipated that she might suffer miscarriages, with all the sorrow and fatigue they bring. Even less had she thought it possible that she would experience prolonged illness, conflicts within her new family, and doubts about how the disparate parts of her life were going to fit together.

These experiences led her to begin to think through the lives of women in a new way. What interested her now were the shared conditions of women. She looked for explanations, interpretations of these conditions. And she thought about all she had heard about the farm women in her own family, about women in factories and shops, women in the countryside and in cities around the world. She gave speeches about women in mining families and worked with women inmates at Långholmen prison. She felt a growing sense of solidarity with all of them. In earlier years she had thought that she and Gunnar would somehow be immune to the everyday problems caused by pregnancy, poor housing, illness, and conflicts between husband and wife. Now she tried to understand what different women had done in spite of these common problems, which ones had hindered them most, on which ones they had foundered. She saw her life as linked with the lives of all other women and therefore as typical in a new way.

This new understanding sparked her proposals for reform. How would it be, she now began to ask, if people decided to bring up girls in such a way as not to make them feel inferior? In January 1934 she gave a speech entitled "Education for 'Femininity.'" A letter condensing the message of her talk explains that

the conventional talk about "only a girl" stamps a girl child forever, pulls away the foundation for her self-confidence, undercuts from the earliest years her power to act, take initiatives, carry responsibility, and—yes, all those good characteristics we tend to look at as typically "masculine." How can we know whether women do not have these traits by nature, when education is systematically aimed at stifling them and at

nurturing a deliciously feminine helplessness, shyness, mildness, etc.?

In articles and speeches Alva also spoke of all that society
could and should do in order to lighten the burdens oppressing
too many women and men. For individuals she recommended
increased knowledge about parenting, new methods of child care,
and choice with respect to pregnancy; but these changes could
not succeed without broad social reforms guaranteeing such benefits as good medical care and decent housing for everyone, study
loans, free access to contraceptives, and child allowances.

Alva advocated these reforms wholeheartedly. She took for
granted they would be adopted as soon as she and others had
made the need for them clear. As a result neither she nor Gunnar
was prepared for the shock with which Sweden would react to
their book, published late in 1934, *Kris i befolkningsfrågan* (*Crisis
in the Population Question*), which spoke openly about how these
neglected problems fit together and concerned everyone:

> The population question is going to raise a powerful political
> demand: that the social conditions in our country be so
> changed that its citizens will once again desire to bring enough
> children into the world to keep our people from dying out.

8

Families

❖ ❖ ❖ ❖

*M*y birth, in December 1934, was announced in the Stockholm newspapers as an ironic commentary on the scandal brewing around *Crisis in the Population Question*. The book had appeared the month before with explosive impact, gaining instant notoriety for my parents. Even Gunnar's mentor, Gustav Cassel, felt called on to denounce it in the press. The conservative Eli Heckscher wrote that he had often wondered whether Gunnar, in spite of his great scientific talent, was not temperamentally more suited to be a "full-time agitator." An academic colleague let it be known that his wife, alas, would no longer be able to speak to Alva. As she traveled about Sweden carrying the book's message, more than one irate listener stood up to scold her for not being at home with her new baby. Merely to take up sexual matters was daring; for a woman to co-author a book on such topics defiled her in the eyes of many. And to call for radical reforms such as housing subsidies for families with children, free school lunches, free health care, sex education in the schools, open access to contraceptives, and a law forbidding employers to fire women who became pregnant—was this not a downright threat to morals and culture?

As a contribution to public debate, the book was a stroke of genius. It riveted public attention by painting a grim future for the nation unless full-scale reforms were undertaken to avert the threat of depopulation. All over the country, discussion groups sprang up to debate the book. The problem was burning, the authors insisted. The question was "not just *how* our people will live but the far more fateful one of whether our people will live at all." The Swedish people now risked dying out, they argued, because so few children were being born: 13.6 per 1,000 in 1933 compared with 30 per 1,000 yearly during much of the nineteenth century. In a few years, the population of Sweden, already sparse, would reach its culmination and then begin to decline.

Alva and Gunnar, now thirty-two and thirty-five, combined terrifying language with statistics and scientific interpretation. With their flair for drama, they wanted to set forth as vividly as they could all that had gone into creating the problem facing the nation and all that was now needed to overcome it and to shape a more humane society. And they wanted to do so together. The book carried both their names as authors, unlike many collaborative works before and since published under the name of the husband alone, with that of the wife mentioned, if at all, in the acknowledgments. In rereading the book I can feel the exhilaration of the two young authors as they planned their joint salvo while walking and debating in the Norwegian mountains. I imagine them relishing each new way of matching problems with solutions, each argument sharpened, each rhetorical point hammered in, each new set of data brought in to buttress their thesis.

In so doing, the two did not hesitate to criticize their opponents as unscientific, unintelligent, even dishonest. While they themselves claimed to argue rationally, their adversaries, on the contrary, were usually only capable of "opining." Gunnar later wrote that one reason the book provoked such a fierce outcry in the press was that "the authors had not been especially polite toward those whom they considered simpleminded and wrongheaded. For the more studied malice," he acknowledged, "I was probably more responsible than Alva."

The book began by contrasting two hostile camps when it came to population issues. One group warned of the danger of depopulation, pointing to the decline in births that Sweden and many European nations had experienced since the nineteenth century, especially in the wake of the War and the Depression. Members of this group, among whom were many conservatives and clergy, urged punitive laws to discourage the use of the contraceptives that unquestionably contributed to the decline in births. More generally, those in this camp also opposed all reforms that, in their opinion, would break up families by giving women more freedom. Members of the second group, often Social Democrats, urged greater freedom with respect to birth control along with better schools, working conditions, and housing. On the whole they did not worry about the risk of depopulation but believed, rather, that it might even help cut back unemployment.

What Alva and Gunnar did with these two positions seemed to the public almost like magic. They wholly accepted the conservative view regarding the great danger that depopulation posed for the country, but managed to draw the opposite conclusion: that this danger presented "the most forceful argument for a profound and radical socialist reshaping of society." Indulging in wishful thinking about the good old days was no longer enough, and efforts to outlaw contraceptives would neither work nor do justice to the rightful claims of families.

The shock was especially great for conservatives, who had spoken for years about the declining population of Sweden as a "plague" brought on by the decay of the family and by general moral turpitude. Instead of preaching and threatening punishments, Alva and Gunnar proposed broad social reforms to encourage the formation of families, and they were bold enough to see the rights of women and children as the foundation for those reforms. Why should parents bring more children into the world, they asked, as long as so many families live in dismal apartments with one room and a kitchen, most often without a bathroom? As long as schooling and working conditions are so poor and there is no money even for the most essential food and clothing? As long as women are forced to choose between confinement at home with their children or childlessness on the labor market?

The two authors succeeded in speaking clearly about matters often thought unmentionable at the time, but they did so in a way that was supportive of families—hardly a sign of the depravity their critics attributed to them. If families were less burdened, they wrote, many would welcome additional children. They even dared to suggest that their proposals were more patriotic, more capable of serving the country, than the harsh and moralizing conservative correctives.

Their message was presented in a tone of pure rationality. The book is in this sense very youthful. Alva and Gunnar claim to know so much with such certainty, even about the future. Their belief in reason and in its coming victory still knows no bounds. Society is in transition, they write, between the past precapitalist tradition and the future "more methodically constructed socialist community built on the broadest democratic foundation." Such a new society calls for reform at every level of human interaction, from marital relations to city planning and school and health care.

Moreover, just as the world's economic crises since 1929 have taught nations that they cannot count on market forces to produce a natural equilibrium without government intervention, so there is no natural equilibrium for population. There, too, social policy is needed to serve the needs of society and individual citizens. And this policy will have to be far more forward-looking than in the past. People will soon have to adjust to new occupations and ways of life, to a more energetic rhythm of life, and to collective cooperation. All the more reason, then, to promote family planning, to allow abortion as a last resort, and to reform the school system so that every child is welcome and given the best possible start in life.

The book's rationalism jars when it mirrors the period's concern for genetic engineering, especially when it proposes forced sterilization—on "racially hygienic" grounds—of those who, because of genetic disease or retardation, would offer children an "unsuitable milieu for child-rearing." At the same time the authors warn against Germany's growing "political barbarism of race and class" and sharply dismiss the notion that some races might somehow be higher or more advanced than others. Instead they maintain that all human groups contain a small number of men and women who ought not to bring children into the world.

The book's radical stance is as tangible as its rationalistic belief in the triumph of common sense. In their desire to change society, Alva and Gunnar point to a problem searing enough to reach the public in order to advance many other reforms at the same time. Only in this way, they argue, can the nation avoid the fateful future of which they warn, while at the same time creating a more livable environment for children and families.

Almost all the reforms that came to characterize the welfare state in Sweden were proposed or hinted at in this book. The practical solutions to the needs of women and children and men—and therefore the nation—gave the book its force. That perspective came from Alva.

To bring about these reforms, the book argues, greater solidarity among citizens will be needed; individuals should not have to cope alone with the problems that society often imposes on them. Nor is it reasonable to imagine that private interests and society's interests automatically coincide. There is therefore a crying need both for social policies that motivate citizens to act for the common good and for new educational initiatives to foster collectivist thinking within schools, families, and marriages. Only by such means will it be possible to undercut the selfishness and "the narrow individualism that now poisons our people's entire life and even threatens its existence." Here especially I hear Alva's voice: Gunnar never shared her reverence for collectivism, nor did he worry much about the selfishness and egocentricity that the book condemns.

"Krisan" or "Little Crisis" was the nickname I was sometimes given as the storm over the book only continued to grow. Later I learned about expressions such as "Myrdal cactus," which equated our family name with abundant offshoots, and "Myrdal buildings," also known as *barnrikehus,* or apartment buildings "rich in children." Intimacy and love seemed to be part of the name's aura as well, I came to think, or why else should love seats be called "Myrdal couches"? All in all it seemed as if my arrival had been not only welcome but in some way patriotic. To be linked through my birth and my family name with the message that children should be wanted and were needed in the country was not at all disagreeable, even if sometimes confusing and apparently in the eyes of many even comical or lewd.

My birth under those circumstances, and the arrival of my sister Kaj less than two years later helped to confirm Alva's theories. She did not wish only to lecture and write about more children—wanted children—in families; she longed to fulfill that requirement herself, the more so as she had concluded that families with only one child present a "difficult, most often insoluble educational problem." From that point of view, I arrived in the nick of time. Jan was already seven and a half years old. Had her miscarriages continued, the fact that Alva had only had one child would hardly have been consistent with encouraging others to have more children. (She was to have two more miscarriages, one as late as 1942. At this last one I felt great sorrow, for I had been allowed to feel the baby move and knew that if it were to be a little brother he would be called Tomas.) The two children that Alva had barely produced when the population debate raged so fiercely were not much to show in the eyes of her opponents, and something so private as miscarriages she could never have mentioned.

Now the time had come for Alva to try out all that she had learned in America and Switzerland about child care and all that she had herself proposed during her years of teaching parents about their role. Ours was going to be a family warmly disposed toward children. Past mistakes were not to be repeated. Ever since her visit to America, she had opposed the rigid advice from pediatricians about letting babies cry in order not to spoil them. This time she was going to take care of her health, hiring help for both child care and housework so that she could sleep at night and not have to feel tied to the home and to a newborn baby. Otherwise she knew that she would never be able to cope with all that she wanted to accomplish. And the financial problems that had darkened the early years now seemed less pressing because of Gunnar's professorship and their income from books.

For us children, Alva wanted to buy what she had called "real toys" in the pamphlet with that name that she published in 1935—stimulating, beautiful, well-made objects in bright colors, never conventionally divided into toys for boys and for girls. Toys were not a luxury, she insisted, but essential for children's development. Every child ought to have a special place or corner in which to keep building blocks and clay and all that was needed to create playthings from scratch. "Horse on wheels for the one-year-old's motor play" is the caption under a picture of me in the pamphlet—and I remember again the sturdy white horse with its seat and backrest and quizzical black eyes, and the wheels that squeaked when I held its black reins and rolled from room to room. Faithful to Rousseau, Alva urged that clothing for children should be liberating, not the confining garments that they had been bundled into for generations. She wanted to give us a chance to live close to nature, climb trees, have a wading pool, a sandbox, even a small slide in the garden. About children who grow up in cramped city apartments she had written in 1932:

> Take a city building, where people in 20 small kitchens above and next to one another cook meatballs, where many little nurseries each enclose one languishing and confined little human being—does this not cry out for a more carefully planned organization, an organization in the spirit of collectivism?

If collectivism were to remedy such debilitating isolation, Alva had argued, it would have to permeate every aspect of life. In her book with Gunnar, she had called for communal nurseries where children would be cared for and educated more in the manner of the extended families of the now-disappearing farming households than in that of small, isolated modern families. A model of the experimental collective dwelling that she had designed with the architect Sven Markelius was finally exhibited in Stockholm in 1936. Yet in planning their own existence, neither Alva nor Gunnar had the slightest desire to adopt a collectivist way of life. There still did not exist an ideal collective dwelling—one that made possible both togetherness and solitude without that cramped living that denies human needs:

> In general, unavoidable togetherness in large and in small matters, in conflicts, arguments, and eroticism, in psalm singing and card games, in grooming and housework, in rest and wakefulness, is enervating for everyone. The well-being in

living together becomes difficult to call forth. Irritation is unavoidable when solitude is not offered as a change from togetherness. No one then has the chance to pull aside. All has to be shared with everyone; all must be experienced by everyone.

In these words I can hear echoes of childhood experience and family stories, of the tensions between Jan and Gunnar in the first, cramped apartments, and of Alva's sometimes desperate need to be alone. One senses her incipient doubts: just how does one achieve both independence and togetherness? And is it actually possible for women to live a life that is free and adventurous and rich in achievement while at the same time finding intimacy and happiness within a family?

Her answer then, as later, had much of her father's "builder's spirit." If one wanted things to have a better chance of working out, one had to begin by reinventing the environment. As she wrote in a pamphlet entitled *Stadsbarn* (*City Children*): "When children do not fit into cities, then the proper path is not to abolish the children but to change the cities."

By designing a new kind of house, she would try to free herself and Gunnar and at the same time help us children develop in that freedom and happiness she so often called for in families. For such a life in common, neither collective nor single apartments would suffice. Instead, our family first moved to a large, rented villa in Bromma, a suburb of Stockholm; and with the help of Sven Markelius Alva then began to plan a villa of her own in nearby Äppelviken. She wanted to put into practice all her ideas about combining family life with a creative intellectual environment with sufficient possibility for both togetherness and independence to satisfy each one of us.

The result was what one commentator called "the most radical family house of the thirties," innovatively designed throughout and planned with equal consideration for the practical needs of children and parents. Built on several levels on a rocky hillside and topped with a large terrace surrounded by a ship's railing, it was widely discussed in the media. Month after month during the first year we would look out at family groups stopping to scrutinize it at length while on their Sunday walks.

On the ground floor of the new house was a sunny, roomy nursery for Kaj and me with an enormous drawing board on the wall, and bedrooms for Jan, a maid, and a housekeeper, along with a kitchen, a dining area, and a family room, all with easy access to the garden. Upstairs Alva and Gunnar ruled. They had a large work room with access to the even larger "ship's deck" terrace, a room for their "archives" with shelves from floor to ceiling, and a spacious and bright American-inspired bathroom. Their bedroom was equipped with a wall on ball bearings that could be rolled out from a closet to separate their two beds so that they could choose solitude when they so desired "as a change from togetherness." The movable bedroom wall aroused further commentary in the press. For a woman—and I believe that it was Alva who needed solitude far more than Gunnar—to provide for independence even in the marital bedroom seemed to many to be going too far.

It was an ideal house for a family with small children. Kaj and I quickly felt at home in our nursery. There were creamy white linoleum stairs on which we could ride mattresses from upstairs down to the floor below, windows we could climb in and out of, a round wading pool under the branches of two weeping willows, and a yard with a lawn for ball games with all the neighborhood children who gathered there during those years. No fences shut out either children or adults. Alva arranged a play school for us along with other children at home and always kept the house open and hospitable. It was the opposite of those places she had described, in which children's rooms each enclosed "one languishing and confined little human being," and such a one I never felt myself to be.

Each time I see photos of that house I rejoice again at the beauty and the perfection of form that Alva succeeded in creating there. This was the first time that her true genius for design came into its own. One cannot possibly think of Alva without seeing her against a background of gloriously composed colors and shapes. Clothes, furniture, even kitchen tools—on everything she put her own bold but never garish stamp. The last apartment she ever furnished, in the suburb of Djursholm outside Stockholm, was much smaller than the house in Äppelviken and other houses and apartments where she had lived, but its forms were as strikingly simple and its colors were the same: white walls with green and black as contrast, glowing orange and yellow and blackish purple vases and decorative objects, and flowers or plants in the light from large windows.

That house and that garden in Äppelviken became the background for my childhood. We lived there for the greater part of the years 1937 to 1947. They gave me that "order of things and furnishings" that Alva felt she had never known as a child. I remember every climbing tree, every hiding place, every rug and painting and chair; the light that streamed in through the leaves of plants in the large window in the family room and the snow that we shoveled when it lay a meter deep on the terrace. We used to call the rug in the family room our "green meadow"; from there my memories are mostly horizontal—on my stomach, heels in the air while playing Monopoly, wrestling with Kaj and other friends, or in various gymnastic poses.

In this house Alva hoped to realize all her ideals about children and family life as well as she could without help from Gunnar and in spite of all her activities outside the home. And since what she did at home those first years mirrored her ideals and all that she worked for in the larger community, that period was the most family-oriented in her life. It offered a kind of stage set, though not meant as theater. Here Alva had her great chance to design a life-style in order to show how a complicated family like ours might live together. And it was she who gave life to the scene: Alva—or Avva, as Jan taught us all to call her—lit up the home whenever she was there.

But it was to be expected that the house would not by itself create an idyllic atmosphere. The old conflicts between Jan and Gunnar only increased while—and in part because—Alva suffered in silence. Inwardly she was also torn between her many activities and the family life she claimed to value so highly. We children competed with one another and often with Gunnar for her attention. These clashes made her feel split apart, pulled in different directions.

I think she knew early on that she had not managed to create the home environment she had hoped for. And since she wanted to combine home life, marriage, and children with other significant work, she felt increasingly underutilized in her work capacity. She was made for great undertakings, but they were a long time coming. I have rarely met anyone with her intense need to give herself totally to demanding but inspiring work. During these years I could not observe as I later did how she could become half desperate without such work. Perhaps she had not yet had time to find its absence as depressing as later in life, but already she was surprised by her lot and somewhat dissatisfied with it.

To be sure, Alva had thrown herself into the population debate that followed the publication of *Crisis in the Population Question*. She traveled throughout the country, giving speeches and conducting workshops, and wrote innumerable newspaper articles. She derived intense pleasure from standing up and fighting for the reforms she saw as so clearly needed, even when she was ruthlessly attacked in the press. "It was probably worst during the mid-thirties, when we proposed, among other things, free school lunches and people said that that amounted to pure communism, the dissolution of the family, etc." Later she wondered whether the anger that she refused to express in personal relations might have been channeled into the energy and eagerness with which she battled the forces of inertia during those days. At any rate, she was far from discouraged by the controversy she and Gunnar had aroused. She had a great many warm supporters and drew courage from seeing the groundswell of popular concern she had helped stir up. Gunnar and she received more letters than they could possibly answer from men and women ready to work with them for better housing, better schools, free health care for all, and the other changes they had urged. Some even wrote to confide that their book had inspired an addition to the family.

But Alva knew that, as a woman, she still did not really count at the policymaking level. It was Gunnar, not she, who was asked to chair the Housing Commission established in 1935, even though she knew much more about the topic than he. That same year, Gunnar was made a member of the newly formed Population Commission, while Alva was merely asked to be a consultant. He was asked to run for Parliament, not she. Even the National Parents' Association wanted him as its chairman. When he pointedly inquired whether the board had not in reality meant the post for Alva its members replied, somewhat embarrassed, that of course they took for granted that she would be the one who would do the actual work.

She was shunted aside not only because she was a woman, and a mother of small children besides, but also because she and Gunnar were so often paired as "the Myrdal couple" that many people thought they could benefit from the ideas of both for the price of one. And in that case, why not turn to the man? It was only in the sixties that people realized that Alva was a better politician than Gunnar—that she was more conscientious, more dependable, more diplomatic, and a much better speaker—but by then she did not have many working years left.

Her principal project during the years in Äppelviken was the training college for preschool teachers that she helped to establish in 1936. By naming it Socialpedagogiska Seminariet—the Seminar for Social Pedagogy—she intended to convey its stress on a socially oriented approach to child development. She saw public policy and education as the two levers of social change, capable of bringing about all the reforms the nation so desperately needed. Schooling, she and Gunnar had written in *Crisis in the Population Question,* had to help children acquire a sense of community and cooperation rather than a narrowly individualistic ethos of egoistic competition, and the purpose of the Seminar was to begin by educating teachers themselves to carry out this task.

Plans for the Seminar had been modest at first. When Alva investigated collective child care in the early thirties she found the personnel ill equipped for the kind of care she advocated. She considered them sentimental, inexperienced, completely without social interests, ignorant about child development, and given to the "spinster model" for teachers, with all that this implied about the rejection of sexuality, of marriage, and of a full life. On this

subject she had written in *City Children,* in 1935. She summarized
its main conclusion in an interview:

> that collective child care was excellent but that the execution
> was inadequate because of the poor training of the person-
> nel. . . . That was when the architect Wallander said: "If you
> are dissatisfied with the training then make it better!" He
> immediately offered to build such a school into the next large
> complex of cooperative apartment buildings he was planning
> in Stockholm for the community of Kungsklippan.

Alva began planning. Now she would be able to work to free
both women and children in a concrete way. Her interest was
"partly in freeing children, in their right to develop in freedom,
partly in the freedom of women, in their opportunity to flourish
in working life." If children could develop without the poverty,
the isolation, and the parochialism that often marked their homes,
their richer common life would train them to be free and fully
mature adults. And that aim required that the staff, too, lead full
lives, lives devoted not just to child rearing but also to their own
participation in society, to their own self-development, including
their own sexuality. For this purpose, the teachers should preferably be under thirty-five, men as often as women, married as often
as not. As for the resident students, Alva encouraged them to go
to dances and meet men, something entirely new up to then in
such schools, and to plan for marriage and a family of their own
so long as it did not stand in the way of all outside work.

Alva used to say that equality based on justice was her fundamental value—equality between children and adults, men and
women, rich and poor, the sick and the healthy, and peoples from
all religions, all countries, all cultures. And that is true enough.
But I believe that freedom actually came first for her. Without
freedom there could be no safeguards for justice, no lasting equality—only the free can keep these values safe. Children's freedom
and that of women and all others from poverty and war and
oppression—she could speak out so strongly for these values because she felt them to be indispensable in her own life. In the

Seminar she hoped to combine freedom and equality: the personnel, freed in the ways she had planned, would come from all levels of society and raise children in a classless spirit to resist prejudice and exploitation of all kinds.

But the freedom of women for which Alva worked was not merely freedom from household slavery and from the "spinster mentality" which meant that many women were fired from their jobs if they got married. It was also freedom for gainful work. And there was an element of pressure in this ideal of freedom. Already in *Crisis in the Population Question* she had objected to the possibility that women might use their freedom for

> sports and beauty care, erotic promiscuity, social activity of a charitable kind, and, among the more intellectual and ambitious, also a lot of "free" literary, artistic, or scientific work of a nature unlikely to bring in income.

Women should, in other words, be freed to do the kind of socially productive work that Alva valued. It is therefore not surprising that a crisis sometimes arose when a student enrolled in pedagogy and child-care courses merely with the intention of marrying and bringing up her own children:

> Against this I fought hard. I kept reminding the girls of what they had cost society and their parents and that it was absolutely necessary that they exercise their profession. It is a professional training, a teacher's training, that we give them. These expensive study years are not meant to make them better mothers and housekeepers! Everyone could use that; but one must acquire it in one's spare time more simply and cheaply.

The only crises Alva remembers from her work in the Seminar occurred with girls who wanted to give up their course of training in order to get married. Alva insisted that it was "wrong to throw away or downgrade training that after all aimed for professional work! In the service of society. And for the welfare of many children—not only one's own." One senses the outrage of someone who, like her, had fought hard for her own education, at the thought that others might not understand its full value and thus not feel responsible for putting it to use. It was not only the cost that she found wasted on students who did not intend to use the training. She planned her courses as means to liberate both students and children. She had had to fight for herself and for the students; it was now their turn to carry on the battle.

The school turned into a larger and more innovative undertaking for Alva than anyone could have predicted. It could not open until after Kaj's birth in late August 1936. She then began in earnest, allocating her time as flexibly as she could between home and the Seminar, along with all the lecturing and political work to which she was already committed. Until then, Sweden had not had adequate training for personnel in kindergartens and other early childhood centers. Alva became the first director of the school. She decided to divide the instruction into separate terms of theory and practice instead of merely having brief hours of practical internship each week which made it impossible for students to enter into a child's entire day.

The theoretical instruction included all that Alva had absorbed abroad; after all, as she pointed out, they were living in the golden age of child study. She hoped to be able to pass on to her students all that she had learned from Dewey, Bühler, Adler, Piaget, Goodenough, Freud, Ilg, and Gesell. But she also hoped, in focusing on individual children, to convey far more than a body of knowledge. There was really only one important thing to remember about any one child, she maintained, whether it arrived in a family as a newborn or in a school class as a beginner, and that was that "the human child is the greatest miracle of creation. Every single child, moreover, is a world of subtle secrets, a personality, a unique occurrence, never to be repeated on this earth." As a result, the air children breathe, the food they eat, the atmosphere in their families, the warmth from human contacts, the toys placed in their hands, the experiences that meet their first gropings in the outside world—all contribute to shaping individuals. There could be no greater or more rewarding challenge, Alva insisted, than to do everything in one's power to give each single child the best possible start in life, whether as a parent or as a teacher.

Alva's diary entries when my siblings and I were born convey that sense of the wonder of it all—no doubt intensified by the disappointments brought by each of her miscarriages. But she also notes the words we were learning, our motor development, what we were eating, and our habits, oddities, fears, imaginary play-mates, and social relationships. After her death I was surprised to discover, among her many abortive plans for books to be written, the outline of one that was to be entitled *Sissela*. The title gave me a mirror-quick sense of careening perspectives and roles. Here I was, finishing a book about her, to be entitled (in the Swedish edition) *Alva,* only to come on her, as a young mother, outlining one about me! Who was reaching out to whom? Trying to un-derstand and capture in words whose life?

I was half disappointed, as I read Alva's outline of this pro-posed book about me, to find that she had intended to cover only my first year of life and to write in the dry tone of a scientific report, so unlike that of her diaries and letters. The subtitle was to be *Close Observation of a Child and Experimentation During Its First Year.* Aiming to show how different psychological theories might interpret similar facts about a child's development, it was meant to encourage parents to keep notes on their own children.

Might such studying of one's children not risk seeming intru-sive to them? I have no memories of feeling that way. At first Kaj and I noticed nothing unusual; later we relished the word games, the chance to draw and do puzzles and solve problems that the tests involved, especially since we sensed so much affection and interest in what we were doing. Kaj was one of the children studied by Frances Ilg for the series of books that she published, with Arnold Gesell, on the development of young children. The 1930s were years of passionate concern to improve the lot of children and of high hopes for all that could be learned from observing them. Encouraged by Ilg, Gesell, and others, parents and teachers were studying children with a new focus on person-ality at every stage of their development. Jean Piaget had never hesitated to use his own children as research subjects. In New

York, Margaret Mead and her young pediatrician, Dr. Benjamin Spock, scandalized many by arranging for the birth of her daughter Catherine to be filmed. All across the United States, innovative schools were being founded. One of them, the Miquon School, was started near Philadelphia by Margaret Bok, a young mother of three who was convinced that schools could do far more to foster a child's creativity and pleasure in learning. Much later, her son Derek would become my husband.

But Alva did not intend her students to learn only about children. If they were to carry out their teaching well, they also needed to learn about society. She was all too aware of how little young people, and especially university students, knew about social conditions: they lived "in a form of social innocence much longer than all the girls who 'woke up socially' in our school."

To round out their education, the students' knowledge about children and society ought, according to Alva, to develop along with insight into their own personalities. Self-knowledge was to be facilitated through instruction in "mental hygiene"—a course that bordered on personality analysis and psychoanalysis—and through personal counseling. It was crucial, Alva thought,

> that future teachers receive guidance not only in thinking about the developmental processes of children, but also in reflecting more objectively about their own.
>
> Actually, I had not really thought all this through in advance. But gradually, I got it all to come together into a system, and then it seemed to be self-explanatory. The board, the colleagues, the students—I believed all were unanimous about this. We had a superb level of collaboration.

At the Seminar, Alva flourished as never before. She herself had helped to create this environment and to choose those who worked there. She who had never received her doctorate, never become a professor like Gunnar, was now in a position to impart knowledge about children and psychology in a manner she considered far superior to the sterile and wholly theoretical courses still offered at universities. We children were welcome at the

Seminar's quarters as well and felt as much at home there as Alva. We were even allowed to do carpentry—something out of the question for girls in the Swedish schools of the day—and we loved the book corner and the toys gathered to demonstrate what children most enjoyed.

Gunnar, however, was growing dissatisfied. Too much time was going to pleading for reforms in housing, sex education, and population policy—all the practical work that Alva stood for and that he was beginning to find tedious. It threatened to slow down his own scholarly work. He was therefore tempted when, in 1937, President Frederick Keppel of the Carnegie Corporation invited him to come to the United States in order to undertake a large-scale study of what was then called "the American Negro problem." At first Gunnar declined, but as the weeks went on he began to regret having done so. Both Alva and he sensed that this was what he ought to do. They saw it as a way to "stretch the personality—to shape ourselves anew after some years during which we risked being squeezed into one-sidedness," as Gunnar later wrote. "The problem is immense in scope and importance, it is as complicated as life itself, it is permeated by the most intense valuations and these valuations clash violently."

Gunnar knew that the sponsors of the study had turned to a foreigner because they wanted a completely unbiased, fresh look. Most Americans who had studied their nation's race problem had already taken sides on its causes, manifestations, and possible remedies. Why not choose instead a highly regarded foreign scholar used to directing collaborative studies of economic and social problems and known to have taken a stand against Nazi and other doctrines of racial inferiority, yet still a stranger to research on American race issues? Gunnar seemed to the sponsors especially likely to bring objectivity and scholarly acumen to the study: "I was asked to be both the subject and the object of a cultural experiment in the social sciences."

To be sure, Alva would have to take a leave of absence from the Seminar and we would all have to wrench ourselves away from the house where we had lived for only a year. And moving the entire household would be expensive and difficult. But to have the opportunity to return to the United States and undertake such a great if perhaps impossible task would surely be worth the attempt, they both concluded.

The press photo showing our departure by train from Stockholm, on our way to the port of Göteborg in the fall of 1938, reveals these high hopes: Alva and Gunnar in suits made from the same broadly striped fabric, he carrying a briefcase, she with roses on her arm, Jan glowing with a giant bouquet of gladioli and carnations, I serious, having just scraped my nose while running too wildly, two-year-old Kaj attentive, safely ignorant of all that lay ahead.

From the M.S. *Kungsholm* Gunnar wrote Gustav Cassel on September 9, 1938, that he and Alva were approaching the Statue of Liberty with all their children, including two twenty-year-old college girls who were to take care of the household. "It feels wonderful for Alva and me to have thrown off all the thousands of practical duties and to be able to turn once again to what we were born for: pure science and the free life of research."

My own memories from the ocean crossing and the period that followed are hazy, filtered through Alva's many photographs. I had no insight then, at three and a half years of age, into how the journey was to affect our lives. Only much later did I understand that this was to be the most intense, stimulating, magnificent period in Gunnar's life. The severity of the racial problems in the United States had taken on new prominence in the public eye because of the persecution of Jews in Germany: how could American citizens castigate racial hatred and debilitating prejudice in Germany while shutting their eyes to them at home? Both Gunnar and Alva realized that they could no longer view one country's problems in isolation, as they had in writing about depopulation in Sweden. Never again would they approach large issues in any but an international perspective.

Gunnar threw himself into the work with all his energy and creativity. He spent the first two months motoring through the South with his Swedish colleague Richard Sterner to get a direct sense of what he was to study, rather than steeping himself first in books about the issue. He reported to Carnegie's President

Keppel that "I didn't realize what a terrible problem you have
put me into. I mean we are horrified." His fear of not being equal
to the challenge came out in many of his talks with Alva and close
friends. He was "shocked and scared to the bones by all the evils
I saw." In the end he traveled in every state and interviewed
"sharecroppers and plantation owners, workers and employers,
merchants and bankers, intellectuals, preachers, organization
leaders, political bosses, gangsters, black and white, men and
women, young and old, Southerners and Northerners."

To Gustav Cassel Gunnar wrote in January 1939 that the
problem fascinated him more and more:

> I feel that I am making contact with certain fundamentals in
> the tragedy of humanity. I cannot yet say that I see clear lines
> before me. I still feel as if I am swimming in an ocean. . . .
> Last time [I visited the United States], I lived my ordinary life
> and worked with my usual problems. Now I *have* to penetrate
> questions that are thoroughly American. I have to dive more
> deeply than ever into a foreign culture. Even if it is tiring it
> makes us happy. After all, it is an extraordinary and rare
> expansion of the personality that we are living through.

Given Gunnar's Enlightenment ideals, worked out since the
early years with Alva, it was no wonder that he would come to
see not only the American racial problem but the roots from which
a solution must spring in terms of a dilemma: that of the jarring
contrast between ideals and reality that he believed most Americans felt in their hearts. The ideals were those of what he called
the American Creed: "the essential dignity of the individual human being, the fundamental equality of all men, and certain inalienable rights to freedom, justice, and a fair opportunity." The
reality was the shameful one of racial segregation and all the evils
it fostered. There was no reason, Gunnar would suggest, for this
dilemma to remain unresolved; the challenge for the nation now
lay in living up to its principles by altering its practices. And social
science could help to bring this about by shedding light both on
the condition and on its remedies.

For this purpose, he assembled a remarkable team of social scientists—among them Ralph Bunche, Franklin Frazier, Charles S. Johnson, Otto Klineberg, Arnold Rose, and Dorothy Swaine Thomas—to conduct meticulous research on all facets of the problem. He knew from the outset that this study had to be interdisciplinary, concerned with every aspect of American life and far vaster in scope than anything he had ever attempted; and he knew how many different ways there were in which he might fail to live up to the task. Much of the time he felt exhilarated by the challenge, but he relied on Alva, as always, to lend support and vitality when he felt that it might defeat him.

Alva saw to it that the arts were part of their learning about black American culture. Sterling Brown and Richard Wright were familiar visitors in our household, bringing friends over and advising Alva on how to assemble a collection of original recordings of blues, work songs, and prison songs. She read their works, along with those of Langston Hughes and others, and brought as much literature by black authors home to Sweden as she could. As a result, it shaped the background in which I grew up, along with the singing of Bessie Smith, Billie Holiday, Paul Robeson, and many others. When I began trying to translate poetry in my teens, it was natural to turn first to the rhythms of Langston Hughes, beginning with his melodious poem about the "golden girl" in "Harlem Town."

After a year's work in New York, Gunnar traveled through the South once again, this time with Ralph Bunche as a companion. Bunche, a brilliant, erudite, and at the time radical young professor of political science at Howard University, six years younger than Gunnar, was one of his closest collaborators. During this trip Gunnar lived and breathed the problems as blacks experienced them, feeling the humiliation when Bunche could not stay at hotels or eat in restaurants because of the color of his skin and taking pleasure, whenever possible, in outwitting those in charge of enforcing such rules.

More than once, the two got into trouble with the authorities. They had to flee the state of Georgia after Gunnar insulted the matriarchal head of an association for the protection of white womanhood. When she claimed that most black men think only of raping white women, he asked in a surprised voice how it could be possible for anyone to have such thoughts about *her*. She called a city official to signal the presence, in Atlanta, of two dangerous subversives. The warrant for their arrest was issued that same night, but by then the two friends had already crossed into another state.

For Bunche, the association with Alva and Gunnar appears to have been a turning point. Having grown up under segregation, Bunche's expectations of relations with whites were low. Now he found that he could work and communicate on the highest, most uninhibited intellectual and social level with at least some whites. Bunche and his wife came to be among Alva's and Gunnar's closest friends. A photo from the period shows Bunche, Gunnar, and Alva sitting on descending stone steps outside the Bunche house in Washington, D.C., their intent faces turned as if interrupted in mid-conversation. They could hardly have imagined at the time that all three would one day receive Nobel Prizes—Bunche as early as 1950, for his efforts in negotiating a truce in Palestine.

With collaborators such as Bunche, Gunnar's capacity to survey a vast set of interlocking problems found its fullest expression. With them he mapped the contradictions and conflicts among whites in America as among blacks and countered as pseudoscientific the commonplace theories about innate racial inferiority. He showed how poverty among blacks and whites tied in with racism, unemployment, poor housing, and education, how each factor exacerbated the others, but also how the downward spiral could be turned around through specific attempts to remedy each of these deficiencies. In so doing, he was making use of what Alva and he had already practiced in their book on population: what he later called the "institutional approach" to social problems. Its central idea, he wrote in *Asian Drama*, "is that history and politics, theories and ideologies, economic structures and levels, social stratification, agriculture and industry, health and education, and so on, must be studied not in isolation, but in their mutual relationships."

Alva used the same approach in working on the book that

was to become *Nation and Family: The Swedish Experiment in Democratic Family and Population Policy*. She intended to treat Sweden's experiences with social reforms as an experiment: one that other nations could examine and learn from, and that they could replicate while adjusting it to their own circumstances. She also meant to stress that the Swedish effort to shape a family policy was democratic, unlike the Nazi pronatalist and racist family propaganda that had sprung up in Germany. She dismissed the writings on population by Germans during the 1930s as pathetic, though perhaps inevitable in a country where freedom of science and public discussion were barred: "One senses the procrusteanization of the German soul."

In discussing Sweden's policies the book was, in many ways, more mature than its predecessor. Alva had had time to reflect on the Swedish debate over family policy and to evaluate the discussions in the population commission and in Parliament. And since many of the reforms that she and Gunnar had proposed had begun to be implemented, there was far less need to fend off opponents. Rather, what mattered was to exercise self-criticism regarding proposals that had failed or that should have failed and to be as persuasive as possible about those that deserved a trial in the United States and elsewhere. Gone, therefore, was any exclusive claim to rationality and any attribution of ignorance or worse to critics; gone, too, was the hortatory tone and the faith in progress as somehow inevitable once the right actions are taken. On the contrary, it was impossible not to see just how powerful the forces of unreason and of social disintegration were. But although both Alva and Gunnar had become more modest about the capacity of reason and social criticism to reverse the darkness engulfing Europe, they retained greater hopes for the United States.

Nation and Family begins by asking what principles might underlie a responsible family policy in any country. In what Daniel Patrick Moynihan calls "a superb feat of pure intellection" in his preface to a reissue of the book in 1968, Alva goes through population trends, changes in the family, questions for parents in planning their families and their expenses, and possible government policies that best serve families and thus the nation. Government policies inevitably affect families; the only question, she argues, is whether these policies will be made consciously, with families in mind, or will affect them haphazardly and destructively.

This time Alva places less stress on the threat of depopulation, one increasingly beside the point as the world's population began shooting up. Already in 1941, fertility and immigration were on the rise even in Sweden. Alva emphasizes, rather, the benefits to society and to families from the reforms she advocates, quite apart from their effect on birth statistics.

Which policies, then, best serve families—and thus nations? In the second part of the book, she looks carefully at what a small country like Sweden has managed to do. She considers such measures as maternity benefits, provisions for the handicapped, and providing adequate nourishment and educational opportunities for all children. She takes up the need for decent housing but also shows how housing loans have had the secondary effect of helping create the modern Swedish design that was beginning to be known the world over; and she insists on the importance of satisfying people's needs for art and for beauty, for recreation and a chance to travel and to buy gifts for others. Society ought not only to counter poverty and suffering but also to promote a way of life that is richer in what people most treasure.

Coming after the lucid exposition of so many constructive programs, the book's last chapter, entitled "One Sex: A Social Problem," strikes a far more troubled note. The reforms Alva has advocated do not go to the heart, she suggests, of the fundamental dilemmas that women confront with respect to marriage itself. The most profound curse on every woman's life, she claims, is the uncertainty of her life plan, given the conflicting hopes and expectations she faces. Is a rational balance even possible between work and marriage?

"The feminine sex is itself a social problem," Alva argues; and any woman, whether young or old, whether married or not, whether employed outside the home or not, is likely to *be* such a problem. The family is the essential social relationship, but so long as family life remains so poorly harmonized to new economic

realities, women will continue to feel torn. Those who choose to
work outside the home while they have children will experience
guilt no matter how they divide their time; those who choose to
stay home will feel isolated by comparison and uncertain of their
status, even of the meaning of their lives once their children have
left home.

Alva raises a cascade of questions hinting at "a complicated
pattern of brooding over riddles, never solved and rarely even
expressed." A family policy like Sweden's, no matter how rational
and how solicitous of mothers and children, might one day be
declared a failure for not having tackled the very problem of
marriage itself. And the efforts to help women combine motherhood and remunerative work will in all likelihood encounter so
many difficulties that there will be a lengthy transitional period
during which women will either have to shun maternal responsibilities that are too heavy or give up outside work.

I cannot help wondering at her insistence that women not
only have problems but *are* problems—that the entire feminine
sex "is itself a social problem." Gunnar, after all, had concluded
that the "Negro problem" which he had been asked to study was
not confined to any one racial group but was, rather, "a problem
in the heart of the American." It was there, he argued, that the
decisive struggle went on. Given the reality of discrimination,
blacks could hardly help thinking of their predicament as problematic; the challenge of living up to the nation's ideals confronted
all Americans. And Alva herself, in writing about anti-Semitism,
rejected the claim heard so vociferously in Nazi Germany and
elsewhere that there was a "Jewish problem"; she argued instead
that it was anti-Semitism itself that was the problem—a contagious form of mass insanity capable of leading to unspeakable
persecution. What did she mean, then, in singling out women as
constituting a problem, even to themselves?

One hint as to why Alva should see the problem of women as
thus unique appears in one of the appendixes to Gunnar's *American Dilemma,* which took on renewed importance for the wom-
en's movement decades later. In it he compares blacks to two
other groups of human beings who are highly visible in every

society because of their physical appearance, their dress, and their patterns of behavior and who have been held down: women and children. The similarity in the problems that the three groups confront, he suggests, is not accidental. It reflects the patriarchal social pattern in which the father of the house has power over the women, children, servants, and animals of his household. Even when this pattern grows weaker, childbearing slows women in the struggle for equality, just as blacks, even after slavery is abolished, "are laboring under the yoke of unassimilability." Gunnar found the barrier against blacks much stronger than that against women in America at the time he was writing; but he referred to Alva's chapter "One Sex: A Social Problem" in *Nation and Family* to argue that the second is more "eternally inexorable."

Alva may have felt the problem of women as more intractable, in the long run, than that of racial discrimination, in part because she saw no evidence yet of a dilemma in people's hearts concerning their treatment. Gunnar could point to the American Creed as creating such a dilemma among Americans with respect to racial discrimination, but Alva could refer to no corresponding creed upholding the rights of women. Neither religious texts, historical traditions, nor laws conveyed an equivalent stress on freedom and equality for women. Even the Enlightenment "Rights of Man" had too often proved, when challenged, to protect just that—the rights of men alone. Whereas Gunnar had found racism to be morally troubling even to many of those who engaged in it, Alva saw no similar discomfort about practices that discriminated against women.

Alva did not, in fact, regard this state of affairs as "eternally inexorable." Change was bound to come. But she closed her book with a warning: "The risk is great that society will proceed so slowly in solving these problems of women's existence that new and even more desperate crises may invade the whole field of women, family, and population."

In these words I hear Alva's fears for all women; but I hear, too, her growing doubts about her own ability to combine parenting, love, and work in the wholehearted, rational, and creative way that she had always advocated. These doubts were strongest during the years when children, husband, and work seemed to pull her in different directions. But they never immobilized her. She saw far too many opportunities for imaginative change, far too many improvements that could be traced to reforms she had helped to implement. And she realized, with some surprise, how fortunate she was in finding a hearing for her views and in coming to know more and more like-minded women who shared them.

Starting in the early thirties, Alva had been a leader in the newly formed Association for Working Women, advocating equal rights and equal pay for women regardless of family circumstances. And in 1937, she had been instrumental in helping to start, and then chairing, the Swedish branch of the International Federation of Business and Professional Women. Through this organization, she helped bring about a change in the Swedish Civil Service—that women could no longer be dismissed because of marriage, pregnancy, or childbirth. In 1938 she became the vice president of the federation and worked during her spare time in its New York office.

Throughout my childhood, I remember different groups of women meeting in our home for these and other causes. Those who came impressed me as being strong, warmly loyal to one another, kind to us children, and endowed with an appealingly earthy humor. Kaj and I could hardly know it at the time, but the examples given us by Alva and by these many women whose lives wove in and out of hers would be indispensable to us as we grew up. Because we had the models that Alva lacked when she was young, we never had to contend with the worry that can beset even many feminists today: the worry that perhaps women are, after all, incurably inferior.

With these friends, we sensed, Alva was in her element. We could feel their exhilaration each time they succeeded in bringing about a shift, large or small. Society was turning into a web of associations for people with shared concerns, she wrote in 1935, urging women to join together to promote their interests. Just as it had once been natural to unite within a neighborhood or community against the outside world, so it had now become natural, instead, to choose where and with whom to belong: "You might say: In the past you were born into a neighborhood; now you choose one." What matters is to do the choosing so as to find friends who are both like-minded and sufficiently diverse to be stimulating. Looking back at what she had accomplished in the company of such friends, she explained to an interviewer how they had had to

> make noise to the conservative male schoolteachers, make noise for equal salaries, for school lunches, for new abortion laws, for collective housing and other reforms. . . . When banks and shops—even the cooperatives—fired women who expected babies, we in the organization threatened to boycott them. That worked right away.

9

Wartime

❖ ❖ ❖ ❖

We had left a Sweden flourishing in peace and fermenting with economic and cultural growth. In jest, we had told our friends that we would come home earlier than planned if war broke out. Yet like most of our compatriots, we had not been able to believe in anything as mad as a new world war in spite of all. Even as our ship left Sweden, however, the Munich crisis was already beginning. After that, the shadow of the risk of war lay over our whole life and our work.

So wrote Alva and Gunnar in "Midseas," the preface to the second book they published together, in 1941, *Kontakt med Amerika* (*Contact with America*). When they had sailed from Sweden in 1938 they still doubted that Hitler had the resources to win a major war and that he would be foolhardy enough to embark on one. Later they would look back at their time abroad as "those fateful years in America that began with the September crisis of 1938 and ended with the invasion of Holland in May 1940."

As always, they participated in world history in an intense and informed manner, following events through both Swedish and American daily and weekly papers. The Swedish papers arrived two weeks late by boat, offering what Alva called "a strange review after the fact." Wherever they were, I remember the newspapers: Gunnar sitting in "his" chair surrounded by cigarette smoke, overflowing ashtrays, and tables piled high with papers and writings of all kinds, Alva moving about from one task to another, or seated with a stack of papers, underlining or cutting out what she wanted to keep.

Letters to friends and relatives in Sweden show their pain as they tried to think through how to respond to the war's inexorable approach. They agonized over the news of Germany's devouring Czechoslovakia and the pact with the Soviet Union that allowed the division of Poland. Gunnar had to force himself to expend all his energy single-mindedly on his book, while Alva devoted more and more of her time to help raise funds for the defense of Finland against the Soviet Union and for refugee aid. But they also began to ask themselves whether they ought to stay in America and finish their books, as many friends counseled them to do, or to return home and do all they could to help prepare for their nation's defense. As early as January 1939, Alva wrote to Gunnar's sister Elsa:

> It is so horrible, the whole thing—I don't suppose anything will ever be all right again. Where do we really want the children to grow up—is there a country for them? Is there any future? . . . one does feel a bit guilty to think that here our kids would fit in, this country could never go under, but would we be able to desert thus, for their sake?

She saw the dilemma as a harrowing personal choice: should they desert Sweden and live in security or make common cause with other Swedes, at whatever risk? And if they decided to return home, should they leave us three children with the friends in America who kindly offered to take care of us, or keep the family together by bringing us along?

The summer of 1939 brought an interlude when it seemed to Alva almost as if their personal time stood still. She and Gunnar rented a small house in Huntington, Long Island, near the beach, for four months. Alva would always look back to that summer—the only one we all spent on vacation together—as a time of limpid happiness when all family tensions seemed suspended. She and Gunnar would work during the mornings while Kaj and I played near the house. Jan was earning money by clipping and pasting newspaper articles for them. Then we all went to the beach in the afternoon. In the cool of the evenings the two of them were free to work once again. After we returned to Sweden, my strongest memories of America would be of the dunes and waves that summer when I was four. In trying to tell my friends of the vastness of American beaches, oceans, cities, I would compare the waves I had seen to skyscrapers stretching far into the blue sky—all equally impossible to conceive and equally magical at such a distance.

When, in September 1939, England and France declared war against Germany after its invasion of Poland, Alva wrote home: "These days are terrible. I feel only an awful paralysis. What will happen? What will become of us all? Never could we have known how patriotic we would feel." It did not occur to her and Gunnar to fear returning, even though their outspoken antifascist activism would place them at great risk should Germany invade Sweden. But they wanted a role when they returned, especially since they had neither work nor a place to live there, their villa having been rented out to friends. Gunnar wrote to the prime minister, Per Albin Hansson, to ask how they might best be "mobilized" to serve the country if they came back. But he received no reply: "It looks as if they are not especially eager to get us back."

Then on April 9, 1940, Germany invaded Norway and Denmark. Alva and Gunnar were in Washington, D.C., on their way to Mexico when they heard the news. There was no more room for hesitation. They decided to return to what they feared would be war even in Sweden. And though Jan begged to be allowed to stay, they felt it was important to bring us all home rather than split up the family. But it turned out to be next to impossible to find a ship for the trip home. All passenger traffic had ceased. In May, we were finally accepted as the sole passengers on the *Mathilda Thordén,* a Finnish merchant ship. Barrels of dynamite were stacked together on the deck. The risk was high that we would encounter German mines in the waters near the coasts of England and Norway. As the ship made its way through a storm more severe than any Alva and Gunnar had ever experienced, some of the barrels slid ominously back and forth across the deck. Down in the radio room where we gathered to hear the news, somber voices described Germany's invasion of Belgium and Holland.

Alva and Gunnar's sense of being in the middle of life as the war intensified was especially strong just then when they were midway home but not yet there. Gunnar was forty-one years old, Alva thirty-eight. In the chapter "Midseas," they told of their emotions when their ship had lost radio contact with America but not yet located the European broadcasts: "It is the middle of May and our minds are heavy and anxious. What cannot have happened at home, before we receive bulletins once again from the sick continent?" At last we arrived unscathed at Petsamo, a town on the Finnish Arctic coast, now part of the Soviet Union, and flew on to Sweden:

We had journeyed home to a war, but the war did not arrive. Every day when the sun rose over our country at peace, we felt a happiness that no somber news from the rest of the world and no worries about the future could more than nudge at the edge. We had returned to duties that awaited us, but none sought us out. It must have been the strong contrast between fateful expectations and their dissolution into a momentarily happy void that made us feel that we were on vacation.

Months passed. Anguish over the fate of Norway and Denmark and fear of an imminent invasion weighed on everyone's mind. Sweden's coalition government had responded to the threat in ways that Alva and Gunnar thought dangerous for the nation's fundamental democratic traditions. Faced with the alternative of invasion, the government had agreed to continue trading with Germany, to allow certain German troop transports free passage through the country, and to impose limited press censorship of news about Germany and the war. Few Swedes would have welcomed a Nazi takeover; but many believed that Sweden, to maintain its independence, had to accommodate in such ways.

Alva and Gunnar found the atmosphere painfully different

from that of the freewheeling debate they had come to take for granted in the United States. Even their own words, they felt, were censored: when Gunnar said in an interview that he was convinced that the United States would intervene in the long run to deny Hitler permanent dominion over Europe, his statement was left unprinted. Everywhere they encountered blackouts, censorship, and political backbiting: "We stagger forward with a minimum of openness, public debate, and democratic controls over government."

In response, they decided to try to arouse their fellow Swedes to guard their freedoms more forcefully: they would write a book contrasting this cramped atmosphere with the far freer debate and the greater awareness of democratic traditions in the country they had just left. When they worked on *Contact with America,* in 1940, Alva and Gunnar could not know whether Sweden would be attacked as Norway and Denmark had been. If that happened, they did not know how democracy and all they had stood for could survive in their country. But they wanted to do all they could to increase the powers of resistance among their compatriots. And by comparing Sweden with the great American democracy that they felt could never give way to the Nazis, they intended to help shape the right kind of resistance.

Contact with America was therefore as personally experienced as *Crisis in the Population Question* and as insistent on the necessity for the Swedish people to understand the crisis thoroughly in order to be able to ward off the threat of catastrophe. Sweden must not allow itself to be demoralized by the danger of war, they wrote; it must not relinquish the normal requirements of democracy, nor give in to the despair and to the "black-out mentality" that risked shrinking everyone's mental horizons. The "semi-censorship" regarding war news that they found on returning home was exactly the opposite of what the nation needed. Many people, ignorant of the prevailing level of censorship, had been led to imagine, for example, that "concentration camps no longer exist, since they have not read about them in the newspapers for years."

Some people may ask, they suggest, whether *any* ideals can

hold up in a time of such crisis. Their answer is that ideals hold up only so long as people continue to honor them. "When ideals tumble, that is only because people let go of them." It was time to guard the nation's democratic ideals and resist all who were trying to undermine them by invoking the danger of war. A small, neutral country like Sweden could otherwise much too easily fall for the temptation to shut itself off from the fate of peoples around the earth by adopting a false air of "normalcy."

But this time Alva and Gunnar were not so triumphantly and youthfully sanguine that the crisis was a transitional one. They could only insist that, however grim the future might look, tired pessimism would not do: "Now we cannot afford not to be optimists." Their conviction, formulated during the year in Geneva in 1930–31, that it was possible to concentrate on reforms in a country like Sweden, regardless of all disunity and madness in the world, had long since been shaken. Even their enthusiasm for collectivism was more tempered: they had seen how masses could grow intoxicated and be driven to barbarism. But in spite of all, they retained their faith in the possibility, however fragile just then, that reason could win out in the end.

Alva and Gunnar always looked back at this book as a hastily assembled contribution to an emergency. When Alva reread it in 1979, she saw much that would require correcting and quite a bit that needed to be entirely rewritten. I find it not merely hastily assembled but also profoundly split. The first and last chapters are written in despair over the war that has just broken out; the rest of the chapters go over previously prepared comparisons between conditions in America and Sweden—between schools in the two countries, for example, or the press, or the role of different social ideals—set forth in order to stimulate reforms in their home country.

The comparisons often favor America, especially when it comes to human traits. To be sure, the authors grant, they have seen greater evil, injustice, and weakness in the United States than in Sweden. But they have also witnessed more goodness, a livelier passion for justice, and more exuberant, creative strength among

Americans than among Swedes. In America, they find, people are more open, more idealistic, more willing to experiment and think innovatively, more interested in psychology, fonder of children. The generations are closer to one another. "People simply seem to remember better what it feels like to be a child and young." Families are more valued, openness and generosity are stronger. "While the Swede is more apt to sit and contemplate himself anxiously or perhaps act out something of a role, the American gives in more uninhibitedly to his simple joy in others." People in America do not speak ill of one another. "The cramped in spirit are almost unknown" and "the tone of conversation itself is naturally more considerate and heartfelt." Even journalists in America are thought to want to say mostly good things about those they interview.

What Alva and Gunnar said about Americans reflected first and foremost their own experience. They had found far greater warmth and openness in many personal relationships in America than at home. But their words were also meant to warn that Swedes now had special reason to overcome their customary stiffness and reserve, for these had contributed to the dour war mentality that endangered Sweden's democratic traditions. Fifty years after they wrote, studies comparing attitudes among Swedes and citizens of other countries corroborate many of Alva and Gunnar's observations. To the casual observer from abroad, the stolid formality and distance are especially striking among Swedish men and seem to have been largely overcome, to the extent that they once existed, among women. Meanwhile postwar immigrants from many different cultures and expanded international travel are slowly bringing greater openness and informality into Swedish society more generally. At the time, however, Alva and Gunnar's eagerness to open up problems for public debate seemed disturbingly "foreign" to many, especially in the government.

Alva wrote the chapter on schools, hoping to encourage a thoroughgoing reform of the Swedish school system along American lines. The reform would involve giving up the existing two-track system in which most children went to public school for seven years whereas a selected elite split off after the fourth grade to train for the gymnasium, which alone opened the door to university study. Such a reform, she argued, should serve democratic and egalitarian ideals throughout the system by giving everyone an equal opportunity for schooling and by bringing a greater proportion of the population into schools of one kind or another.

In advocating the American system as a model, Alva often presents it uncritically. Although she claims to have studied schools throughout the country, she draws many of her conclusions from well-run public schools, often in the Midwest, from the numerous experimental schools that had been started during the last decade, and especially from the school she knew best— the progressive Lincoln School in New York, where Jan had been a student. One looks in vain for traces of the many miserable segregated schools that Gunnar had been studying or for more traditional private schools.

In America, Alva writes, schools doubtless realize the democratic ideals of fraternity and equality of opportunity better than in Sweden. Competitive examinations do not play nearly the same role that they do in the Swedish gymnasium; rather, cooperation is emphasized throughout the curriculum. Textbooks are so lively and well composed that they can serve students all through life. Boys and girls learn to take care of children, cook, keep careful accounts, understand the importance of science, and practice citizenship in political affairs. She finds that America, generally speaking, has developed "a school that is more suited for real life than ours, that reaches further in perfecting the human material, and that makes childhood, during this process, into an experience of happiness."

Having come to know the variability among American schools at close range, I could only write in the margin, when I read this chapter, "Illusions, illusions—how *could* Alva believe all this?" To be sure, she was writing about America's more generous, hopeful attitudes toward children and education in the late thirties. By now, research has shown that the time adult Americans spend with children has been going down steadily for decades, along with the proportion of resources devoted even to children's most basic survival needs. If she could have witnessed the makeshift schooling for homeless children during the 1980s or the hopelessness and brutality in so many inner city schools, she would surely not have written in a tone of such unqualified praise. But the euphoria of her chapter would have been excessive in any period.

My doubts about Alva's chapter connect with a larger question concerning her writings and Gunnar's. How could they be so certain, I have often wondered, about what is right or wrong, humanitarian or dangerous, factual or sentimental? In this book, as in *Crisis in the Population Question,* the most astounding points of view, sometimes emanating entirely from their own hopes or fears, are presented as facts. All writers are prone to such overstating, but Alva and Gunnar were so especially certain that what they said was "scientific" and therefore incontestable. They could present hypotheses regarding the future in the same tone of self-evidence in which they put forth population statistics, and offer personal interpretations of abstruse matters as obvious to all who had their eyes open.

At the same time one feels, in this as in their earlier book, how sharp their aim could be, how much they understood of problems that most people would never be able to sort out, how often they were in fact right, and how forcefully they conveyed the large outlines of a problem, while capturing the links between so many circumstances. It was this forcefulness that others felt and found inspiring, whether it concerned social reforms or research, prospects for the future, or efforts for peace.

In deciding to return to Sweden, Gunnar had hoped to be able to work within the government. Once home, however, he found that no one seemed to need him. The grand gesture of returning home for patriotic reasons began to seem pointless. A number of his bitter comparisons between leadership in America and Sweden probably took form during this period. In the book, he wonders what Lincoln's fate might have been had he been born in Sweden. After detailing the petty obstacles that the Swedish community would have placed in Lincoln's way, he asks even if our more rigid society had not hindered him in any external way, would we ever have allowed that man to become his people's leader? And would we have idealized him afterwards—a man who, still at the age of 45 could say about himself that he had failed at everything . . . and who did not have much more to go on than a burning sense of justice, a mind clear as crystal, and an ingeniously fluent tongue?

Gunnar came to feel that his abilities would not be rightly used in Sweden no matter how threatening the situation became. Of course he took part, with Alva, in political debates and in putting together *Contact with America;* at the same time he engaged in the work of ideological resistance by writing searing articles about the nonexistent foundations for the Nazi theories about race. But it all felt to him like treading water. His true work lay unfinished on the other side of the Atlantic.

Alva, meanwhile, was putting the finishing touches on her book *Nation and Family,* to be published first in English, then in Swedish as *Folk och familj.* The preface mirrors, once again, the tension and danger throughout the world:

> As I sign the preface of this essay on efforts and plans for preventive social policy in peaceful and democratic Sweden, devastating totalitarian war is ravaging the Old World and threatening the New. . . . It may be that before this book is published our form of free and independent democratic government in the far North will have perished. This book, begun and in the main written in time of peace and in a confident spirit, would then come to stand as an epitaph of a defunct society. Even if that should be the immediate fate of our Scandinavian democracy, this essay will have been worth writing. Our house may be burned, but this will not prove that there were basic faults in its construction. The plan will still be worth studying.

If the countries of Europe become free once again, moreover, true democracy will have to be rebuilt from the ground up. At that time the major question will be whether "we shall have enough humanitarian zeal, calm reason, and cooperative will to carry out huge social programs and at the same time preserve social peace." Children will have to be protected and family policy will be central. Sweden's approach to social policies could then be a model for other nations.

I can see her before me as she sat at her large birchwood desk across from Gunnar's during the dark winter of 1940–41 and wrote about children and families and the future. She was determined to persevere, even though no one could know at the time how the war would end. As it turned out, *Nation and Family* was published to very little press notice in America: it appeared shortly after Pearl Harbor, when, quite understandably, few were interested in Sweden's social policies. But the book lived on within universities, and in 1968 a new edition appeared with a preface by Daniel Patrick Moynihan, then a Professor of Education at Harvard University. Urging that America had every reason to try to benefit from the reforms that the book described, he saw to it that it was taken up more seriously in the American debate about social policy.

In Sweden, Gunnar was growing more and more restless. His own unfinished book in America and all the coworkers who waited for his return weighed on his conscience. No one could know how long the war might last or how it would end. Meanwhile, the danger of invasion was abating for Sweden. Fearing that if he postponed his return too long he might become incapacitated or lose the sharpness of his insight into the problems with which he was struggling, he decided to return in February 1941. And right away he began to press Alva. How soon could she join him? She alone, that was, since it would be far too dangerous to try to travel with us children. Up to then, he and Alva had never been apart for more than short periods of time. That must not happen now either, especially since the war made it impossible to plan for a definite date of return or even a safe journey home.

Gunnar made his case over and over again before he left and then wrote, urged, begged her to come. Without her, he insisted, he could not even think, much less write well. Alva did not understand, perhaps, why it was so essential to him that she should abandon work and family in order to risk a journey that was, by then, extremely dangerous. But I believe that she sensed that he needed her clarity and vitality in order not to drift into depression or manic and fruitless activity, and that he craved her effervescence of ideas and her sensitivity and understanding in order to be able to bring to an end the work that otherwise might devour him.

To begin with, Alva answered that she could not leave before the spring term was over. And she agonized. That spring her beautiful, shy sister Maj became ill. Maj had gone against her mother's wishes by marrying Olle, the stepson of Alva's Aunt Mimmi on the neighboring farm. Lowa had never intended that this daughter, whom she had protected since childhood, should move away from home; and she regarded Olle as somewhat backward besides. But for once Maj pushed her decision through. The two were asked to live in one of the wings of the farmhouse belonging to her sister Rut and her husband Elon. Olle worked on the farm as an inspector.

From all evidence, Olle and Maj lived a true idyll. But they agreed to move back with Lowa and Albert when he asked them to help with a new project. Albert wanted to start a chicken farm with Olle's help, while Lowa and Maj would be in charge of the household. After some time of this new togetherness, Olle fell into a deep depression and required psychiatric attention. Maj was pregnant at the time. Lowa thought she was too weak to have a baby and feared that Olle, then hospitalized, would be an inadequate father. Perhaps his problems might even be hereditary. Alarmed, the family, including Alva, persuaded Maj to seek an abortion, only to learn, after it was carried out, that she had intestinal cancer. After still another operation in April 1941 she died.

Maj's death at the age of thirty-one—like that of "the lily of the valley"—shook her family deeply. They could not help wondering whether she would have lived had she not undergone the abortion, and whether the physicians in charge had informed them fully about the causes of her death. Lowa no longer wanted to live. Alva grieved and worried about the abortion decision, and all the while Gunnar pressed her ever harder to join him in America.

Alva hesitated and kept postponing the decision. She knew that nothing would be the same between her and Gunnar if she did not go: he required her presence unconditionally. She longed to be with him, too; but she did not want to leave her work and the family. Jan was almost fourteen years old, at the threshold of puberty. He had pleaded to be allowed to stay in America when we left in 1940 and had had a hard time returning to school in Sweden after his two years in the free atmosphere of the Lincoln School in New York City. Brooding, rebellious, contemptuous of teachers and most adults, he would be held back in one class after another. I was six, about to begin school in the fall, Kaj only four. We all needed her; she knew that we would feel abandoned if she left.

True, she could ask Gunnar's mother Sofie, a widow since 1934, to come to look after us in the Äppelviken house. But Sofie was now over sixty and, as we children thought, prematurely aged. She still lived in the old-fashioned world that Alva and Gunnar had left behind. After her husband had died she had settled in the little town of Säter in Dalecarlia, near all the relatives in the county of Gustafs. To come to our hypermodern home was surely not something she longed to do. And we three children were self-willed in a manner she found quite disturbing. Kaj and I grumbled at the news that she might take Alva's place. Although we could feel her devotion, we found her nagging and weepy and a dreary contrast to Alva with her quick, lively, bright manner.

Alva herself knew that Sofie was hardly the maternal ideal that she had promoted in her courses on parenting. Could she also foresee that her mother-in-law would become neurotically anxious about us children? That she would lie sleepless each night and worry that Alva and Gunnar might never return? Did Alva realize what a contrast the change would mean for us, what coercion about food and warm underwear, what bundling up even in early summer, what endless going-over of each new reason for worry, all with the best motives? At any rate, she could not feel

even a fraction as hopeful that all would go well as she had been
before the trip to America in 1929.

In spite of it all, she finally left. "At the time, my sense of
obedience to Gunnar was decisive—as usual," she wrote in a letter
late in life. "Did I therefore put marriage before parenthood? Yes,
but not without gnawing guilt and an inner sense of mutiny."
Alva later looked back at that journey as her life's second great
mistake. The first had been leaving Jan when he was two years
old. This time she was confronted with an ultimatum. If she had
not gone it would have represented a de facto separation, perhaps
stretching over many years, depending on the outcome of the war.
Gunnar would have seen a choice favoring the children and her
work over him as a betrayal. Divorce would, she thought, have
been unavoidable. It was a possibility that she was not ready to
consider.

With the help of Aleksandra Kollontai, who was the Soviet
envoy to Sweden at the time, Alva received a visa to travel by
train through the Soviet Union and Siberia, as Gunnar had done
the previous February. But on the day before she was to leave, in
June 1941, Germany invaded Soviet territory. Her trip had to be
postponed and rerouted. After several months she finally managed
to catch a clandestine flight to England, where she stayed until
she could find a plane to take her farther.

In England, Alva had her first experience of a country at war.
Though the Blitz was over, there was no reprieve in the German
bombardment. Night after night, she later recounted, she would
lie awake, when in London, shaking at the sound of bombs falling.
Later, when she traveled in the British country-side, she would
marvel at seeing most homes and industrial regions undamaged:
"And one's eyes meet with special gratitude the massive and yet
frail cathedrals—York, Durham, Peterborough—rising whitish
gray against the gray-gray sky."

The articles Alva sent home to newspapers from England
were later collected in another quickly assembled book of essays,
Stickprov på Storbritannien (Samples from Great Britain). They
speak of her awe at the way in which the British had come together
in response to what began as a nearly overwhelming threat. She

writes of the widespread confidence, evident in the fall of 1941, that the war would be won, of the grace in self-sacrifice that she sensed everywhere she went, and of the lack of militaristic bluster in a country so intent on armed resistance. She recounts seeing remarkably little hatred of Germans as such. About the enemy, she reports, the British say "he" much more often than "they"; she quotes a little boy as saying that "he thought he would get us last night, so he bombed our house; but we were in the shelter, so he didn't manage." Everywhere, she adds, children have, in Hitler, a new name for their darkest horrors.

Pointedly, Alva informs her fellow Swedes that even though public debate is more open in Britain than in their own neutral country, there is very little disloyalty to be seen: "The political seismograph that one carries as an observer can only register this: the unity and the common will with respect to the war is even stronger than one might have expected."

After the next stage on her journey, taking her to Portugal to connect with a plane that could take her across the Atlantic, Alva had to wait for weeks once again. Lisbon was sunny and hot and her hotel overflowed with individuals who, like her, were waiting for one of the rare clippers that were available for the flight to the United States. She wanted to cable Gunnar to let him know she was still coming. But as she did not know when she would arrive and could not, for security reasons, explain where she was, she settled on a suitably vague but affectionate hint: "So near thee!" Gunnar, however, was utterly mystified, for the cable that reached him read "So near three."

Alva was fortunate in securing a seat on one of the last planes that left Portugal for the United States. When the day arrived, however, it turned out that she was last on the list of passengers and unlikely to be included. But as the crew enforced strict weight limitations, all the passengers had to be weighed. The man ahead of Alva was declared to be too heavy, and so his seat fell to her. The flight went to the Azores first, and then to Bermuda, with additional periods of waiting at each step.

Three among Alva's fellow passengers interested her especially, and she decided to approach them for interviews for her

Swedish newspaper column. One was the actress and writer Erika Mann—pencil-slim, her black hair cropped short, and her sardonic face as capable of the purest wide-eyed pantomime as of dead-pan Hitler imitations. She had been forced to leave Germany in 1933 because of the stinging political cabaret, The Peppermill, that she had founded with her brother Klaus in Munich. When, two years later, she was deprived of her citizenship, she had married her friend W. H. Auden in a "passport wedding" to secure British citizenship. Now she was on her way to join her parents, Thomas and Katja Mann, in America.

Alva also interviewed Jan Masaryk, then a member of Czechoslovakia's government-in-exile, later its foreign minister, who would plunge to his death in Prague after the Communist takeover in 1948. The third of Alva's "interviewees" was the burly historian, reporter, and world traveler Louis Fischer, whose vivid, thoroughly informed *Men and Politics,* dealing with the causes of the present war, had just been published. Once the war was over, he predicted, a European union would be bound to follow in the long run.

The four stayed together for the duration of the trip, sharing views about the war, its coming end, and the prospects for Europe and the world—all as they got on and off the clipper, sat on sunny lawns in the Azores and Bermuda, dined under the stars until late at night. Alva always remembered the journey as an extraordinary coming together of four whose lives seemed, just then, to be held in abeyance.

In mid-October, at last, Alva reached the United States and a jubilant Gunnar. Earlier that month he had written to his mother from Dartmouth College that he had been working from sunrise until midnight each day, seven days a week—"Weeks have passed when I have not spoken to a single person"—all in order to make the book as good as he possibly could and then to be free to return home once again. Now he looked forward to Alva's arrival and planned to take a few days to walk with her in Vermont's Green Mountains before moving to Princeton, where his collaborators had already set up "headquarters" for finishing the book.

In Princeton, the two settled into a small flat in a house at

341 Nassau Street, near the university. Alva fully realized that her main task would be to lighten Gunnar's load and to support him in an effort so vast and many-dimensioned that it could otherwise prove to be too much for him. She did this not by taking over the writing of parts of the book, but rather by debating each one with him, providing an environment in which he and his collaborators could feel at home, making it easy for him to keep up with friends and colleagues, and generally "humanizing" his existence.

At the same time she was working on a book, never completed, that she intended to call *Women and Wars*. Begun while in England, it drew on her observations of women's role in the war effort. Looking at it from the point of view of her later work on disarmament, one sees the same concern for factual details but not at all the same purpose. Here she was writing about a war that she took for granted was not only necessary but fully justified by the threat posed by totalitarian states to the survival of democracy. She stressed the contrast between all that women contribute in wartime and the little that they are entrusted with in peacetime. Later she would write about the danger of the militarization of the world and the threat posed by nuclear weapons to all of humanity.

Gunnar's book, *An American Dilemma,* became his greatest achievement, often described as one of our century's foremost works of social science. He wrote with a combination of passion and objectivity that brought Americans face to face with the contradiction between their ideals of equality and liberty for all and the oppression of blacks that the Civil War had not succeeded in eradicating. While conducting his study, he had concluded that the decades during which little improvement had taken place in the relationship between the races were coming to an end. He saw reasons to hope for changes that would bring the nation's practices closer to what he had called, at the outset of the book, the American Creed: the respect for the dignity of each individual, for equality, and for the inalienable rights to freedom, justice, and a fair opportunity.

The sense that there was new hope after so many years gave him the strength to carry this gigantic task to its conclusion. The group of younger collaborators who had helped with the research, written preliminary studies and drafts for a number of the chapters, and edited the book became like a family for Gunnar. To be sure, there were tensions, even quarrels, over what direction to take and what to include or leave out; but he would never forget the rare intellectual camaraderie that he experienced with these coworkers.

As Gunnar often pointed out later, *An American Dilemma* ends with the word "Enlightenment." He had been impressed early on, in reading the great British thinkers of the nineteenth century and others, to see with what meticulous care they often chose the last word of their texts. I remember his telling of how the economist and philosopher Henry Sidgwick first ended his *Methods of Ethics* with the word "failure," only to change it, by the seventh edition, to "scepticism." Gunnar never saw reason to change his own last word. He stood to the end of his life by the convictions expressed in the last paragraphs of *An American Dilemma*:

> Social study is concerned with explaining why all these potentially and intentionally good people so often make life a hell for themselves and each other when they live together, whether in a family, a community, a nation, or a world. . . . With all we know today, there should be the possibility to build a nation and a world where people's great propensities for sympathy and cooperation would not be so thwarted.
>
> To find the practical formulas for this never-ending reconstruction of society is the supreme task of social scientists. The world catastrophe places tremendous difficulties in our way and may shake our confidence to the depths. Yet we have today in social science a greater trust in the improvability of man and society than we have ever had since the Enlightenment.

At home in Stockholm, meanwhile, we felt safe, however confined, in the anxious care of our grandmother Sofie—but also abandoned. We sensed the need to learn to be independent, since the war made it far from certain that we would ever see our

parents again. Sofie could not conceal her nervousness on this
score: it was contagious. In my imagination I lived through a
thousand dramas of being orphaned. They blended with thoughts
about the war and about Nazi tormentors. I wondered how I
would be able to withstand hunger, imprisonment, torture. To try
to find out, I had to evade my grandmother's hovering solicitude:
in secret, and far away from home, I would risk frostbite on the
coldest days and make scratch wounds to look like tattoos on my
skin. Sometimes I felt wholly cut off from the rest of the family.
An early poem speaks of these feelings:

> *The door bangs closed and I am alone*
> *Alone as never before*
> *No one knows what loneliness can mean*
> *Behind a big, closed door.*

I could hardly tell Alva in my letters how I felt. She seemed
infinitely far away. At her end she now lived the close, relaxed
"student existence" with Gunnar that they both cherished, and
was engaged in writing, lecturing, and seeing their large circle of
friends—all with her usual energy. She always had a special ability
to concentrate on what lay before her, to cut off everything that
would otherwise scatter her thoughts. The risk, of course, was
that all who were thus cut off and set aside did not wait passively
until she had time for them again—least of all children and relatives. Her capacity to be incisive, clear, and focused on finding
creative responses to the problems that lay nearest at hand only
served to increase the distance felt by those who were set aside.

From Princeton, Alva wrote a letter to me at Christmas 1941
that shows the distance between us during the uncertain war years
and her hopes that all would soon change:

Dear, sweet Sissela,
Here comes yet another little letter. This time it is you who
will receive it and pass on my greetings to the others: to
grandmother, who is so *cozy* and takes care of you, when you
would not otherwise have any relatives near you, to Jan, who

usually receives the telegrams, since he is clever and knows English, to Kaj, who can't read herself. . . .

Things here are just as they were. Uvve's [our nickname for Gunnar] work goes so well, that we are sure to be able to return when we had promised. And what jubilation there will be then! Then we won't separate any more in this stupid way but rather live together and be like a real family.

Now I have begun knitting a darling pink sweater for you; Kaj's blue one is already finished along with a brown skirt, though I am not sure whom it will fit. When I receive the measurements, I'll decide and then knit another skirt for the other one of you. I also include a little photo that shows how I stand outside and look for Gunnar, when it is time for him to return home. Mostly, we walk together, holding one another's hand and not taking many steps away from each other.

Yes, now you must hug the others and read the letter to them. Then you yourself get a kiss and the very warmest greeting from your own

Avva-Mommy.

In a letter to Sofie in June 1942, Alva admits that she should perhaps have returned home earlier that spring, in part because of the work that she knew awaited her there. But that could not be, even though Gunnar's work was taking longer than they had at first hoped. For they had decided once and for all, when she came to join him in the United States, "to *absolutely stay together.*"

The time of departure finally came in October 1942, a year after Alva had joined Gunnar. His work was then sufficiently close to being completed so that he could assign the remaining tasks to coworkers and plan the return trip.

It had been the most absorbing work he had ever undertaken. When Kaj once asked him, years later, what had been the greatest moment in his life, he was silent for a long while; then he replied that it had been when he stood at the Princeton train station after his work was over, "with the manuscript for the *Dilemma* in my hands—ready! All that I had lived for." Now both he and Alva longed to be home again; Alva especially dreamed about the

family life that she could then resume. They had vowed on all
that was holy, she wrote to Sofie, to spend lots of time with us
children. Flying home over occupied Norway in a plane with its
lights out, they barely escaped being downed by German planes.
At last they landed in Sweden, still secure and neutral, and hurried
to return to the beautiful house in Äppelviken and to us children
with our own needs and expectations and illusions.

Reunions after long trips are seldom easy. This one must have
been especially difficult, for them as for us. For them, the war
was a reality far more tangible than for many in Sweden. They
wanted to work out guidelines for postwar recovery, join with
refugees from different countries to promote international cooperation and practical reforms, and help Sweden plan for the future.
In spite of all her protestations to the contrary, the family no
longer occupied a central role even for Alva. She and Gunnar
came flying back with so many experiences and such vast plans,
which we were unable to share. Our own world in Äppelviken
simmered with tensions that they hardly noticed at first, only to
find them increasingly entangling.

It turned out to be a particularly painful time for Gunnar
and Jan, then fifteen. They fought over everything, from schoolwork and table manners to politics. During the preceding year,
Jan's school performance had gone from bad to worse. He rebelled
increasingly against Alva's and Gunnar's rationalism and reform-
mindedness and was vocal in his support of revolutionary ideologies, in particular of communism. To Gunnar, used to careful,
informed debate, this fifteen-year-old's arguments seemed shallow
and impudent. He, who had set much store in being the firstborn
son in his own family, striving to go further in the world than his
own father had, found Jan a great disappointment. And yet he
also resented any evidence that Jan was challenging him on his
own terrain, let alone trying to outshine him.

The arguments at the dinner table grew ever more savage.
Instead of saying that she had had enough, Alva tried to mediate
and smooth over. Both Jan and Gunnar then felt misunderstood,
betrayed—yes, "displaced." With all that she had learned—and
taught—about the psychology of adolescence and family conflicts,

Alva must have seen the anguish on both sides, yet found no way to defuse it or to work things out. Her silent but visible suffering instead of taking a position depressed us all. She used to say, "I cannot get angry. I can only get sad." Alone in her room, she wept. But we never saw her show truly explosive anger. Here, it would have cleared the air.

Alva's suffering did not stem only from the fights. She was beginning to wonder whether her dreams had not been largely illusions. The old quarrels that had poisoned her parents' home about money and sexuality and ultimately about power, and that she had wanted to ban from her own wholly re-created life—how *could* they surface once again? And so coarsely expressed, at times through Gunnar and Jan coming to blows, something she had never experienced even as a child? Kaj and I could hear tumult and anger upstairs, but tried to block it out. We, in turn, wrestled and quarreled vociferously, in part to get Alva's attention—and this contentiousness, too, was something she had never experienced with her own siblings.

By comparison, the Seminar must have seemed to her a haven of serenity. To teach and write about child rearing was a holiday compared to trying to deflect the family quarrels at home. In the long run her smoothing over, her silent suffering, her retreat to neutral ground became an incurable habit that would hurt her more than all the rest of us. She set aside the problems at home in order to be able to continue to write and teach. As late as 1944 Alva would clinch her arguments for six-hour workdays for both husbands and wives by appealing, without a trace of irony, to the idyllic parental togetherness that would then be possible: "Just imagine what glorious leisure they can then have together! At home and together with their children, for the enjoyment of all and mutual help."

Like Alva, Gunnar found work was not only absorbing in its own right but also an escape. And why not? Among colleagues and students he was admired. With them he felt he could press ahead in his research and share his magnificent intelligence and his creativity without the undertone of alternating teasing and bitterness that often made conversations with Jan impossible. Tore

Browaldh, one of the students Gunnar especially appreciated, gives a sketch of Gunnar as "an admired and popular teacher in economics":

> wearing a colorful, elegant tie and a jacket of typically American cut, Gunnar Myrdal stands, insolently young and charming in the lecture hall and speaks about economics in a way that captivates his students. His ability to use a rich flora of examples to bring life to abstract concepts is as much appreciated as his unwillingness to use intricate mathematical formulae to make his knowledge seem more exotic.

By 1943 it had become clear that the Allies would win the war. At that time Gunnar traveled once again to the United States to study postwar planning there, with Tore Browaldh accompanying him. This time, knowing that he was returning in a few months, he did not demand that Alva come along. It is possible that both at first drew a sigh of relief at this respite; yet her letters convey her loneliness during his four-month absence and her longing to re-create the all-encompassing intimacy of their early years.

Gunnar used to ask, only partly rhetorically, whether it would not be better for him to move to a hotel. Much later Alva wondered if that might not have been for the best. At the time, however, it was Jan who left. He would storm away from the dinner table again and again. Finally he decided to move out altogether. As he remembers in an article written when he was fifty, he knew that the moment had come one day when Gunnar was chasing him around a table on the upper floor:

> I kept the table between us and ran around it the whole time so that he could not get to me. At last I noticed that I had stopped and had lifted a chair and I said: "One more step, old devil, and I crack your skull." . . . It was the first time I had managed to make him back off. Then I knew that I must leave home.

Jan's plan was to leave Stockholm to find work with a provincial newspaper. To Alva, who had ached to be able to continue
her own schooling at the same age and who had since been so
vocal in promoting better schools, his dropping out of school at
sixteen carried overtones of a personal verdict. But she tried to
help him with advice, contacts, and money. Behind the scenes she
quietly supported his need to make his own decisions when Gunnar castigated him for incompetence at school or derided his
dreams of a career as a writer.

After Jan had left, her sense of guilt and defeat as a mother
mingled with immense relief at no longer having to endure the
daily battling. She stored the books and belongings he had left
behind and turned his room over to me. Now Kaj and I each had
our own rooms, which alleviated our squabbling. But was this
change carried out too suddenly and too soon? I often thought
so later, after considering how my own children would have felt
had I eliminated their personal territory in that abrupt way. When
I asked Alva about it, she replied that she had thought that Jan
needed to feel that his decision to leave had been fully respected
rather than seen as a momentary whim. Once on his own, he kept
writing stormy letters home and visited from time to time, living
in a basement room that we younger children found romantically
dark and muffled.

With Gunnar, Alva still had to walk a mine field. His threats
to seek refuge from family life hung in the air. They concerned
far more than the arguments with Jan, which had only served to
intensify his resentment at not having Alva all to himself. How
could she placate Gunnar, she wondered, make him feel that he
alone counted for her in the midst of all other demands on her
time? Yet do so, somehow, without rejecting those demands?

A few letters saved from 1943 give a glimpse of what it took
for her to try to convince him. She wrote of a honeymoon she
hoped they might take that would allow them to be alone with
one another in utter peace and stillness, and to have time to talk
over "what I shall do with my life and how you should plan your
publications." And at home, she promised, she would do all she
could to keep their own top floor all to themselves, free of family

pressures, a sanctuary for them both. This effort could never fully succeed, she confessed, presumably because Kaj and I and other members of the household recognized no such unspoken boundary at the top of the stairs. For these interruptions, Alva took all the blame. In a passage that blends great love with almost total submission, yet without giving in altogether, she claimed to realize that all depended on her "own poor self" being such

> a double creature, who wants to have *all* of me turned toward you and yet *half* turned toward the children and a house open to others. But of course you must know that the first is most important even for me. . . . It is not in any sense excessive that you, whom I take to be a very glorious man, should have my entire life at your disposal.

When she wondered, late in life, how she had come to "displace" herself in order to fit in with other selves, I believe that she was referring to such periods of struggling to fit everything together. The accommodation with Gunnar succeeded, but at a cost in submissiveness and in smoothing over problems in need of airing that she would later regard as having been too high.

The spring of 1943 also brought the upheaval of unexpected death in Alva's family. Lowa, who had never recovered from Maj's death, came down with a severe case of influenza and died. Albert, deeply despondent, died three months later of a sudden heart attack while fishing on a riverbank. Their deaths came as a great shock for Alva. She grieved for them, especially for her father. And she felt guilty. There was so much that was unfinished in her relationship with them.

I do not believe that Alva ever hoped for friendship with her parents. Her childhood still lived as bitter, even "hellish," in her memory. She could not forget her mother's near-hatred in response to her pleas to be allowed to pursue further studies. It should nevertheless have been possible for Alva to learn to see her parents as fellow human beings, to feel for their problems, perhaps truly to acknowledge them not just as parents but as equals and thereby become fully adult herself in relation to them.

But that would have taken time. Alva had always postponed spending time with them, always been in too much of a hurry, always thought that she would find time for them later. In so doing she also postponed the kind of settlement with them through which she could have overcome her childhood contempt and defiance. And I wonder: Was this not yet another of the "completely preposterous displacements" between what she had become and what she could have planned that she sought to trace at the end of her life?

Alva's desire to be radical—to start over from the roots up—may have been part of the trouble. With children and grandchildren, even great-grandchildren, she sought to realize the goal of closing the gap between generations, as she claimed was done in the United States; but she could never do so with her own parents. When it came to them she could not bring herself to call forth the warmth between human beings that she experienced so strongly in America but found wanting in "our frozen land." There she felt too entangled in old childhood patterns.

As Alva's grief and guilt receded, and as Jan's departure removed the anguish of the fights with him, life with Gunnar gradually seemed to get back on the old tracks. And with Kaj and me, she later wrote, "plus the Seminar, plus the joy of sharing in so many battles for progress, everything became so much happier." Although she took refuge at the Seminar as soon as she returned from America, she had to wait for over a year to resume its direction, having appointed a substitute to take her place until the fall of 1944. She devoted her free time to lecturing and to writing columns for *Aftontidningen,* one of Stockholm's daily afternoon papers.

In these columns she had a chance to discuss every domestic and foreign issue that came to mind. She spoke of the niggardliness she often sensed among Swedes toward refugees, toward children and adolescents, and toward the handicapped; she criticized society's shutting women out of certain occupations as well as many women's acquiescence in notions about their lesser capacities; she castigated the government for its feeble moves in the direction of school reform; she took up the threat the Soviet Union posed to

Finland, the plague of anti-Semitism, the coming overthrow of totalitarian regimes; and above all she discussed plans for the postwar period in the same many-sided way in which she had earlier treated family policy. She warned both of unproductive pessimism and of naive illusions about how all would improve of itself once the war was finally over:

> In reality, the risk is immense that the peace will not lift the world out of chaos and crisis. Perhaps the peace will only turn out to be the second act of a desperate drama of fate that will continue to grind on for the rest of this century until there is no more West.
>
> But neither does pessimism do as a working hypothesis, other than for historians who work retrospectively. We who live now and want to work in the future must hold down the doubt that borders on despair. Above that, we must study, plan, and act, as if we believed in the capacity of human beings to achieve that good life together that we know they desire.

This combination of almost desperately clear vision about the problems of the world and wholehearted optimism as a "working hypothesis" would remain Alva's position from the beginning of the war onward. But as the years passed her clear-sightedness would also deepen. In 1943 she could still write that, if the peace was sabotaged this time, it could not be because of ignorance since "the world's best brains" had by now charted what was needed; "human nature" could no longer be blamed since peoples were not "the same unenlightened and irresponsible masses as in 1918" but, rather had greater knowledge and an "inner preparedness to realize the international ideals"; and no sabotaging of the peace could occur, either, with heads of state like Roosevelt, Churchill, and Chiang Kai-shek leading the planning. Her trust in "the world's best brains" would gradually dwindle. Through her work for the United Nations she would come to doubt the spread of enlightenment and idealism in the world, and far fewer leaders would inspire her confidence.

She worked at plans for the postwar period together with

Gunnar, who chaired Sweden's Commission for Economic Post-war Planning. He was then writing *Warning Against Peace Optimism* to caution against the naive assumption that the Allies would necessarily continue to cooperate after the war and to warn of a possible worldwide depression at that time—the latter a prediction that he would shortly revoke as overly hasty. She herself was a member of the Social Democratic party's postwar committee and of the Committee for International Aid. Once again she and Gunnar pooled their forces and made use of one another's insights. Both took for granted that the planning must concern all that human beings do and need—education, human rights, agricultural production, industry, politics, cultural life, and family policies—and that it must build on international cooperation. Their strength, as always, stemmed from their ability to encompass all these factors and see how they affected one another.

Alva had been one of those who had helped Count Folke Bernadotte plan his trips to Germany in white Red Cross buses during the war in order to bring as many individuals as possible from the concentration camps to Scandinavia. When he returned to report to the government commission that had sponsored his journeys, he concluded his statement with a "Mission accomplished." At that point, Alva related, she stood up to reply that the mission could not be considered even half accomplished. True, the former inmates were now free. But their need for health care was desperate and little had been done to plan how they might best be reintegrated into society—how they might be helped to find jobs and schools for their children and to reestablish their lives. She worked to organize these efforts and also launched a series of radio broadcasts in many languages to inform all who needed assistance of where to go and how to proceed. In May 1945 she started a newsletter entitled *Via Suecia*. Its articles, in four languages, served as a forum for refugees. It also contained lists of persons still missing, addresses of those living in Sweden, poetry, memoirs, and news; and it provided information about Swedish formalities and customs, including its democratic traditions and the role of women in society.

In 1946 Alva was invited to join the Swedish School Commission, which was set up to reform the entire school system—in part because of her discussion of the advantages of the U.S. school system in *Contact with America,* in part because of her public criticism of the minimal reforms proposed so far by commission members. This preoccupation with schools, beginning with the visits to America, once again combined family and professional interests. When she had first had children, she wrote about parenting and toys and the rearing of small children as well as about what families needed. As we grew older she turned to reforms that would help schoolchildren and young people get more out of life while also educating them about society's need for their contributions.

It mattered especially, she insisted, to think through what schools actually do with the human beings placed in their hands and all that they might be able to do. The dreary old educational routines must cease; instead one had to think of students as individuals. In Sweden, as elsewhere, it was also important for schools to provide an egalitarian education and to offer everyone the same opportunities from the outset. She urged a comprehensive public school system modeled on that of the United States to replace the old two-track system separating a largely well-to-do elite and all others from the fifth grade on. Ability, not parental income, should decide who would have access to higher education, and no one ought to have to make do with education that ended at fourteen years of age.

Alva's articles and studies still had the same energetic, lucid, rational tone as her earlier works. She wanted, above all, to persuade. Her sentences often begin with expressions like "It ought to be clear to one and all," "It ought to be clearly stated," "Let it be said so that no one can misunderstand," "It ought to be as self-evident as the multiplication tables." If only people *understood* and could join in support of what she saw as so necessary, she thought, then of course they would change their opinion and adopt her proposals.

When she looked back in her eighties at all this activity, her energy astounded her. Was it not in part a means to displace other longings or compensate for her home life? Or even to challenge Gunnar? In one article she urged reforms "to make the men enter into a fuller existence within the intimate family world, where most women now stand abandoned, alone."

10

Upbringing

❖ ❖ ❖ ❖

What do you like best in human beings?
Openness and generosity.
Least?
Opportunism, cruelty, and indolence.
What don't you like in children?
Well-mannered hypocrisy.
What do you like in them?
Everything else.
FROM AN INTERVIEW IN 1944

While writing this book and trying to enter into Alva's life, I have come to reflect again on the questions I have heard so often from others: How did it feel to grow up with Alva and Gunnar? What was it like to have parents as forceful, as intense, as ambitious, and as extravagantly gifted as they? Now that I have read through all that Alva wrote about children I must also ask: How did things turn out in this home that she tried to make so radically new and creative, such a source of happiness? What did she mean when she wrote in the note I found in *Contact with America*: "Show the cultural analysis to Sissela. Says much even about us personally, for instance *myself* as parent"? And how did I find life at close quarters not only with her but with the parent that she passes by thus in silence?

Starting about 1942 my own memories begin to help me enter into and understand Alva's life. But these early memories are flickering and unsure. They have more to do with my own feelings and with impressions of colors, moods, objects, persons than with happenings within this family where so many went their own way.

If I nevertheless try to convey how I experienced the years 1942–47, before we moved to Geneva, I do so with two reservations. The first has to do with my brother Jan's writings about his childhood (see Chapters 16 and 17). I have no desire to contest his feelings. I was not even born during his first seven and a half years and remember nothing from my own earliest years, least of all about his experiences. In 1942, when he was fifteen, I was only seven—it felt as if an eternity separated us. He was often away, tried one school after another, and finally left home when I was about eight. Therefore he figures very little in my childhood memories. Now, as I look back, I understand how difficult those years must have been for him as well as for Alva and Gunnar. But at the time, this slid past Kaj and me, perhaps pushed aside as something unfathomable but frightening.

In the second place, it is of course not childhood itself that I or anyone else can get a grip on, but rather those years reflected through a thousand prisms and later experiences. One shapes one's childhood in the very process of thinking about it and creates it many times over as one writes about it—choosing and setting aside different words, sentences, images, thoughts, clusters of memories—seeing that world in lights and nuances taken from one's life as it has since become. In this way one transforms the past just as when one tries to capture and reproduce a dream. As for myself, moreover, I don't have much confidence in my memory. Those who can rattle off dates and names and events from the past impress me even as they make me wonder. How can they be so sure? Is even the present so easy to seize and to set forth?

I do, however, have no end of diaries since the age of fifteen that help me to come closer to the past, if not to grasp it or get it to stand still as if for a portrait. And in September 1984 I discovered yet another trove of clues: a pile of papers I had left behind when I married and that Alva had saved. Among them I found nineteen closely written pages from when I was seventeen, with the dramatic title "At the Turning Point." The turning point had come because I was considering breaking my engagement to a young man I had loved, because I had finished school but not yet begun my university studies, because I felt I was neither a child nor an adult, and above all, because I felt immature and afraid.

The reason for writing the essay was to "briefly relate my life as it mirrors itself in my soul." I quoted Henri Bergson's words about our inability to experience anything twice, even in memory, since we undergo constant change; but I hoped that I might at least "reexperience my childhood better now than in thirty years."

When I sat in the sunlight on Alva's moss-green couch slightly more than thirty years later and read what I had written, I agreed gratefully with this prediction. I found much that I had forgotten—if also much that I had left unspoken at the time. Most of all I recognized myself as I was and in how I thought so long ago. Now I could come closer to my memories about my childhood and about Alva's role in it and try to understand how they had come to be layered and reshaped.

With my essay in mind I have gone back to the chapter on education in *Contact with America* that according to Alva says so much about her as a parent. And now I see her idealistic, sometimes naive presentation of the condition of children in the United States in a new light. It offers more than a comparison between the Swedish and the American situation at the end of the thirties. Deeply anchored in Alva's own experiences as a child, it is meant as a kind of declaration of independence, as a challenge to her relatives, to all that was narrow-minded in the schooling she herself had received, to the past, and to Sweden.

Children should be allowed to be free and strong, this challenge declares. It is not necessary to treat them harshly, to subject them to the coercion then so common in Swedish schools and families, least of all to physical punishment. Coining a phrase, she rejected the idea that children should be brought up to be "obedience persons" (*lydnadsmänniskor*). Rather, they should be made to feel as warmly welcome in schools as in their families and in the community. Their need for warmth and joy should be generously satisfied rather than stingily suppressed. Education can make childhood into an experience of happiness if children are loved and respected as individuals from the very beginning.

Conversely, children should be encouraged to resist the automatic obedience that grown-ups often demand. They should learn to think critically, to see through superstition and stereotypes, to act independently and stand on their own two feet as soon as possible. As early as 1933, Alva had written that it was particularly important, in protecting democracies against totalitarian demands for submission, to educate coming generations for criticism, opposition, and a healthy independence.

Alva tried to live up to these ideals with us children as well as she could. Of course she could see that many forms of oppression remained even for us in our schools and our community, and of course she came to realize that tensions within the family exerted an even stronger force; but we must never turn into "obedience persons," come what may. And one can hardly say that any of us did.

But this goal was far from enough; Alva did not wish to introduce just any sort of freedom. When I read her pronouncements on this score I become wary. She writes that children should be "socialized" so that their freedom finds its expression in energy, not sloth; they must become useful members of society and "properly suited for living" (*livsriktiga*), not parasites or deniers of life, and fully mindful of others rather than egocentric. Radical reforms must be introduced in families and schools in order to bring about a "reshaping of human beings" to "perfect the human material." Every situation, from cooking classes in schools to science or nature walks, must rear children not only to independence but to greater usefulness—all for the sake of increased personal happiness and the benefit of society.

When I read this chapter I cannot help thinking of Jean-Jacques Rousseau's educational ideals, so warmly admired by Alva and her father Albert. Poor little Emile was to be formed, perfected, in just this way by his tutor. Every walk, every conversation, every question was meant to help him become the kind of person that Rousseau most admired. Officiously accompanying the boy, the tutor would guide him toward understanding life and nature. Luckily for Kaj and me, Alva did not go along with Rousseau's oppressive notions about how to educate girls. If Emile evokes my pity, it goes a thousandfold to Sophie, who was to be brought up to become his obedient companion through life. Nor did Alva follow Rousseau's advice to isolate children from society or to keep books away from them until the "right time." But her notion of taking advantage of all situations in order to "perfect the human material" sounds disquietingly like Rousseau, not least for me as I contemplate my lot of having provided the human clay to be shaped in just this fashion.

Worst of all, Alva could have tried her hand at such reshaping much more methodically than Rousseau. He himself had failed utterly as the tutor to the sons of a nobleman. In his *Confessions*, he recounts how, each time he had a child with Thérèse Levasseur, he took it, in spite of her tears and protests, to the foundling home in Paris. In contrast, Alva was eager to put her ideas into practice with us, and she was sure that during the last decades science had brought forth improved methods of perfecting the right kind of strong, socially conscious, happy individuals.

It is therefore the more fortunate for me that she did not undertake such a task in earnest. True enough, we children did not become "obedience persons." But we rarely felt socially useful, least of all "properly suited for living." For one thing, Alva's ideal of liberty turned out to jar with the task of perfecting us. She could talk about both concepts in the same breath, but in practice she saw that reconciling them was much more complicated. The perfecting could not be carried out through coercion. She did not follow Rousseau so far as to claim that human beings should be forced to be free. And the more we were encouraged to think critically and to stand on our own two feet, the more easily we could answer back when it came to the guidance of our upbringing.

It must also have been the case, at least when Kaj and I were growing up, that Alva lost track of us as "human material." We were no longer at the center of her ideals about education. She had too many other interests in life and found expression for her ideals through the Seminar for Social Pedagogy, her writings, and the Swedish School Commission, and she was not with us long enough each day even to begin to try to form us. Had she taken her educational role with deadly seriousness and been ever-present, entirely focused on our reshaping, Kaj and I might well have had to offer the same prayer for supernatural intervention to which she herself and her sister Rut had resorted as little girls: Dear God, please let Mother get a job!

Instead we were allowed to drift. We could dawdle and bicker and fight. No one objected if we took school too casually or tried new formulas for stirring up gunpowder in the basement. Our upbringing was much less programmatic than the regime to which someone with Alva's energy and superabundance of ideas might otherwise have exposed us. Many people thought we were wild and ill bred. Our daily hygiene was haphazard: I remember the ignominy of having my tangled hair brushed in front of the class by a frowning grade school teacher. And we staged a common mutiny against Alva's energy and devotion to beauty and culture with a delight hardly appropriate to "well-formed human material." During a car trip through France, for example, Kaj and I demonstratively sat on the floor next to the backseat and played cards, yawning whenever Alva tried to point out something she found worth admiring.

Finally—and perhaps most important among the reasons why nothing went as programmatically with our upbringing as it might have—Alva's high hopes had come to be undermined more generally during the forties. To begin with she had not only longed to make great contributions in life but also hoped for a radiant love life, an intimate intellectual friendship, and a home where children were to grow up more free, more fitted for a full and productive life, and more happy than ever before. But career opportunities for women were late in coming and the home situation had begun to splinter and break up. However rending this was for her as well as for Gunnar and Jan, it may have saved Kaj and me from the danger of impossibly high expectations.

Yet the larger question remains. How did it actually feel to grow up with Alva and Gunnar as parents? All children of exceptionally gifted and forceful parents—I think for example of Margaret Mead and Bertrand Russell and Gandhi and Thomas Mann, whose children have all written about life with them—share dangerous childhoods. They live near fields of force that can draw them in and risk turning them into hapless satellites, parasites who live on their parents' resources and strength, or self-pitying, bitter antipodes like Gandhi's son Harilal. How can they share in the energy and richness of such lives without being undone as independent individuals? To what degree must they in that case find ways to guard themselves? My own answers to these questions vary from one period to another in my life. When I think back on my childhood, I must, as always in this connection, consider Alva and Gunnar separately.

If one looks at Alva only as a mother of small children, she was captivating but not ideal, in spite of all her knowledge about children and their development. She spoke and wrote about those who are "naturally gifted" as parents—who have the ability to live almost on the level of children and who are phlegmatic, with an outgoing, live-life-smiling attitude. Obviously, she knew that she was not one of them. Nor did she in the long run want to be such a person: she foresaw too great a danger of getting stuck at the level of small children and of losing contact with them as they grew up. It would be better, she suggested, to combine knowledge about children and their education with a feel for what they need at different stages. But when it came to caring for small children, she probably did not have the right sort of inner calm or patience. It was hard for her just to *be* with children without doing anything with them, and she was often away from home even when she was not abroad. After the stay in America 1941–42 she was even less focused on taking care of children than when we were small, and her image of herself as a mother who combined child care with professional activities by working at home is one that I find idealized.

But when she was home and had free time she was a joy to be with. Then she would read, draw, and take long walks or bicycle trips with us; she would sew clothes for us and help us with our stamp collections and cut out costumes for families of paper dolls and play word games for hours. With her we could talk freely; with her we could do puzzles and fantasize. And our lives were enriched through Alva's having inherited her mother's talent for storytelling. Just as Lowa could come home after going to the theater during the years in Stockholm and perform passages from the play she had seen with such feeling that all the family could see each scene as if with their own eyes, so Alva had the ability to make us see and feel the dramatic quality in the smallest event she described. Over and over again we asked her to tell, for instance, the story of how she and her sister Rut had gone to a birthday party in a neighboring village wearing fancy new dresses that they had sewn somewhat narrowly in order to economize on fabric; how to their horror both dresses had begun to burst in the seams as they walked back along the highway, hers in back and Rut's in front; and how they had arrived at a desperate solution: that Alva should carry Rut the whole long way home—on her back.

Time spent with Alva was nevertheless always a luxury for us. I have no memories of her doing such ordinary things with us as putting on Band-Aids, helping us take baths, baking Christmas cookies, or consoling us when we were sad. And even when she was with us we could never be sure that Gunnar would not make loud, insistent calls for her presence.

Did Kaj and I suffer from this? Yes, of course we were sometimes alone, hungering for love. But for the most part I cannot say that we fared badly during those early years. There was always a nurse or someone else to whom we could turn for lasting tenderness and daily needs. We always had one another, too, no matter how often we squabbled and fought. And in 1942, when I was seven years old and Kaj five, Karin Anger came to us as housekeeper. With a warm embrace, laughing wrinkles around her eyes, and a face that all children knew understood them, she became our substitute mother for the eight years that followed. She provided all the love and care we longed for, and her thoughtfulness gave everyday living depth and security. She admired our adventures and hardships, dressed our wounds, laughed at our stories, and put us to bed each evening with songs and hugs that we wanted to prolong forever. In "At the Turning Point" I described Karin as

> this wonderful, harmonious, angelic figure who has brought light into the lives of so many people thanks to having succeeded in forgetting her own misfortunes. Karin told us fairy tales and dog stories, Karin ran up the stairs with us on her back, Karin gave us goodnight kisses and Karin gave us good food. I think we loved her more than our mother. She received our confidences with such mild gravity, and all our friends adored her.

Loved her more than Alva—yes, at that time we did, but that is not to say that we ever tired of Alva. Alva was more distant and we could never count on her daily presence; but she was fascinating, always intensely alive. When she came into a room it was more real for us all.

It was also important that we felt so proud of what Alva had managed to accomplish as a woman. She had had to fight her way forward, without models, without money, without the kind of support she so lavishly gave us, and she had fashioned her own life more than most women we knew. She was living proof that women can reshape their lives, escape from the conventional role that we saw so many other mothers play.

Alva's fight to free women and children must therefore also be weighed, not only when one thinks of her life in general, but precisely in assessing her role as a mother. By her example, she removed for Kaj and myself many sources of worry about our own lives. So many girls we knew lived with models for women from which Alva had freed us both. Most families I saw were ones I would not have wanted to grow up in—especially not those in which the lives of daughters were planned in detail, with prohibitions and fences blocking off everything I wanted to do in life. Nor did I carry the all-too-common burden of knowing that my choices in life meant everything for my parents—that they wanted to live vicariously through my life. No wish could have been further from Alva's and Gunnar's thoughts; they had their own lives to live.

Alva's engagement and concern, together with the deep security and tenderness I received from Karin Anger, gave me a feeling of great expanses to explore and a jubilant sense of independence. Alva's need for freedom was also mine. Freedom could have its frightening sides, but it elated me. In particular I have always looked back at my life at the ages of eleven and twelve as paradisal: a time of total independence, even where looks were concerned—no one interfered with my reluctance to wash, comb my hair, or brush my teeth—and a time of warm, unproblematic friendships, experiences of mastery and joy, and boundless hope for the future.

Kaj and I knew of the criticism Alva received about the free way in which she brought us up. To us it seemed so self-evidently better that we never questioned her choice, if we even saw it as a choice rather than as something entirely natural and instinctive. Only in retrospect have I understood just how experimental Alva intended our upbringing to be. She wanted both to make use of the most imaginative contemporary conclusions about child rearing and to free us from the prevailing stereotypes for girls and women. Not until 1986, when I first read her speech "Education for 'Femininity,'" did I understand just how explicit the latter aim had been. I noticed that she had given that speech in January 1934—just before the time she became pregnant with me. And I was struck by her questions regarding the energy, initiative, sense of responsibility, and other good traits usually seen as typically "masculine": "How can we know whether women do not naturally have these traits when education is systematically aimed at stifling them and at nurturing, instead, a deliciously feminine helplessness, shyness, mildness, etc.?" And what would happen, she continued, if one were not to educate young girls thus? But I was struck too by her honest, cautious answer: "I do not know. Science and thinkers do not know. Woman such as she is in her essence does not exist."

Not that Alva thought such women could come to exist without support from society and culture. But if she could at least lighten the burden within her own family—if she could counteract the sense of inferiority she herself had experienced through being told that she was only a girl, that she should not do this, could not accomplish that, had not enough strength for this, did not understand that—it would be a step on the way for us. That step was one she did all she could to help us and other young girls take.

Gunnar himself had long been an outspoken feminist, but in a somewhat different way. At home we received ambivalent messages on that score. We noticed that whatever he thought about equality in principle and however strongly he supported Alva's work plans, it was always his work and well-being that came first. And where exceptionally talented women were concerned, he preferred to restrict their ambitions to the intellectual plane. In his eyes, women should not aim to "have it all." He underlined their rights in his books and fought to make way for them in the workplace, but if they had some special talent he thought that work and marriage should suffice to fill their lives; having children would only make most of them apathetic. Each time a gifted woman of his acquaintance got married, Gunnar would predict in a gloomy voice that soon enough she would be sitting at home with a fat baby, and that would be the end of her contributions to her chosen field. Kaj and I thought this sounded ominous. An abyss of uncertainty threatened when we began to think about the values that lay behind such pronouncements. But at the same time we could never quite take them seriously, perhaps in part because we thought that it had been our exceptionally good fortune that Alva had nevertheless insisted on having a family.

About Gunnar our views were split from early on. It was impossible not to notice and slowly begin to feel awe of his playful and luminous intellect, his profound knowledge of society, his inventiveness, and his charm. We knew that not many could have such a father. But precisely as a father he was in our opinion so much less satisfactory than the fathers of our friends. He was the opposite of the fathers Alva called for in her talks about parenting. He had never taken the slightest part in caring for us, never arisen at night when someone needed help. As the years passed he came increasingly to turn away from the family and toward his work.

This tendency would never change. At first it may have been his books that gave him reason to work seven days a week without recreation or hobbies. In the end, this pattern became a lifelong choice—one that he pointed to with ever greater pride, to Alva among many others. She had taken each of us children on week-long bicycle trips around Sweden and used to invite us—often one by one for more intimate togetherness—to come with her on train journeys when she was going to give a lecture out of town. If Gunnar took time off, however, it was with Alva alone, in order to be able to work in peace and quiet. We children were often sent to stay in the countryside with relatives during the summers, much to our delight.

I have been told that I was very attached to my father when I was little: each morning when he went off to work I would sit on a rock ledge outside the house in Äppelviken and weep as if I had been abandoned for life. And abandoned by Gunnar we probably were. Unlike most of the stiff adults we knew, he could create warm and immediate contact with people in a minute—and then as quickly turn his attention elsewhere. Our sense of abandonment stemmed not just from our knowledge that he did not share our interests or seem to see us as the individuals we felt we were rather than as periodically amusing and cute objects; we also experienced him as one who could injure those who were weaker than he—one who, like the lion in Gunhild Tegen's poem about Gunnar, could go out in his morning "to play and strike."

Absorbed in his work, already deeply egocentric and with an inner insecurity that drove him to downgrade anyone who might be a competitor, he often said that children simply did not interest him. Children were a sort of nuisance. One might possibly think of them as toys for the moment; but "throw out the little devils" was the half teasing, half aggressive refrain we were to hear whenever he wanted to have Alva to himself.

Gunnar's egocentricity was nevertheless of an unusual kind. True, he thought that the world circled around him. But his world was so much more spacious than that of most others, so much richer in insights and possibilities, so much more coherent. This made him far more fascinating to talk with than more doggedly

narrow-minded egocentrics. But it also gave him a head start in
his competition with relatives and all before whom he felt the
need to assert himself. Was it not quite true, he might ask, quite
"scientifically" true, that he was much more praiseworthy than
most? Why should he not boast? Why should he repress the truth
of his own brilliance? Would it not in fact be better for others to
have their views expanded by seeing how exquisitely well an
intelligence might function?

Gunnar's capacity for aggressive teasing was well known.
Even when he was little, his grandmother used to say that he
could tease so as to cause boulders to shake. He seemed to have
an unerring instinct, in talking not only with us children but with
many others, for discerning just what inward kernel of disquiet
his words could attain to greatest effect. Jan and Gunnar's brother
Robert along with competitors and younger colleagues came to
experience this trait in an especially hard way. It was as if he
calculated these cruelties, but as if, at the same time, he was
oblivious of their effect—as if he were an unaccountable small
child when it came to fellow human beings.

In retrospect, I now think that had Gunnar chosen to remain
a bachelor, as did Immanuel Kant and Jean-Paul Sartre and so
many other thinkers, or had he been married but remained childless like John Stuart Mill, no one would have asked why he
worked all day each day or why he was not playful and understanding with small children. Surely the ideal life for Gunnar
would have consisted in an intimate and collegial marriage with
Alva, with a stimulating circle of friends but no responsibility for
children, so that the two could travel freely and study and work
wherever they wanted. Instead he ended up not just with Alva
but also with a role in the full, rich life she herself sought as a
professional woman, a wife, and a mother. It grew to encompass
three children, a large house and garden, extensive entertainment,
and household help, friends, refugees, and relatives who often
lived at home. Perhaps he felt at times a stranger in the midst of
all this—and to be able to growl or to travel far away with Alva
must then have seemed to him a vital necessity.

I have only gradually come to understand my response to

having Gunnar as a father. It was twofold. I began, first of all, more and more to think of him as if he were indeed a child: to be sure in many ways a grown man, but one who at any time and often quite unexpectedly could act like an unfathomable, unaccountable little boy. On a drawing done when I was ten years old I have lined him up with Jan, Kaj, and myself as four rather small tots next to Alva as mother to us all. In this way I deposed him, not as an adult in general, but precisely as a father.

If I deposed Gunnar as father I also knew that he in turn could deny us as children. Of course he could take "peasant pride," as he sometimes said, in having children in his house. But he used to explain to us that it would take time before we would really count. One could not talk with small children, he often said. Not seriously. Only when they were about thirteen years old or so and could converse and reason in a clear manner was it worth the trouble. It would be irrational to try to surmount such natural obstacles earlier. He seemed unable to think of us as persons in our own right, and we were equally unable—then—to understand the depth and the scope of his own thoughts. "Absent-minded professor" was the most positive expression I thought I could apply to him.

Instead I learned simply to walk around him, not expect anything from him, and never confide anything personal to him about which he could laugh with others. These tactics were my second protection against Gunnar. It was not only that I trans-formed him in my thoughts to one of Alva's children whom she would have to struggle to educate; I also slipped aside, dreamed myself away in imagination, wandered far from home even when I was very little. This distancing had its drawbacks, but I think it saved me from being pulled into the openly brutal or darkly suppressed tensions in our home.

In these ways, I neutralized Gunnar. But even if I no longer saw him as a real father, I could still respect him as an intellectual parent, possessed of striking originality and force in coming to grips with seemingly intractable social problems, and one whose books I eventually thought through with profit, often with great admiration. Even at the intellectual level, however, I had to be careful to guard my independence. For many years he talked with me about my becoming an economist so as to follow in his footsteps and carry on his work. This idea never took root. At the time I thought of such proposals as rather amusing expressions of his egocentricity. Even more farfetched, in my eyes, was his suggestion, once it had been discovered that I learned languages easily, that I should study to be an interpreter so that I could devote myself to translating his books and speeches into different languages. Here it helped to have been taught not to be an "obedience person."

But if we did not acknowledge Gunnar as a father, we did what we could to find substitutes. It seemed natural for Kaj and me to turn to other men as secure father figures. In the early years it was especially my uncle Elon, Rut's wise, warm, strong husband, who played that role for me. He would pick me up at the train station with a sleigh when I arrived in Nibble, near the town of Västerås, where he and Rut had a farm, and I delighted in being wrapped in bearskin rugs and blankets and then driven home through the winter darkness with him as coachman.

I also admired the fathers of my friends, especially one who laughed a great deal and told stories and played chess and Monopoly with us and went on yearly summer vacations with his family and lived "normally," in my view. About that father I had a daydream. What if his boring though beautiful, Ava Gardner–like wife and Gunnar—hopeless cases both—could travel away. Far away. They might get married if they so wished, but at any rate they would disappear to the outer limits of our existence. Then Alva and my friend's impressively cheerful father could marry and she and I become sisters.

With such thoughts of fathers, and with Karin as a mother substitute, three or four firm friends, and cousins and other relatives to whom we felt close, and with Alva who stood for the whole and gave it life, my childhood existence felt full and secure. In addition, life in our home was enhanced by the many who visited it. Women's groups and other organizations met there and friends and relatives went in and out. Several young women whom Alva wanted to encourage helped her with library and archival work; they became part of the family. Two refugee children lived with us for longer periods: Gitte Borgschmidt, a beautiful girl with dark curls whose father saved her from the Nazis in Denmark and treated her like the little princess she resembled, and Julie Bernard, a short, quietly truculent French girl who came to us from a bombed-out part of Lille just after the war. I remember the suspicion with which Julie surveyed the milk we drank at dinnertime and how she rejected offers of water—she would have wine or nothing at all.

A circle of socialist refugees calling themselves the Little International used to meet with Alva and Gunnar at our house to discuss postwar plans for a democratic Europe. Among the members were two young men who were to become heads of state in post-Hitlerian Germany and Austria: Willy Brandt and Bruno Kreisky. The group worked out detailed plans for "restoring freedom and civilization after the Nazi holocaust" and for urging the Allies not to insist on the vindictive peace treaty that had been so debilitating after the First World War. Since Alva was a member of the Swedish Refugee Commission, our house became a gathering place for groups working with refugees. Kaj and I did not yet understand much of their discussions, but we knew that they touched on large questions. When it came to the war itself and the struggle against Hitler we were deeply engaged. From the beginning, Alva and Gunnar made clear that it was possible to come to grips with world problems, that one ought to have the courage to speak out critically when the need arose, and that boundaries—national, ethnic, professional, and most others— were there to be crossed. As the years wore on I realized that they took part as few others did in what was happening in the outside world, in the end entering the history of our entire century.

I have often thought that the role of parent does not only include that which Alva did least well and Gunnar not at all: to provide personally for children's nourishment, comfort, and care of every kind. Even these needs were ones that Alva arranged very responsibly for others to help meet. But to the parental role belongs also the effort to give children insight into how societies function and what individuals can do to contribute rather than merely be free riders. Above all, that role calls for parents to convey a sense of the values needed to do one's best in that regard. And here, setting an example seems to help far more than preaching and coercion. Although, as I have mentioned, Alva fortunately never had the time to "shape the human material" in her children in the directions she thought most socially useful, her example, with that of Gunnar, was powerful. It would be wrong to think of the two of them without feeling the force of their courage, their generous engagement, their joy in working, their openness and willingness to take risks. And to grow up in a home where the adults truly felt the full attraction of the Enlightenment ideals of reason and human potential could give a nearly dizzying sense of the depth and the scope one can experience if one only dares to think freely.

To be sure there can be peril in growing up with parents as forceful as Alva and Gunnar, who invoke such ideals so boldly and unquestioningly. Children may then feel that they are in the presence of centers of energy that can draw them in and over-whelm them, at times disable them, all in the name of reason and social utility. Yet I never felt thus disabled as a child. True enough, our family was unusual, outspoken, often split. But so were others, in a manner that seemed to me more oppressive. Had I read Tolstoy's words at the beginning of *Anna Karenina*—that all happy families are alike but all unhappy families unhappy each in their own way—I would have appreciated the response that those words inspired in a critic: "*All* families are Russian novels."

11

Departures

❖ ❖ ❖ ❖

*D*isquiet was in the air for us all *in 1946. Alva felt her life too full of disparate tasks—committees, talks, articles, conferences at home and abroad—without a strong guiding aim. The previous year many had mentioned her for the post of Sweden's minister of education. But she had withdrawn her name, knowing that Gunnar might be named minister of commerce and that they could not possibly both be in the government at the same time. When Gunnar was asked to serve he accepted, eager to put his plans for postwar economic growth into practice. But a year later he had already run into heavy weather. His quick way of toying with ideas and of saying anything that came into his head irritated many and made it easy for misunderstandings to arise.

From then on, views were split regarding his contributions in the government. His good friend and colleague, Ernst Wigforss, on the one hand, later wrote in his memoirs that those who are strangers to the delight of allowing ideas free play in order to have the stuff for further reflection "find it hard not to misjudge personalities like Gunnar's, for whom such an atmosphere of imagination and toying with ideas seems to be the breath of life itself."

Herbert Tingsten, on the other hand, a former friend and the editor in chief of Sweden's most powerful newspaper, *Dagens Nyheter,* took the lead in hounding Gunnar. He criticized many of Gunnar's decisions as opportunistic and unreliable. In his memoirs Tingsten claimed that the happy love for himself in which

Gunnar lived "makes him identify an objective with his own advancement. The resulting sense that all means are allowed provides the background for his unreliability."

Gunnar himself looked with contempt at what he took to be partisan polemics. But of course he could not avoid feeling the heat. And he found his government colleagues, such as Wigforss, strangely unwilling to take seriously his warnings about the nation's economic policies. When his suggestions within the government were met with silence, he opted for speaking out in public about the need for stronger import limits and for a devaluation of the Swedish crown. Criticism was immediate, the more so as imports rose sharply. After he had concluded what he saw as a favorable trade agreement between Sweden and the Soviet Union the attacks against him grew stronger still, fueled in part by the incipient cold war and by pressures from the United States.

In March 1947 the government felt forced to reintroduce rationing of coffee, tea, and cocoa—an unwelcome reminder of wartime scarcity and a great shock to the coffee-loving Swedes. Gunnar and other ministers were accused of poor management, and a scandal erupted that put in question Alva's integrity. A number of papers insinuated that she had relied on advance information to stock up on coffee the day before the rationing was to be introduced. She could not deny that she often made large purchases, nor that she had bought coffee, among other things, the previous day. But for her, such shopping in bulk was nothing out of the ordinary. When she had worked with Sven Markelius in planning our house in Äppelviken, she had added a storage room next to the kitchen that would allow her to make fewer but larger purchases. In that room there was row upon row of cans and jars: shrimp, asparagus, lingonberries, applesauce, exotic imports from abroad.

Alva felt deeply wounded that such purchases could be thought of as hoarding. She recalled her own parents' dispute about the wheat her mother had wanted to set aside for the children during the famine of 1917. The daily press pursued her with innuendo. "Halva Dyrdal" was the name one editorial gave her (*halva* meaning "half"; *dyr,* "expensive"), and anonymous

letters flooded in. Sometimes stinking meat arrived in greasy pack-
ages, which the police had to open. On days when the criticism
had been especially severe, she would arrive at the Seminar wearing dark glasses to hide any signs of having wept. Ten days after
it had all begun she published a complete accounting of her
purchases and offered to show what she had in the family storage
room. "But let me ask, in closing," she added, in a tone that
showed how bitterly ironic she found the criticism, considering
Gunnar's indifference toward everything having to do with the
household,

> are all means now permitted in the political battle? Will public
> persons be systematically made the subjects of scandal? . . .
> Will we find ourselves in a system based on spying and in-
> formers? In this case, it is not even me personally that people
> want to get at, but my husband, who has been absolutely
> silent about the rationing plans and who happens to have
> much less concern for the family's private household matters
> than most.

Kaj and I sensed the anxiety. For us, the public pointing to
the name Myrdal no longer stirred faintly amusing thoughts as
when used in expressions such as "Myrdal cactus" and "Myrdal
couch"; now we saw our name clearly singled out, denounced,
and in turn defended. We heard accusations we knew were
groundless and others we were not sure we understood. Some
opened a kind of abyss: could people really think such things?
About our parents?

Because of the scandal we gained new, outside perspectives
on what might be going on inside our home. Our private lives
were openly discussed. Our family's food purchases and views on
child rearing, even our parents' personal traits—all could evidently
be evaluated and disputed in a way we had not understood up to
then. Just as Alva had learned through the debates in her childhood home and in her family's two newspapers about subjects
such as the cooperative movement, social democracy, the right to
vote, and the Great War, so we received, early on, a feeling for

the many-sidedness of views and for differences between appearance and reality; but for us the lessons became bitingly personal.

In this way, Kaj and I experienced for the first time what so many other children of well-known parents go through. We noticed that adults, especially at school, seemed to treat us differently depending on their views about our parents. We began to understand that Gunnar had a polarizing effect, as did Alva in her own way. People seemed either to admire or to detest them, and in some unfathomable way this spilled over onto us. Some teachers seemed to resent us for political reasons: Kaj remembers, for instance, being sent out of the classroom one day that winter after having asked questions that the teacher found too persistent. "You are just as impertinent as your mother!" she was told. At the same time, some of our friends' parents treated us with increasing coldness as the newspaper criticism grew. Why it should have anything to do with our schoolwork or our friendships we could not understand, but that is how it was. We in turn took Gunnar and Alva's side wholeheartedly and lived intensely through each new development in the public debate.

Gunnar later wrote that these attacks, much like those after the publication of *Crisis in the Population Question*, "left a bitter aftertaste that I have only gradually and slowly been able to overcome." He felt misunderstood and insufficiently appreciated and began, once more, to wonder whether Sweden offered the right environment for him. His life's greatest work, *An American Dilemma*, which was already a classic abroad, had not been translated into Swedish, or even properly reviewed. And he was less interested, when all was said and done, in Sweden's postwar problems than in what happened in the rest of the world. Already in 1946 he had begun to look around for other opportunities to work abroad.

When Trygve Lie, the newly appointed secretary-general of the United Nations, offered Gunnar the position of director of social affairs in his secretariat, he turned it down, explaining that his central focus was on international economics rather than on social affairs. Immediately, Alva received the offer in his place; but she too said no, explaining that, challenging as she would have found such a position, she could not put an ocean between the family and herself. A second UN invitation tempted her sorely: Julian Huxley asked her, early in 1947, to be assistant director of the newly formed UNESCO in Paris, which was to become, under his leadership, a world center for international cooperation on problems of education, science, and culture. Huxley had worked with Alva when she was a Swedish delegate to early meetings of the International Labor Organization and of UNESCO. In her usual inventive manner, she had written reports about all that might be done after the war to rebuild and improve school systems and cultural institutions the world over. At the same time she had, since July 1946, worked to start a new international organization to further research and reforms having to do with early childhood education: OMEP, the Organisation Mondiale de l'Education Primaire.

Alva saw the UNESCO offer as a fantastic opportunity. She who had for so long had to make her own way and create her own possibilities for work, was now being asked to assume an extraordinarily stimulating position—one that seemed tailor-made for someone with her energy and creativity. Had she been free she would have accepted it right away. But at the time she found it natural, once again, to decline because of the family. Gunnar made it clear that he did not want to move to Paris.

He had, however, asked Alva to insert a message from him in her cable turning down the first offer: that he himself would be interested in heading the UN Economic Commission for Europe (ECE) then in the process of formation and to be based in Geneva. Its task would be to address the vast economic problems faced by a Europe reduced almost to chaos by the long years of war and deprivation. Gunnar knew he was being seriously considered for the position and felt ready to leave Sweden for the commission's much larger endeavors in Geneva.

The offer came, and Gunnar weighed it during the very weeks in March 1947 when the newspapers were urging his resignation and the campaign against Alva was growing stronger. Early in April he accepted the position. He knew that the intensifying cold war and the Iron Curtain tightening across Europe imperiled the

ECE before it had even had its first meeting. In an interview some thirty years later, Gunnar recalled the circumstances under which he and Alva had debated whether he should accept the appointment:

> We felt very uncertain about what was going to happen . . . but we said the risk we are going to bear is that we are going to put everything we have into making a success of this adventure. My sane judgment was that more probably than not, this whole thing would explode but [if it did it would not be] because I did not put in everything I could of my brains, of my money . . . everything in me should be at the disposal of this adventure.

"Now the snooties are sore!" gloated Kaj, then ten, about all those who had carped so vociferously at our parents, in a poem written when the news about Gunnar's resignation and new position appeared in the newspapers:

> *Now we're off to Geneva*
> *to have a good time, and woe*
> *to anyone barring the way.*
> *That one I'll just punch, Boss.*

For us, it turned out to be a definitive departure. It contributed to the dissolution of our family that had begun when Jan left home so early, and to Kaj's and my becoming expatriates. But of this we knew nothing at the time, nor did we understand how deeply torn Alva felt. Outwardly she seemed her usual active self. She went about her work, arranged to show the house to potential buyers, began French lessons with Kaj and me, and planned furnishings for our new home. But inwardly, I later learned, she felt utterly thrown off stride. She was having to leave our home in Äppelviken, the Seminar, her work on school reform and so much else, without having any firm plans for what she would do in Geneva when she arrived.

Writing to Gunnar, who had gone ahead to Geneva while she was winding up her work with the School Commission and taking care of the details of our move, Alva explained that all seemed to be going well with the furniture and the house, but that the "psychological move" was faring worse. She knew so little about what she was going to do. "It can't be that I am exhausted? Or wiped out? In fact, I don't really want to do anything except plan furnishings and be with you. In every other respect I feel low."

Our new home in Geneva was called Les Feuillantines, Alva told us, showing us drawings of the house. It stood in a park facing the Place des Nations and the UN's white palace overlooking Lake Geneva. Gunnar confessed to Alva that he worried about having an official residence for the first time in their lives, but that he also thought it necessary. In the struggle for survival that the ECE experienced from the very beginning, with no certainty from one week to the next about which nations would even agree to take part, it was important to be able to use the house for informal negotiations on the spur of the moment and to entertain delegates and other visitors generously. Not wishing to saddle the UN with great expenses, he and Alva planned to spend most of the proceeds from the sale of their house to furnish their new residence. This was part of what he meant by saying that he would place not only his brains but his money and all that he had at the disposal of "this new adventure."

House planning and furnishings now took over completely for Alva, helping her push aside the uncertainty about what she would actually do in Geneva. To plan for a house was always, for her, to work out how one would live. This time she wanted to make it possible for friends to stay with us for long periods if need be. And large spaces were needed for entertaining guests. The move was an immense affair—all that our family owned and masses of newly bought furniture were packed. It seemed as if Switzerland would be our home base for life, so great was Alva's labor.

As for myself, I was blissfully happy about the move, in spite of tinglings of melancholy at the thought of having to leave my friends. To go abroad, speak new languages, have all manner of adventures—what could be better? Kaj and I shared elaborate fantasies about a treasure that might lie buried in our new garden. We drew tunnels criss-crossing the plans for the garden that Alva had given us and decided who was going to get to dig where, longing for the opportunity to begin. In addition, I was eager to be free of the annoying sense that people reacted more to me as Alva and Gunnar's daughter than as the person in my own right that I wanted to be. I rejoiced at the thought of breaking away from the sluggish Girl Scout group I had been too shy to leave. And I felt ill at ease in my school, the Bromma Läroverk, with its severe and chilly atmosphere, the more so because teachers kept comparing me with Jan and taking for granted that I would follow in his stormy tracks rather than—once again—be myself. It is no wonder, therefore, that I saw the opportunity to move abroad as a veritable coup.

The train trip, in August 1947, lasted three days. It took us through bombed-out German cities and starving crowds at each station. Hundreds of thousands of families were still migrating after the war, and Soviet actions in Eastern Europe sent ever more people on the refugee trail. Food was hard to obtain and the catastrophic weather that summer had spread the threat of famine still more widely. Europe's industry and commerce were recovering from the war slowly, with high tariffs making trade even more difficult. The Marshall Plan, announced in June, had barely begun. Hungry children begged along the railway carriages for food or cigarettes. We hardly dared look out the windows. Since we had just celebrated Kaj's eleventh birthday, we made up packets of candy and sandwiches even though we knew they were hopelessly inadequate gifts for the hands reaching toward us.

Unlike our house in Äppelviken, Les Feuillantines was not a modern villa ideal for a family with small children. It was, rather, a palatial, languorous older house with a view, on clear days, of Mont Blanc behind the park and the glittering Lake Geneva. On the ground floor Alva decorated the large salons, library, and dining room with contemporary Swedish furniture upholstered in rich, glowing colors, blending with warm antiques and shimmering, pastel-colored Venetian chandeliers. The second floor had comfortable rooms for her and Gunnar and two guests, and on the third floor, along with a spacious attic, there were large rooms for Kaj and me, Karin Anger, and a maid.

Much later, Alva wrote me that we may not have been clear about what the changes meant for us all when we moved to Geneva—the broken bonds of friendship and the sense of estrangement at first in a new language. I wrote back to say that that was not how I, at least, had experienced the transition. For me it was liberating. I saw it as a journey to seek my identity and as an adventure of a fresh kind. And the new house that was causing Alva so much trouble was for me a pure joy. True, Kaj and I gave up our plans for extensive tunnel digging in the garden as soon as we went outdoors with our shovels in the heat of the late summer day and began to have our doubts about the existence of the treasure. But to live in a park with mossy benches, paths, a little stone bridge over a dried-out brook, a thicket of bamboo where the stems sighed and cracked as one hid among them, an abandoned tennis court, and huge trees in which we could build cabins was like having a whole kingdom to explore. And the lively world of Geneva with inhabitants from every nation, with the mountains so near and the lake in which, at the time, one could still swim at many beaches—I found it all dazzlingly novel.

Gunnar saw the ECE as facing an immense challenge: to counteract the increasing split between Eastern and Western Europe by assisting European nations to recover agriculturally and industrially. He had warned, earlier, against excessive postwar optimism and intended to propose strong practical measures for international cooperation. Now he had a chance to promote these ideas in a manner quite different from that of a scholar or a minister of commerce. If it were possible to restore economic links between East and West before the cold war made this impossible, both sides would benefit. From the outset, he knew that the task would be difficult; but the cold war was to limit the opportunities even more than he had been able to predict.

Gunnar became totally immersed in the problems confronting him. He began by assembling what by all accounts was a remarkable group of colleagues from many nations to work in the ECE secretariat and infused it with a rare spirit of collegiality and creativity. As a result the atmosphere in which he worked seemed utterly unlike the mood of distrust and backbiting he had experienced during the last years in Sweden. Here he had an exceptionally talented team to help him and great opportunities for important contributions. Perhaps he had arrived, this time, as the right man in the right position, just when the need for innovative political action based on careful studies of the economic situation was greatest.

Gunnar's daily schedule came to exclude all that did not concern the ECE—and, for the first time, even Alva. His work routine was grueling, from early morning through meetings and gatherings almost every evening. Alva warned him not to exhaust himself, but to no avail. Less dependent on her clear-sightedness and support than before, he thrived on the collegial atmosphere in which the commission's work was carried on. His coworkers, for their part, saw him as a brilliant administrator. They admired, too, his warmth and informality and total commitment, and his refusal to accept a chauffeured limousine or other status symbols dear to many high officials. His secretary was Anika de la Grandville, a young Hungarian-born widow of a Frenchman who had died in the war. With her regal bearing and dark, high-cheeked beauty, she was not only a marvel of efficiency but also deeply knowledgeable about the history and languages of Europe. All gave Gunnar the admiration and loyalty he had not known since the days of similarly collegial and dedicated work on *An American Dilemma*.

Gunnar was increasingly treated as a great man—with grandeur in his ideas, forceful, charismatic, and courageous enough to withstand all cold war pressures from both East and West. Internationally, the work of the ECE came to be highly regarded, not only for the objectivity of its research but for keeping alive the idea of East-West cooperation at a time of such seemingly lethal divisions.

Absorbed and inspired in these ways by his new challenge, Gunnar must have found Alva's methodically fervent concern with furniture, bills, moving out of one house and into another trivial by comparison. Gradually, Alva felt the full force of the change in their lives. She had foreseen that the move would be trying and that she would experience regret at leaving the Seminar. "But only after a year did it dawn on me that I did not, this time, have the marriage to turn to," she wrote. "ECE became everything for Gunnar, the family and I nothing." The story about the spouses who lived happily forever after had been shattered. The two who had written together, worked through so many ideas together, discussed all they did in minute detail with one another, suddenly had much less in common.

Alva never understood why she had been so abruptly excluded from the partnership with Gunnar that they had both taken for granted until then. She herself had sacrificed much in order to accompany him; this time, however, it had come to nothing. All that she had believed and written about marriage—the full-fledged companionship, both as spouses and as partners in work—had now been abandoned. And not a word of explanation had she received or even demanded. Once again she suffered in what I find inexplicable silence. She told me much later—just as surprised as I when she reflected on it—that she had never asked Gunnar during the forty years that followed what exactly had taken place.

Worst of all, her second dream, of going into the world to seek her fortune, seemed equally likely to remain unfulfilled in Geneva. True, she was now abroad. But she had been obliged to sever all professional links with Sweden after turning down the offers to work for the UN in New York and Paris. And, being a foreigner, she was not allowed to work in Geneva, except precisely at the UN, where she was excluded from all employment because Gunnar's high position there might otherwise arouse suspicions of nepotism. The situation of women in Switzerland was, in her opinion, degrading. It was not just that Swiss women had neither the right to vote nor what she regarded as minimal rights within their families and communities; they also seemed to accept their inferior status in a cowlike manner that Alva had never seen in other European nations or in the United States.

Much like the other wives in the city and in the UN, Alva was now, suddenly, solely a housewife and a hostess. Everyone took for granted that she would concentrate on her husband, her children, her home, and entertainment. Without work of her own she entered a period of desperate powerlessness that I did not recognize at the time but understood later, when I saw her respond to a similar lack of challenging work. She looked back at the move to Geneva as "a breaking-up that pulled away the foundations for all meaningful work on my part."

Here was Alva, still youthful and strong, without the slightest channel for her creative powers. Was her life now to shrink, as did the lives of most wives when their children grew older and their husbands less attentive? She who had vowed since childhood never to be "tied to a housewifely existence that would center on a man" was now trapped. She felt, I believe, buried alive, locked into the superficial role of hostess while shielding a wifely role that had become nothing but a mask. These roles gave her no consolation. She had always enjoyed inviting friends home and creating an atmosphere of beauty, good food, and lively conversation. But that had to be on the side of her essential existence. It had to reflect a genuine togetherness, not an empty shell.

Her suffering seems to have passed us all by, in part because of her silence and self-effacement. Had she made scenes, quarreled, thrown flowerpots, we would surely have paid attention. As it was, Gunnar remained so preoccupied with his own concerns that he took for granted that she, like the rest of us, would take care of herself. And she kept up appearances. "I can't get angry, I can only get sad," as she used to say—but this time, she concealed even her grief. Kaj and I, who should perhaps have understood at least some of her feelings, only experienced greater distance on her part at the time. It was as if her inner light had gone out. She took less and less part in our lives, but we did not connect this with her personal problems.

In addition, our own experiences were so novel and strange that we hardly had the energy or the imagination left to enter into her anguish. Our solitude at first among so many new persons speaking unfamiliar languages and the fact that both Alva and Gunnar had disengaged from our concerns threw us together in a new way. Kaj, barely eleven when these changes struck our family, began experiencing our new home as alien, empty, devoid of love. Karin was still our dearest friend, but she never felt at home among the Genevans, in the new language, or with all that was foreign, and she was shaken when Alva, who had always given shape and stability to our home, drew apart from us all more and more.

I too drew away. I fell into a period of fantasizing and writing and succeeded in creating a world of my own in the house and the dreamlike garden. In addition, I experienced my first—if utterly unrequited—love. I relished standing by my window each evening and looking out over the trees silhouetted against the meadows in the mists beyond them. I wrote poem after poem about these experiences, unaware of Alva's anguish one floor below.

The International School—Ecolint—that I had longed so to join bewildered me at first. I knew neither English nor French, the two languages most in use. A completely unaccustomed silence gripped me. During the first fall weeks at school I was near tears most of the time. I walked from classroom to classroom almost paralyzed with shyness among all these children who were able to speak so effortlessly. I now had to rethink the significance of speech and silence, of meaning and expression and explanations in a wholly unanticipated way. I felt driven to learn both English and French as rapidly as I possibly could. This task was the more complicated since English was being taught to the French-speaking children in French and French to the English-speaking children in English. Even now I remember how at first I experienced what was said around me as a fog that covered everything, and how I gradually began to distinguish outlines in the fog, lights, signals, so that in the end, after the winter holidays, I was able to maneuver within the two languages and overcome my self-imposed silence.

To have mastered French and English gave me a sense of new powers and of greater closeness to my friends at school. I enjoyed life there more and more; it became a home for me, its tangible reality a contrast to the equally indispensable imaginary life I had woven around the garden at home. The school life was stimulating in a way I had never before experienced. It was just as liberating and as warmly humane as the ideals for schooling that Alva had advocated in her writings and in the Swedish debate over education. With slightly more than three hundred students from around the world, the school was small enough to function as a kind of extended family, so that stiffness and formalities of all sorts were completely excluded. Its ethos was one of internationalism, of cooperation, and of respect for cultural and other differences among human beings. This allowed me to discover religions, nationalities, languages as realities more personal than they had seemed when I heard them debated in Alva and Gunnar's adult world. And I found a new father figure in one of the teachers. He used to take his family and a group of students on a two-week ski trip in the Swiss Alps each winter. To my indescribable happiness, I was permitted to come along, that first Christmas holiday, to Verbier, then a small, peaceful village unknown to most tourists. I was captivated by his warmth and humor as he guided us up the mountains on sealskins or sang with us around the fire after the evening meals.

But about all these experiences—my muteness, my rediscovered ability to speak, my sense of happiness and belonging—I talked very little with Alva, just as she concealed her despair from us. This period must have marked the low point in our relationship. My letters to her from ski trips and bicycle journeys describe my activities, remind her of books, games, clothes I needed, but say nothing about what I thought. We were then only conventionally mother and daughter, though not the slightest bit hostile.

The light in our home was dying out. This happens slowly, not as when a candle's flame trembles and goes out. Gunnar led his life entirely apart from the rest of us, Alva was subdued, Karin anxious and without her usual joyful force. Gunnar forgot birthdays altogether and social life was determined by his official needs. Kaj and I found the hum of voices that rose to the third floor from his and Alva's cocktail parties absurd and did not enjoy the elegant meals for guests to which we were occasionally invited. More and more we sought our security and our real lives else-

where. It would take a few years for our home in Les Feuillantines
to dissolve completely. But long before that, we had had to think
through how we wanted to live and how we might manage for
ourselves. Kaj even began, gropingly, to look around for a new
family.

Even during this difficult period, however, Alva was not entirely deprived of opportunities to work. She continued to write
articles about family policy and education. And together with
Lady Marjorie Allen, who had done so much for children in
England and who became one of Alva's closest and most warmly
admired friends, she worked to get UNESCO to take OMEP
seriously. This undertaking required considerable international
travel. Each time she went away on such a mission her spirits
revived. On one such trip she wrote to Gunnar how much it
meant to her to be working on genuine problems, with colleagues
she respected. She added that when she was out maneuvering on
her own, away from his immediate vicinity, she became much
stronger and more capable; but that she still wanted, most of all,
to be near him.

When Alva was asked to give a lecture to UN officials in
Geneva she chose a topic close to her heart: "The Surplus Energy
of Married Women." Once again she was using her own situation
as a foundation for the contribution she hoped to make. The very
title of her talk, though it concerned women's need to work, was
sexually ambiguous. One of those present wrote to me after her
death about the title's apparent double meaning. Here stood this
beautiful, brilliant woman who spoke about how married women
have energy in excess. Her insistence on speaking about problems
in the labor market, he said, disappointed the less serious-minded
among her male listeners.

It was also during this period that Alva began thinking about
the book she would later write with the sociologist Viola Klein,
Women's Two Roles. But for her, writing was never as profoundly
satisfying as for Gunnar. It could not take the place of practical
work. Rather, it was something she preferred to do on the side
or as a spur to the reforms she sought. She never learned to

immerse herself, as he could, in writing projects, preferring to surround herself with people. Having a book under way was therefore not much help against her gnawing unhappiness in Geneva.

But writing turned out to provide her with a new opening. She had pointed in a series of articles to the outrageous differences in standards of living among nations and proposed a form of "social taxation" that the UN might levy in order to help even out the disparities. She had also lectured at several conferences about the conditions in which children lived and about the need for school reforms. These writings reached the UN secretariat in New York as a reminder of everything she had earlier written and done. Perhaps someone there had also heard that she now regretted having turned down the previous offers to work for the UN. Finally she was given another chance: in the fall of 1948, Secretary-General Lie asked her, once again, to go to New York to head the secretariat's Department of Social Affairs.

That letter arrived as something of such "dreamlike satisfaction," Alva said, that she could not resist it. Only a little more than a year had passed since her departure from Sweden and all the plans for a new life in Geneva. The move had seemed to her definitive at the time. Now she wanted to go away once again, perhaps not with the same finality, a bit more tentatively, but with the freedom she craved. She wanted to flee the illusion, now a caricature, of the complete partnership she had clung to for so long. By now, making her way out into the world to lead her own life required nothing short of such an escape. But letters to Gunnar when he was away from Geneva show that she had in no way given up on the marriage itself. Rather, she wanted him to know just how much the new opportunity meant to her:

> I walk with my back straight in a completely different way from before. All day long and in my sleep, my unconscious works over the impending job—which gives a vigor that has long been absent—and in the evenings, my eagerness almost contracts into a little anxiety. But essentially, I am only happy.

I can even fulfill functions as your wife and go to cocktail parties the week long. . . . Gunnar, I feel sheer bliss about this opportunity.

From the very beginning, Alva admitted, she felt that he had had little regard for her obligations when they conflicted with his, and she had, up to that time, halfheartedly gone along. No longer. "For the *first time,* I shall hold up my work as against yours." She did not believe that saying so would detract from their love, she added, any more than the temporary separation that her new position required. It is as if she wanted neither Gunnar nor even herself to suspect that her crossing the Atlantic to live and work in America could hurt their relationship. She wished, rather, that the reverse would be the case: that they would again be "newly in love."

Alva's departure was perhaps a little like leaving her parents' home and her siblings to join Gunnar in Stockholm when she was young. Now it was Gunnar and the family in Geneva that she left behind—once again wholly without open criticism, much less rupture, and surely burdened by the thought of all who would miss her, but still most of all with inner exaltation. She used to speak about the dizzyingly sensuous enjoyment she always felt when planes took off and ships weighed anchor. That feeling must have been especially intense when she set out for New York and a free life of her own on February 1, 1949, the day after her birthday.

12

Career

❖ ❖ ❖ ❖

*I*t *was when she turned forty-seven,* then, that Alva felt that
her real career had at last begun. She had come to view Gunnar's
career path as a straight and spacious track, shaped by his creative
power and his exceptional capacity for hard work. But the path
of her own work, she later wrote, was, rather, like "a meandering
ribbon running alongside of his." Without ever having been much
in demand or having had a full-time job, she had managed to
"create certain larger or smaller loops" with this ribbon and to
develop independent projects and achievements, almost never for
much pay.

Now she was setting off on her own spacious track. In New
York she was employed for the first time in a position of exceptional responsibility. Having been asked to head the UN's Department of Social Affairs, she became the highest-placed woman
in any international organization. She could hardly wait to begin.
"Now I see clearly," she wrote much later, "that I first became a
free person in 1949. And so *happy,* in New York, in Paris, in
New Delhi!"

In her new position, she had the opportunity to act for her
ideals with the international perspective she had increasingly
found to be indispensable. But now that perspective opened up
still further. All the issues that she had dealt with earlier—the
position of women and children, schooling, housing conditions,
population—she could now consider with the whole world as a
background. This shift affected her deeply, especially with respect

to the poorer nations. It was as vast a shift as the one she and
Gunnar had experienced during their first trip to America, when
they felt they had had their eyes opened politically, or when the
coming of the Second World War forced them to rethink their
optimism regarding the future.

One can feel this transformation in comparing two of Alva's
speeches. In the summer of 1948 she lectured at a conference in
Prague on the different obstacles in the way of schooling and child
rearing. She began by stating that she would not take up the
extraordinary obstacles posed by wars, migration, and starvation
that social planning could not easily remedy. Instead she intended
to focus on more ordinary circumstances such as housing conditions, the structure of families, and the standard of living. Choosing many of her examples from Sweden, she compared the state
of affairs in Europe and the United States.

Two years later, Alva lectured at Mount Holyoke College
about how the UN could help improve social conditions. This
time she no longer touched solely on a few industrialized nations.
Nor did she choose to exclude the effects of war, hunger, and
migration as beyond the reach of planning. On the contrary, she
began by comparing the optimism at the UN's founding with the
realities in 1950:

> It is hard even to imagine the depth and breadth of the black
> misery still besetting this world. It seems incredible that more
> than half of this world's inhabitants go hungry today . . . ;
> that about half of them, because of their illiteracy, are unable
> to participate in the life of our century. It might as well be the
> year 1350 as far as they are concerned; at least some 200
> million people have no roof over their head or any abode
> worthy of the name of home.

Of course she had been familiar with these facts before and
often felt overwhelmed by them, but never with any sense that
she could do much about them personally. The League of Nations
had had as its members mainly European nations. Not until after
the Second World War had the question of equal standing between

different nations and continents come to the foreground. Now it was part of her mandate. Through the UN it was possible to work for all the goals that now became "hers" officially: human rights, the plight of refugees, population, standards of living, addiction, and for the first time in the international forum the UN offered, the status of women. And it was possible to bring about results. That same year, for example, two additional nations had, with UN assistance, introduced women's suffrage.

It was also in New York that Alva could first put her great talent as a diplomat to full use. Her subtle way of entering into discussions and taking them seriously made meetings a new experience even for practiced civil servants. Her ability to dramatize what was at stake forced them to confront choices that they would otherwise easily have slid by. She had patience enough to wait for results but could also discern solutions where others saw nothing but chaos or bone-hard conflict. She used to say that she looked at negotiations as a game with mirrors: she enjoyed all the intricacies and the moves of the game, so long—but only so long—as she perceived possibilities for agreement, even if it would take years in coming.

Now that she was living alone, she was also cheered by how much easier it was to make new friends of her own. She no longer needed to serve as a hostess for the gatherings that Gunnar had increasingly sought to dominate. She was free to decide how she would spend her time and with whom, and at the UN there were countless chances for contacts of the stimulating sort she relished. To Gunnar's sister Elsa she wrote, in January 1950, that her life was

> so full, even with friends. After all, I have never had this same chance to do what I can and be what I am; it is an "unfolding" that almost astonishes me myself.

From that time onward, she had friends wherever she traveled. When she met people, young and old, whom she could imagine as close friends or when she came across friends of long standing, one could see a spark of intimate recognition in her glance—one that transcended barriers of age and experience without ever denying them.

Alva's gift for such close relations with others may have sprung, in part, from her strong sense of "the unavoidable isolation of the individual." She had known this closeness with Rut, with Märta Fredriksson, through correspondence with Per Sundberg and Andreas, with Gunnar, and with a number of colleagues. She could feel suffused by it when working closely with others for causes she believed in, such as the rights of women or of refugees. Only in certain embittered or petrified situations did she find friendship impossible. Friends should be chosen, she insisted, and friendship could thrive only if it was mutual. She often used the German word *Wahlverwandt* or the English "kindred spirit" to express the bond—familial yet chosen rather than based on the accident of birth—that she felt with such friends.

Alva could nevertheless not concentrate fully on her work and on her lively new social life. Our family was in her thoughts more than she had perhaps imagined it would be. She had left Geneva without coming to a full understanding with any of us about her reasons for not staying. In her desire to escape her despairing sense of powerlessness in Geneva and her problems with Gunnar, she had at first given over all responsibility concerning household matters to Karin, hoping that she would continue to handle them smoothly. Alva also had theories about how her absence would make Kaj and me more independent and more responsible about schoolwork and pocket money. But without the deeper explanation that was needed, we did not find the theories especially inspiring.

Nor had Alva considered fully Gunnar's need for someone to help him keep the house open for dinners and cocktail parties. In struggling to have the ECE go on functioning as an all-European organization despite the cold war, he found it indispensable to continue bringing delegates together at home for meetings and informal discussions. In Alva's absence he turned increasingly to his secretary, Anika de la Grandville, to make all the necessary arrangements and to serve at his side as a hostess. We grew used to seeing her arrive for Sunday luncheons and other gatherings, always elegantly attired and ready to welcome the guests. When Alva returned for visits, she seemed to accept this change as well. But although she claimed never to have challenged Gunnar on this score, her letters to him show increased distance and occasional wistfulness. It is clear that her hope, expressed as she was preparing to leave Geneva, that their temporary separation would make them "newly in love" was receding.

Alva invited me to stay with her during the spring term of 1950 as a concession to her own longing for more family life and to her role as a mother. She had rented a small, semi-detached house on Barstow Road, a quiet street in Great Neck, Long Island, not far from the UN's first headquarters in Lake Success. I had a room of my own with the luxury of a radio and began attending Great Neck High School. By comparison with the International School in Geneva it seemed a crushingly large school in which I felt lost at first and overwhelmed by shyness. And Alva's cheerfulness irritated me. Her visible pleasure in her many new friends—especially the men among them—made me uncertain and grumpy.

I felt challenged, and I wondered what this newfound happiness might portend for our family. My response was a surly unwillingness to go along with whatever amusement Alva proposed. I refused to go with her to Broadway shows, refused to drive with her to visit friends who invited us for weekends in the mountains or by the sea, refused to talk with her about anything other than my journey back home, for which I longed more each day. Instead I sat by the radio and ate all the cookies I could find and fantasized about friends in Geneva and about the garden at home. I have since thought of those months with guilt. I must have been an unsatisfactory guest for Alva. But then I did not really want to be her "guest."

That summer she moved to Paris to head the Division of Social Sciences at UNESCO. She had already stayed longer in the United States than she had originally intended and found it hard to be so far from the family. Paris might offer just the right distance from home, she wrote to Gunnar's sister Elsa: "Just sitting in Geneva is not for me." In a press interview she said that she thought Kaj and I needed to have our parents "a little closer and a little more together."

Closer? More together? We saw no signs of that. We were still alone in the Geneva house with Gunnar, who was more immersed in his work than ever, and with Karin Anger, who had fallen ill during my absence. Exhausted, isolated, and severely depressed, she had decided to return to her hometown in Sweden. Kaj was thirteen at the time, I fifteen. We suffered over what was happening and did not understand the reasons. It was hardest for Kaj, who while I was abroad had been alone during Karin's gradual collapse and finally had seen her lying in bed day after day, too tired to move.

We noticed that people began to feel seriously sorry for us. Many believed that our parents' marriage had foundered and saw us as two abandoned beings without either father or mother. We felt the ambiguity in our situation. We knew nothing for certain about their relationship. They did not live together, to be sure, but visited each other as if nothing had happened and often talked about how good it was to be separated only by "the distance of an overnight train journey." How should we evaluate our own situation? Would it be better to accept the compassion offered us or to keep up appearances in a more nonchalant way? Mostly, I think, we avoided thinking about the matter, while feeling warmed by the sympathy from several families.

Whatever she thought inwardly, Alva herself kept up appearances, as she had in Geneva when she realized that the consummate partnership with Gunnar was over. She would not question her attitude until late in life. Then she spoke of the personal sacrifices often demanded of persons in public life. She might well, otherwise, have considered divorce—much less common at the time—had she not been concerned about how it would "appear."

Kaj and I have often wondered why Alva didn't bring us along to New York and Paris when she first left Gunnar. Or why couldn't we have lived in Ecolint, which was part boarding school? How could she leave us so entirely without supervision? Even though we shared the same house with Gunnar, he was often absent or having company. Now there was no one at home who took an interest in our studies or even in the most ordinary matters such as visits to the dentist or outgrown clothes. We learned to take this into account in our letters to Alva. One winter, for instance, I wrote that I needed a bathing suit for the summer, adding that it was perhaps a bit premature to mention this, "but after your April visit, one never knows when you'll return." When such advance planning was needed just for a bathing suit, there could not be many confidences about thoughts or friends, and Alva's brief visits gave us no chance to come closer to her.

During this period, it was as if Kaj's spirit drained away. She wrote heartrending letters to Alva about her loneliness without a mother. Sometimes she lay in bed, like Karin, for days on end. At last she found a way out that may well have saved her from prolonged despair: she managed, with ingenuity and tact, to be invited to live with one of her teachers and his artist wife on a small farm outside the city. With animals to care for and only light farming chores, they and their children struck Kaj as leading the right kind of life, close to the earth. After her arrival they took in additional youngsters as boarders. Kaj relished being part of this extended family and regained her joy in living.

My own response to this isolation was to try, rather, to be my own father and mother: to find my own principles for living, my own life-style, above all to find myself. I was deeply attached to Les Feuillantines and to its magical garden and had no desire to live elsewhere. The solitude became something I both enjoyed and found threatening. It nourished me and gave me a chance to think through my life. But I feared that, if I were not careful, I might perhaps fade away altogether, so misty and unreal did I feel myself to be. "If only someone could see me, prove that I am still alive!" I wrote in a story I began the summer I returned from America when I was alone in the house for a few weeks. "But all the shadowy beings with which my imagination has peopled the house these last few days seem to stare right through me."

The following spring, a playful but absorbing love began for me with Michel, a rangy, dark-haired Swiss high-school student three years older than I. He lived with poetry and for poetry in a richly imaginative way that seemed to me to suit his brooding good looks. Perhaps I escaped somewhat into this love, but it gave me devoted closeness and a deep-rooted certainty of existing in the eyes of another. It saved me, I believe, in the same sense that Kaj's new family saved her, from a situation so bleak that we might not otherwise have had the strength to cope with it. The peril was no longer, as when we were small, that of living near parents so forceful as to overwhelm us. It was, rather, that of feeling abandoned, left entirely to our own uncertain devices too soon. But now, my entire life came to focus on Michel. Family, school, everything else fell into the background. When our relationship, after little more than a year, grew stormier, it was, if possible, even more all-absorbing.

Even though Alva was away much of the time, and even though my own life now diverged so deliberately from hers, I did not turn against her. I sensed, as did Kaj, how she felt torn between work and family, especially in Geneva with its laws against foreigners' being employed. To some extent we were able even then to identify with her as a woman and as someone who was trying out paths that had always been reserved for men. And even if we had no desire to imitate her when it came to family life, we were still proud on her behalf. To be sure, we could not fully grasp at the time how desperately important it was for her to find her own way, to escape Gunnar's dominance, and to seek her fortune even if it took her far from us all; but we knew that the stakes were high.

Many in Geneva now spoke to us of Gunnar as a great man, perhaps hoping that this might make us understand him better. They mentioned his phenomenal capacity for work, his ability to analyze the world's economic and political problems, his contagious faith that the nations of Eastern Europe would one day renew full contacts with the West, and his tenacious efforts, in the face of opposition from many quarters, to increase and buttress such contacts as remained. They also stressed his courage when it came to standing up for what he knew was right. He defended his Eastern European colleagues vigorously, especially émigrés who risked being forced to return to Hungary or Czechoslovakia. He was, so far as I know, almost the only head of any

UN agency who refused to allow any government to intimidate officials whom he considered to be international civil servants, protected under the UN charter from such pressures.

It was important for Kaj and for me, when we began to be old enough to understand more about his work, to see what an example of integrity and courage he set when the cold war made cowards of so many others. We could see that grandeur of intellect that others admired in him and the force with which he cut clear through the most entangled problems. And gradually we came to have more understanding for his situation, even though we remained unable to feel that he was much of a father.

For when we stopped to think, how many of the men who have been regarded as great have also been good fathers? Some abandoned their children, as did Rousseau and Strindberg. Others, like Marx and Darwin, had wives and children who arranged everything to suit the "great man." The question of why these men worked so hard or why they were not more accessible to children simply did not arise.

At the time, no one called Alva great in the same manner. But we thought of her as Gunnar's equal. I remember, for instance, being interviewed by Eleanor Roosevelt, who was traveling to different schools and taping radio programs with young people. She began by asking me, encouragingly, whether I was not Gunnar Myrdal's daughter. When I answered that I was, and Alva Myrdal's daughter as well, this seemed to me a mere formality: of course I was not just his daughter and it clearly couldn't be the case that only he was worth mentioning on radio. But my reply was surprising enough to be quoted later in *Newsweek*.

We could not avoid noticing how happy Alva was with her work in Paris. Sometimes she said that she felt "airborne from sheer inspiration." Among her responsibilities at UNESCO was that of giving new life to the different scientific institutes destroyed during the war and creating entirely new institutes and universities in the newly formed states. She also brought in experts such as Margaret Mead and Otto Klineberg, whose work challenged the concept of racial superiority. Once again, Gunnar's interests intertwined with hers. The result was that UNESCO took a position against all talk of "higher" or "lower" races and sought to eliminate from school textbooks the parochialism that often led to conflict between nations and cultures.

But when it came to the study of population problems, Alva encountered obstacles that she had not fully anticipated. In 1950 the world's population was approximately 2.5 billion, up by one-fifth since 1930. (By 1990, it had more than doubled in four decades, to reach 5.3 billion, with nearly one additional billion forecast for the year 2000.) The 1950s were the crucial decade in which pressing ahead with family planning programs could have stemmed the population explosion, with all that it contributes to poverty and to environmental problems. Along with the World Health Organization and the United Nations Population Commission, UNESCO could have led the way in this effort. Instead, communist and Catholic governments joined forces to block all efforts to address population problems. As Gunnar would later report, delegates from the Soviet bloc and Catholic scholars vied with one another at the World Population Conference in Rome in 1954, arguing that there was no real population problem anywhere in the world but only a need for huge social and economic reforms. Maoist China, though not a member of the UN, concurred. It was already the world's most populous nation with 540 million inhabitants, and growing rapidly; but Mao Tse-tung still resisted any attempt at family planning on the ground that a large population, if properly led, had to be a great asset in the realization of socialist goals. Even in India, one of the factors hampering the family planning programs instituted after independence in 1947 was the legacy of Gandhi's advocacy of sexual abstinence in marriage and his opposition to contraceptives.

That so many forces should be united to deny women access to family planning without their having the slightest say in the matter seemed, to Alva, an injustice of worldwide proportions. She could see the results in her travels. Everywhere the poorest were the first to suffer, and the multitudes of starving families only continued to grow. She had long seen access to contraceptives and sexual education as a basic requirement for the empowerment of women and families and for the welfare of nations. And although she agreed with those who claimed that, with a higher standard of living, women would ultimately find a way to limit their families, she thought it unconscionable simply to leave the poor and the illiterate to their fate. I rarely saw her as wrought up as when she described to us what she saw as the cold-blooded maneuverings by public officials from many nations to strangle all reforms in that area.

When it became clear that Alva and Gunnar would live separately for longer than they had intended at first, they decided to break up the home in Geneva. I grieved over the loss: once again it seemed to me a sign that they, in their zeal to work, were blind to the intimate reality that I experienced in the house and the garden. Gunnar rented a sterile little apartment on the other side of Lake Geneva and Alva found a larger apartment on the Boulevard Jules Sandeau in Paris, with rooms for us all where she hoped we might feel at home. The rearrangements required two moves, a monumental labor that Alva directed, this time, from Paris.

"Things, things, things," I groaned, as I witnessed the dismemberment of our home at Les Feuillantines. The furniture standing crated in every room, the richly colored handwoven rugs all rolled up, the piles of monogrammed sheets and towels and clothes in cartons, the antiques from flea markets all over Europe carefully wrapped along with the paintings and the miniature Swedish vases in luminous colors—I saw them all as encrusting her life, preventing her from coming and going as freely as she might have wished, dependent on others for packing, cleaning, hanging, and putting everything together.

Once the vast, laborious move was over, however, I had to admit that she had triumphed again. The new Paris apartment, near the Bois de Boulogne, had seemed, to begin with, a heavier, more traditional big-city environment than any Alva had previously inhabited. But once she had seen that everything was placed where she wanted it, she managed, once again, to give it light and airiness, attuning it to her own vibrant sense of color and form. It was, in one sense, our home re-created once more, and she hoped to tempt Kaj and me to move there as soon as possible.

This would clearly take time. Kaj still went to school in Geneva and refused to leave her new family. And I could not envisage leaving Michel. I was therefore invited to stay in Geneva for the time being with Melvin Fagen, Gunnar's kind and gentle ECE colleague, and his irrepressible wife, Lena, who during the war had helped rescue anti-Nazi intellectuals in occupied France.

It was while I was at the Fagens' that I received the first reports, in November 1952, that Gunnar had been in an automobile accident while driving to Sweden with his colleague, the economist Ingvar Svennilsson. Alva heard the news in Paris. She hurried to Sweden and found Gunnar convalescing in the university hospital at Lund. In spite of a severe injury to his right hip, he seemed in good spirits. He was stoically determined to pay as little attention to his injury as possible so as to be able to return to work. He had no desire to allow himself the time either for the physical therapy or the operation that his physicians prescribed. His courage and his desire to work warred against what would be in his long-term best interest.

The very next month, Alva had been asked to travel to India on behalf of UNESCO. Once again she agonized—how to be in two places, fulfill two incompatible obligations? She hesitated, but left at last on December 14, three days after Gunnar's return to Geneva. She asked me to move into his small apartment in order to take care of him and the household while continuing my studies at the university. In these tasks, I did not succeed particularly well. "Gunnar wants to commit suicide because I am so careless," my diary from that period states without further elucidation. My housekeeping may not have been the main issue: Gunnar felt depressed when the symptoms of the hip injury did not go away, anxious about his life, and lonely without Alva, whom he now realized once again he needed. And while I cooked dinner as well as I could when he hobbled home from the office and gave him the help he asked for, my studies and growing difficulties with a jealous and moody Michel led me to cut corners when it came to the details of housekeeping. It would have taken someone far more experienced than I was to persuade Gunnar to seek medical help for his increasing disability. Neither he nor I perceived, that winter, that a great and prolonged crisis had struck him.

Alva did not see the coming crisis either. She sent postcards from India asking me to do what I could for Gunnar, "who sits immobilized in a chair while I get to have this wonderful trip." In a letter written on Christmas Eve 1952, from New Delhi, she asked somewhat distantly whether I had managed to find a place to sleep in Gunnar's apartment and how long I intended to stay there. And she spoke about my impending move to her apartment in Paris:

> My dear Sissela, how good it will be for us to be together for a while. You are much too frail, not merely physically. Even a rearrangement such as that which became necessary just now drains your nervous energy so much. You truly need to have: 1) a comfortable, lovely place to be (and when you come to me you'll get to make your room as cozy as possible, new paint if desired) 2) a plan for your studies.
>
> By the way, Sanskrit [which I was then studying at the University of Geneva] and all that connects so directly with this land that is *partly* a paradise to enjoy and *partly* a purgatory to improve. I go around wishing that I could be eighteen and begin planning my studies. Wonderful fate that awaits you, Sissela!

Alva's intense enjoyment of India and of its culture while Gunnar's convalescence stalled gave her one more reason to feel guilty later on. Why did she not postpone the trip so that she could really care for Gunnar? She might have been able to persuade him to accept the medical care he so clearly needed. As it was, accustomed to their separation and to his past indifference, she remained frozen in her career role, unable to shift gears so as to enter fully into his problems. Meanwhile, her discovery of India was so overwhelming that she could not wish that that particular trip had been canceled. In India she experienced the shared humanity and sensuality that seemed to infuse the entire society, but also witnessed suffering the like of which she had never seen.

It was during this trip that Alva met Jawaharlal Nehru, who became a close friend. A framed photo of him followed her to her last sickroom—his finely chiseled face smiling and his hand reaching out toward a panda cub crouching on a branch. This is how she described meeting him:

> It was Christmas 1952. I was UNESCO's director for Social Sciences and sent to take part, in that capacity, in a conference about Gandhi.
>
> But first we had to be photographed. I had already been placed at Nehru's side in a wide circle on the lawn. Then Ralph Bunche comes sauntering in, sparkling as usual with interest in everyone and everything. I rushed up to him; forgetting our surroundings we hugged and kissed one another. Somewhat embarrassed, I returned to my place by the side of Nehru and mumbled apologetically: "We are such good old friends." And Nehru with a smile in the corner of his mouth: "Don't explain. Don't make it worse."
>
> The next episode concerned our speeches. Nehru's inspired as always but not memorable. I took up . . . the theme of Gandhi and the call of conscience. How absolute it had to be. And according to my accustomed principle I inserted something that would have an inciting, challenging effect, preferably somewhat personal, caustic. Something like: "And the truth must be the same, in whatever circumstances one speaks it, whether it concerns Korea or Kashmir."
>
> At the word "Kashmir," Nehru startled—he had dozed off, as usual during long rows of pretty phrases obliging speakers to nothing. But that a word of truth had to be spoken about Kashmir was of course the whole purpose of my speech.

Alva had weighed what she wanted to say about India's role in Kashmir and about Gandhi, but at the same time she had listened to Nehru and thought about what he had said concerning his years with Gandhi. She referred to UNESCO's goals as Gandhi's goals—to try to relieve tension between nations and make it possible for nonviolence to conquer even internationally. She spoke of the research she had started through UNESCO on how tensions arise and grow. And she ended by agreeing with the premise of Gandhi's to which Nehru had pointed just before: that goals and means are inseparable and that the wrong means can therefore not attain the right goals. But when she mentioned Kashmir in that context, she dramatized her point in a concrete way that Nehru had probably not expected. After her speech, he came up to her, saying that he had been struck by her reference to Kashmir and inviting her to lunch the following day. "Thus began a series of conversations that lasted, that time, a week. After I decided to be stationed in New Delhi the talks and the times together stretched across five years."

For Gunnar, the car accident was a great turning point. Having always been active, he became suddenly sedentary at age fifty-three. He gradually recovered somewhat, but would never again be able to move freely. As the years passed he walked ever more slowly. He, who had always prided himself on his youthful manner and his powers of sexual attraction, now had a sense of having aged quite suddenly. This awareness made him newly uncertain vis-à-vis with Alva. He increasingly experienced her absence as a form of personal rejection and urged more and more insistently that they move back together again. He needed her far more than she needed him.

When I think back, I wonder whether it was not then that Gunnar's sparkling originality and genius began to be less in evidence. His self-confidence seemed to diminish and the tendency to boast and to downgrade others became more marked. He often joked about his bad memory and about the risk of becoming senile, as if he hoped to be contradicted, to be told that this fate would never strike him. We grew used to the contrast—at times we witnessed his originality and magnificent intelligence, but over the years his thoughts traveled more and more often in their old accustomed tracks.

His loss of mobility also made it harder for him to do research: he became increasingly dependent on others who could scour the libraries for the texts he needed. Many have remarked that Gunnar often cites himself in the notes to many of his books.

But that had not always been true. *An American Dilemma,* which appeared in 1944, cites his own work only once, while it refers to Alva five times and to the sociologist W. E. B. Du Bois over twenty. Now, however, rereading and citing himself became a passion. It is natural for scholars to refer increasingly to their past works as they mature, rather than restating their conclusions in detail in each new book; but Gunnar's diminishing physical activity, besides making new research more difficult, may also have contributed to weakening his memory and made him rely the more on his earlier writings.

Earlier that year, Alva had begun to insist more forcefully that Kaj and I move to Paris. Kaj was still reluctant to leave her newfound family in Geneva, but I was eager to go once I had decided to apply to the Sorbonne. At eighteen I was, as Alva had said in her letter from New Delhi, frail. Wildly unhappy at times, serene at others, with a thousand daydreams and shifting moods and interests that pulled me in too many directions, I was exhausted from all the crises with the increasingly jealous Michel. Yet I was unable to break off what had by then become my engagement to marry him in some never fully contemplated future. When I finally traveled to Paris with him in tow, I found Alva packing her suitcases: she was about to take a two-month trip around the world, on UNESCO's behalf, stopping in New York, Honolulu, Tokyo, Bangkok, Karachi, Beirut, Jerusalem, and Rome. Remaining behind in the Paris apartment was what I viewed as a nightmarishly dour Danish housekeeper. She reacted with ill-concealed spite to my arrival, to my coming down just then with the flu, and above all to Michel's visits. My diary for March 18, 1953, notes: "Alva travels around the world today. I am lonely." On the same day, Alva sent me a postcard from Ireland: "Dearest Sissela, You must not be sad. Too bad to have to leave just now, when we were going to begin having such a good time together. Please give my greetings to Miss Elsa, who will surely take care of you until you recover your strength."

The first leg of Alva's trip took her to New York, where she was to deliver a speech that day at the UN Commission on the Status of Women. But at Idlewild airport she was stunned to find that she could not enter the country. The immigration officials claimed that they had orders to deny her entry, in spite of her diplomatic passport and a valid visa recently issued by the U.S. embassy in Bern. For the life of her, Alva could not imagine on what grounds the officials based their action, and they offered no explanation. To be sure, this was the height of the McCarthyite era in American politics. Anonymous accusations of communist allegiance and tenuous chains of alleged guilt by association were the order of the day. But Alva could not see how they might apply to her, least of all since she had visited the United States so many times and lived there for long periods. The only way in which she could keep her speaking engagement at the UN was by signing an agreement granting her "temporary release on parole." Concluding that this strange request may have resulted from a bureaucratic snafu, she signed the agreement and went on to her various engagements.

Gunnar, however, was furious on hearing the news. Whenever he saw Alva as threatened, whether by illness or by personal attacks, he became fiercely protective. In this instance, the lawyer in him also objected to what he regarded as a miscarriage of justice. He thought that she should not have signed the parole agreement, but rather should have issued a protest right away, no matter that she would not then have been able to fulfill her commitment to speak at the UN. For U.S. officials even to require such an agreement was a violation, he felt, of the legal right of international civil servants with valid visas to enter the United States in order to take part in activities at UN headquarters. Alva, moreover, should insist on her right to know what information lay at the bottom of her being denied entry; it was even possible, he believed, that it may have been some false insinuation aimed indirectly at him. During the previous months he had been widely mentioned as a possible successor to the UN's secretary-general, Trygve Lie, and had felt wounded in his pride when the person finally chosen was Dag Hammarskjöld, a brilliant fellow economist from Sweden whom he and Alva had known since their student days, but not widely experienced internationally, and his junior as an economist to boot.

Gunnar immediately asked Hammarskjöld to take all necessary steps to correct the error regarding Alva on the part of the U.S. authorities. One of Hammarskjöld's first acts after taking office in April was to issue a statement stressing the agreement between the UN and the United States, which specified that U.S. officials should impose no impediments in the way of officials of specialized agencies going to and from UN headquarters. In Sweden the press kept speculating. Why had it happened? Could it be that some public official had confused the Swedish Social Democratic party with the Communist Party? Alva was not the only Swedish public official to have encountered difficulties of late. Or could the problem be that she was the mother of Jan, then twenty-six years old, widely regarded as a communist or a fellow traveler, and just then helping to organize a youth festival in Bucharest?

In a statement prepared after she returned to Paris in May, Alva addressed both possibilities. The first was so farfetched, she argued, that no senior American official could be expected to make such a mistake; if a lower-level functionary had done so, she urged that the matter be rectified forthwith. As to her being the mother of someone with Jan's political views, she pointed out that although she and her husband had long differed with him politically, they held it as an inviolable principle that their home should always stand open to him and to their other children. She would consider it "the worst—the most un-Christian, deeply immoral and inhuman—type of 'guilt by association' if a mother were to be discriminated against" unless she denied her child for whatever reason, even if, unlike Jan, he had committed a crime.

No further charges were ever made. On July 29, Ambassador J. J. Wadsworth, deputy representative of the United States at the UN, wrote to Secretary-General Hammarskjöld that he was "authorized to state that Mrs. Alva Myrdal is persona grata to the United States authorities" and that her visa had been properly issued. Secretary of State John Foster Dulles sent a telegram reiterating this message to the American ambassador in Paris and asking that UNESCO be so informed. A small victory had been won in behalf of international civil servants.

During those same years, Alva was working with her friend, the sociologist Viola Klein, on the book *Women's Two Roles: Home and Work,* which would finally appear in 1956. Based on the first set of careful comparative statistics in the field, it was intended as a set of arguments against all those who still looked askance at women's desire to combine family and work. Alva had begun to plan the book after the war, especially during the year in Geneva when she was so painfully aware of the unused surplus energy of married women. It was to be a study of the conditions under which women in the United States, England, France, and Sweden faced choices concerning family and work. But once she began her UN work and devoted closer attention to the problems of women in poorer nations, she set the project aside. It was only with Viola Klein's encouragement that she finally returned to the task.

Initially the two had entitled the book *Women's Two Lives.* But their publisher, arguing that this title might be misunderstood as implying some form of clandestine double life, persuaded them to call the book *Women's Two Roles* instead. It is nevertheless the idea of the two lives that constitutes its central theme. The authors point out that women in industrialized nations no longer have just one lifetime at their disposal, but nearly two, measured against the life span of earlier generations; and that they have at the same time acquired the liberating possibility of limiting their families to the number of children for whom they can provide good care. As a result, women in their forties who have taken care of their children and then turn to the labor market can hope to have as long a life before them as young men at the beginning of their working lives one hundred years earlier. Women have time, therefore, for both family and work, taken consecutively.

The book's message to women is that, yes, you can "have it all" so long as you do not insist on having it all *at the same time.* Instead of feeling split in two when the children are small, why not instead envisage the stages of life as capable of constituting different parts? Then you can live fully and harmoniously at each stage while preparing for the next one so as not to find yourselves stuck in an early one for life.

Merely to accept the prevailing pattern of dependent, home-bound women is to contribute, moreover, to a needless squandering of human resources. And those who join the work force will not only benefit society; they will also become happier personally while avoiding making nervous wrecks out of their husbands and their overprotected children. Working outside the home after a period of child rearing, the authors hold, is like beginning a new life. But at the same time, it seems clear to them, especially as a result of psychological research during the recent war, that children need their mothers and can be injured by too early a separation. Contemporary psychology, they write, has given new support and justification to a point of view that may for a time have seemed outmoded,

> that children's future happiness depends on the loving care that mothers give them. . . . It is evident that mothers cannot work away from home if they are to follow these new, demanding principles for motherhood. This has to be accepted now that we know that love and security are essential for the development of a harmonious personality.

Toward the end of the book, the authors express the hope that fathers will one day share the responsibility for housework and child care. For the present, however, the book places the entire burden of the conflict on the shoulders of mothers. Should they, then, give up all hope of working? No—and here the idea of the two lives comes to their rescue. It is possible to choose the role of mother first, ideally until the youngest child is around nine years of age—that is, during the nine to fifteen years when the children are little—and then still have time to join the work force. "Our 'average woman' would then be about 40 (i.e. assuming, overgenerously, an average marriage age of 25) and would have another 35 years of life ahead of her." Depending on the age at marriage, the number of children in the family, and the length of time spent at home with them, the number of years left will vary. But for most women, there will be an opportunity for decades of productive work.

To be sure, it is possible to remain exclusively a housewife after that time. But labor-saving devices have created conditions utterly unlike those in cities and on farms in the past. The authors point to research showing that, for women without small children, there is much less left to do in the home. This makes it easier for women to slip into depression or to concentrate on a sterile social life.

Once again, Alva was driven to write about a personal problem in a way that could explain it for others, enlighten them about possible ways out. Love, children, opportunities to work—she saw these personal challenges at once as obstacles and tests, similar in that respect to those encountered in the heroic quests of myth and legend. They helped her think her way forward, find her genuine mission in life and, as she often said, many years of happiness in spite of all difficulties.

Just as Gandhi writes about everyday issues in his autobiography, *My Experiments with Truth*—what one should eat, how men and women should live, how children fit into chosen ways of life—hoping to show himself and others how one can find life's meaning, so Alva writes here about housekeeping, sexuality, work, and family. But unlike Gandhi's, this book is far from confessional. The style is dry, bordering on the tedious, something that happens the more easily when two friends collaborate on a book, since it is tempting for each simply to avoid correcting the other's problems of style or construction. Nor is there anything overtly personal in the book: the word "we" refers throughout to the authors' conclusions, never to their lives.

And yet it is a book that has to be read in a personal manner, at least by Alva's children. How did it come about that the father's role in raising small children has been so completely bypassed? In a sense, fathers are as absent from the book as Gunnar was from her own household during the years she was working on the book. And what did Alva mean, we have to ask, by claiming that mothers should remain with their children until the youngest is nine? She herself never adhered to such a maternal standard. Is this, then, a repudiation of her own chosen life? A form of *mea culpa*? Or did she perhaps believe that she did indeed fit the pattern she prescribes since what she saw as her real career started only in 1949—that is, when Kaj, the youngest, was twelve years old?

When I read the book with such personal questions in mind, it is as if I hear Alva's voice speaking from the vantage point of her late fifties to herself at thirty—straining to combine family life and all that she longed to do in the world, ill and exhausted at times, feeling that nothing quite fit despite her efforts to accommodate and make do. In that earlier period, she had put forward one idea after another to solve the seemingly impossible equation. She had conjured up collectivist dwellings in which food arrived via dumbwaiter and skilled professionals cared for infants while women, like men, were free to devote all their energies to productive work outside the home. Now she was thinking of an alternative solution that would, once again, streamline and rationalize living conditions.

But just as Alva had shown no inclination to adopt the collectivist solution when her own children were small, so I believe that she would not have wanted to postpone work outside the home in the manner that this book sets forth. Nor did she suggest such a clear-cut "either-or" to Kaj and myself and other young women as we confronted similar choices. Her own life when we were little bore witness to a suppleness and imagination, when it came to work, that seems contradicted by the book's admonition to mothers to work professionally only after forty or so. It is surely possible for many women, as it was for her, to have small children and do flexible types of work as well. Alva urged women to keep in touch with their fields even while their children were small; yet she acknowledged that much more was required from those who want, for instance, to be doctors. For them, as for scholars and many others, the forty-year line might be tantamount to excluding them altogether either from having children or from a career.

In addition, it was clear even then that many women who began looking for work after forty, having devoting fifteen years or so to family needs, would not find any, no matter how well prepared they might be. The book contains a number of suggestions for ways in which society might begin to change this situation. Alva and Viola Klein advocate training programs for reemploying women returning to the labor market and a shift toward greater employment of older persons. They speak of the need to improve living conditions so as to facilitate combining the two roles of family life and work, including establishing more flexible working hours and extended maternity leave, constructing housing designed for working women, lessening the burden of shopping through better distribution of goods, rationalizing housework, providing nourishing meals in the schools, and creating a network of day nurseries and nursery schools. During the war, they remind their readers, urgent steps were taken to make the employment conditions of men and women alike easier; there is no reason not to press for a similar program of change in peacetime. In all this, the authors were ahead of their time. But until the programs they recommended were in place, their advice to women was fraught with risk insofar as it encouraged them to stay at home with their children in the expectation that jobs would be open to them when they finally entered the labor market.

When Alva reread the book in her eighties, she noted that it made a "strange impression":

> The book, over 25 years old, can of course not be of use in today's debate. . . . But first, a couple of "explanations." The book was written with a specific aim: to demonstrate how much unutilized time women had then. The task had been given to me and my collaborator (an unmarried academic, which also helps to explain things).

This judgment seems too harsh to me. It is true that Alva rethought some of her proposals concerning women and work in the decades that followed. But if one reads the book from the perspective of the 1950s, one sees what a wealth of new ideas it contains. She was speaking, in many ways, about a world of choices that opened up to women only decades later, and the contrast between combining child rearing and work all at once or consecutively can aid anyone contemplating a lifespan likely to be much longer than in earlier generations. In this book, as in her earlier books, she was a "spray can" of ideas; I see them as meant to start a debate rather than to be adopted in literal detail.

By now, moreover, the book's message about women's two lives may have new relevance. A majority of women in industrialized nations now work outside the home while their children are small. The price they pay in fatigue, guilt, and, too often, depression is high. Too many have children in their teens, before they are mature enough to care for them; others are eager to make a good home for their children but cannot do so because of financial or professional pressures. The various provisions that Alva and Viola Klein advocated—for access to family planning, better schools and preschools, improved health care, housing built with families and working parents in mind, and more flexible work opportunities—are still lacking in many nations. Over time, Sweden did institute many such measures, in part because of advocacy by Alva and her colleagues. And the reform process continues. A system of "parental insurance" grants 12 months of leave for the parents of every newborn, with 90 percent compensation of lost income, to be split by mother and father as they prefer. Even the option of a six-hour workday no longer sounds as strange as when Alva first proposed it in the 1930s. She lived to see that a trickle of Swedish couples, by choosing such hours and then staggering their presence at home, could spend a great deal more time with their children.

At the time, Alva discussed few of the issues in the book with me, probably because I showed so little interest. Otherwise, we could have had much to discuss together regarding the problems that it raised. I was, after all, one of the many young women she had wanted to reach in writing it, one who faced choices about how to live yet who felt uncertain about who I was and what I wanted to be. "How do I become myself?" was as pressing a question for me as it had long been for Alva. But in spite of all her attempts at greater closeness, I kept my distance during the years in Paris. Perhaps it was partly self-protection. However uncertain I felt about the direction I should take in life, I did not then want to rely on her forcefulness, her expertise, all the statistics she could set forth about the very choices I saw before me. To be sure, there were quite a few models of women as martyrs or parasites that I abhorred as much as she did; but neither did I want to live her life or adopt her values.

Instead I drifted along in my old role as daughter in which I did not see her fully as a fellow human being but rather as a stable, admirable, yet rather alien "grown-up." If I was going to become an adult myself—and I was not at all sure that this was what I wanted—then my life would have to be entirely different from hers. I wanted to live freely without being burdened, as she was, by objects and furnishings; to live guided by feeling whereas she seemed so eminently rational; to be anonymous whereas she was well known, and outspoken whereas she was discreet and, from my point of view, entirely too diplomatic. My diary expresses a disdain for her values as I saw them. Never must I forget life's mysteries, I wrote, never be swayed by her clear and cogent ideas; I had to retain my love for shadows, for all that was secret, for poetry and nature. In one way I saw her clearly; in another not at all.

My impatience expressed itself through silent criticism even in small matters. Alva's interest in clothes irritated me, as did her blond hair rinses to cover the gray. As an eighteen-year-old, I found her, at fifty-one, far advanced in years. I thought her attempts to appear feminine at her age were artificial and saw every sign that she took the slightest interest in anything having to do with sensuality as disagreeable. Neither my limitless admiration for her during the forties nor my irritated defeminization of her during the years in Paris show genuine understanding for her life as something ongoing and generative. I was then so absorbed in my own lines of thinking and in my attempts to find myself in poetry, religion, politics, friendship, and love that I overlooked the deeper layers in her personality almost entirely.

The change came gradually. To begin with, the greater world of Paris could not but impress itself on me even during my first few months of solitude and near-despair, rattling about in what seemed an echoingly empty apartment while Alva traveled around the world. After Geneva, Paris offered a heady political and cultural atmosphere, perhaps especially tumultuous because of the ongoing agony of France's war in Vietnam. At the Catholic Centre Richelieu, near the Sorbonne, I could listen to fine-tuned scholastic expositions of the church's attitude toward abortion, divorce, socialism, and colonialism and explore the meaning of religious faith with student friends. I could go with others to hear Jean-Paul Sartre speak out against the war in a crowded lecture hall nearby, or listen to the "worker priest" Abbé Pierre preach about what it might mean to live up fully to the Christian gospel of honoring the poor and the outcast. Nearby, Juliette Gréco sang of freedom and betrayal and love, and Yves Montand performed in shirtsleeves before enthralled music hall audiences. But there was danger in the streets, too. Pitched battles between communists and ultra-rightist royalists reached into the courtyard of the Sorbonne. After France lost the battle of Dien Bien Phu in Vietnam, I saw the police clash with demonstrators and Vietnamese students bleeding from an ambush in a subway entry. All these were experiences I felt I had to share with Alva as I tried to sort them out in my mind.

I turned to confide in her about even more personal matters after the summer of 1954, when, at nineteen, I met Derek Bok, a twenty-four-year-old American who would become my husband the following spring. He had just graduated from Harvard Law School and received a Fulbright scholarship to study at the Ecole des Sciences Politiques in Paris. I sensed immediately—as did Alva when she met Gunnar and as many others have surely sensed—that this was something indescribably new and wonderful in my life. When she returned from a trip, I told her that a miracle had happened. I think that she understood instinctively what I meant. I did not burn my diaries and writings, as she had after meeting Gunnar, but I had the same impulse of wanting to start all over with myself—to try to become mature enough, adult enough at last to be able fully to take in all my new emotions and insights.

Alva's response was immediate but discreet. She wanted to help me through what she realized might be a great upheaval in my life without resorting to high-flown phrases. A haircut and a new suit were her first, quite casual suggestions. She took me out to explore Paris on such errands, marking the start of a much greater understanding between us.

The happiness and confidence I experienced with Derek made it possible for me to turn to her and to others in a new way, rather than to agonize like the chaotic shadow I had often felt I was until then. Only when I could be more certain of the contours of my own life, apparently, could I begin to see her as the living and, while obviously not unproblematic, still warmly well-intentioned and fascinating person that she was, rather than staring at her through a distorting lens of ingrained reactions. Only then could friendship take over from the periodically rocky mother-daughter relationship during my Paris years.

From then on, our friendship continued to deepen and evolve over the decades. It may well be that the nearly doubled life span that Alva had stressed in *Women's Two Roles* also makes possible friendship between parents and their adult children in an entirely new way. During all the centuries when so many died before the age of forty, such friendship rarely had time to develop. And then as now, many of those who have lived longer have remained mired in an immutable and unimaginative parental role that does not permit the equality, the generous sharing of oneself, and the mutual respect that lasting friendship requires.

Such a rigid parental role Alva never sought. She maintained warm, often intimate contact and entered into my experiences without ever attempting to control me, own me, live through me. Always, she knew the art of giving advice as an older friend rather than as an anxious parent or condescending expert. She reached out in the same way to Derek and, later, to our children. And about India and her own life and the doings of relatives and world politics she wrote unforgettable letters. As I reread them, it seems to me that she must have preferred the role of mother as friend, combining all that is special in family bonds with the freedom and openness that friendship allows, to the role of being solely a mother.

Sometimes it is children who find it difficult to shift into such a relationship. Friendship places new demands on them as well. Learning to see that parents are complex and fallible beings, while still granting them the humanity that one grants others has to be one of the central tasks of growing up. The mutual respect inherent in friendship allows children to work at breaking free of the burden of the past without denying their roots in that past. Alva knew that she had not carried out this shift in her relationship with her own parents by the time they died; she was the more eager to encourage it in our generation.

An opportunity arose when Derek and I announced that we were planning to marry in May 1955, before he returned to the United States to do his military service. After each of his parents, Curtis Bok and Margaret Kiskadden, wrote that they would fly over for the wedding, Alva persuaded us that we needed to have a ceremony more commensurate with their effort in coming than the brief appearance before the local *mairie* that Derek and I had first had in mind. We did not want a large, overly elaborate or otherwise conventional wedding, and in this she concurred. But it ought nevertheless, she suggested, to be more than a mere formality and to be warmly inclusive of family and friends. Perhaps she also wanted to forestall even a particle of the kind of hurt that she and Gunnar had inadvertently inflicted on their own parents by marrying without inviting them.

Alva proposed one location after another, beginning with the small Swedish church in Paris. None of them filled us with enthusiasm. Finally, she made a suggestion that struck all of us as inspired. She would ask Pierre Mendès-France, with whom she had often conferred on UNESCO matters, to officiate at the wedding. Like many French politicians, Mendès-France was also mayor in his local district—in his case, the small town of Louviers in Normandy. Two months earlier, in February 1955, he had been forced to resign as prime minister after extricating France from her corrupt, brutalizing war in Vietnam and initiating a rethinking of her colonial policy in North Africa. We knew him as a man of vision and rare integrity who had risked his political career during the preceding months in order to do what he thought was right for his country. When he generously agreed to perform the marriage ceremony in the Louviers town hall, Derek and I were elated.

To be married by someone for whom we all shared such respect and admiration marked the occasion as entirely different from the drearily conventional large wedding into which we had resisted being drawn.

When the day arrived, a small caravan of cars drove the fifty miles from Paris to Louviers, where the town hall had been decorated with flags, festoons, and great vases of flowers in the French red, white, and blue. "The sun poured down on the idyllic little town of Louviers," Alva wrote to Gunnar's sister Elsa, who had not been able to come, "and the chestnuts were blooming along the streets." Her greatest pleasure, she added, was in meeting "the new relatives," Derek's parents. She and Gunnar felt immediately drawn to Margaret Kiskadden, Derek's mother, and to his father, Curtis Bok, who was both a judge and a writer. Both were as free-spoken, generous-spirited, and deeply committed to social reform as the Americans Alva and Gunnar had always most admired, beginning with their first visit to the United States in 1929. Inside the town hall, Mendès-France spoke, praising each of the four parents, according to French custom. After Derek and I had signed the formal marriage agreement, the whole party drove off to Les Saisons, a nearby country inn, for a wedding reception in the shade of hemlocks and weeping willows.

Neither Jan nor Kaj came to the wedding. Jan, who at twenty had married Nadja Wiking, an architectural student some years older than he with whom he had had a son, had by now divorced her and married again. He was planning to come to Paris with his new wife, Maj, later on that year, but had no desire to be at the wedding. And Kaj was still on somewhat hesitant terms with Alva and Gunnar. She had spent part of the previous year at an agricultural school in northern Sweden and had every intention of shaping her life in a way unlike theirs. They seemed to her to be constantly rushing about without giving themselves time for the closeness with nature or with the deepest needs of individuals that she had relished in her "adoptive" family. At the Swedish school, she had fallen in love with a young German university student, Horst Fölster, whom she found far more capable of such closeness. She did not want to leave him to travel the long way to Paris for the wedding. She remembers having felt, at eighteen, rebellious scorn for such occasions, regarding them merely as empty formalities.

Alva and Gunnar worried that Kaj had tied herself down too early in life. When they finally met Horst in August they found him serious, intelligent, kind, and clearly very fond of Kaj. But because he was also quite silent and shy with them, they did not find it easy to communicate with him. And his first name proved a stumbling block. Inevitably, it brought to mind the Nazi song "Horst Wessel." The young man felt nothing but a sense of recoil from his nation's recent past; but Gunnar decided to call Horst, from then on, by his middle name, Hans-Hermann, only to settle on his family nickname of "Hotti." While Gunnar looked on this rebaptizing of Horst as a felicitous compromise, Alva tried to talk him out of dwelling so much on the issue of names. For Kaj, the incident was yet another expression of Gunnar's tendency toward wounding condescension.

While Alva was talking with me about plans for my wedding, she also revealed her own great decision: to go to India as Sweden's ambassador. During the winter months she and Gunnar had tried to think through the possibilities that remained for a shared future. Where might each one find sufficiently absorbing and captivating work? Geneva offered no such prospects for Alva, nor Paris for Gunnar. Gunnar knew that he could not leave his work at the ECE for a few years yet. But ever since his hospital stay after the automobile accident in 1952, he had dreamed of undertaking yet another big book. After having visited India himself in 1953 and learning that Dag Hammarskjöld had been named secretary-general of the UN, he began to make preparations for the work that would become *Asian Drama*. He therefore proposed New Delhi as a city where he would be able to write about underdeveloped nations, and urged Alva to seek a position there. He could think of no other city, he wrote her in January, that would not involve a lengthy separation between them.

The suggestion of New Delhi turned out to fit perfectly with Alva's prospects, for after discreet inquiries, the Foreign Office in

Stockholm had asked her to consider several posts as Sweden's first woman ambassador. Among the possibilities was that of becoming Sweden's envoy to India, Burma, and Sri Lanka, then called Ceylon, with the embassy located in New Delhi. Alva could think of nothing more enticing. When the formal invitation finally arrived in the summer of 1955, she accepted with pleasure, hoping that she would be able to persuade Kaj to join her there and be fully a part of the family once again. Just as when she had received the UN offer seven years earlier, she felt suffused by that sense of delight that new, demanding assignments gave her.

She was nevertheless not entirely sure that she wanted to go back to living with Gunnar. That spring and summer, it was a little as if he were being put to a test. He did everything he could think of to show that it would work. When he visited Paris, they made excursions to Montmartre and other places where they had walked in their youth, visited common friends, and went to art exhibits. Alva relished it all and described their "talk-fests," some-times lasting all day long. Increasingly, both took for granted that they would live together permanently, beginning as soon as Gunnar could join her in India for good, then continuing in Sweden where they both wanted to end their careers. But it would still be years before they would do more than visit one another; Gunnar felt that he had much left to do at the ECE.

All seemed settled in August. But unexpectedly, as Alva's departure approached, Gunnar was overtaken by one period after another of severe depression. They may perhaps have been brought on by his decision to go on a strict diet at the same time that he tried—and failed—to stop smoking. He worried, too, about the scope of the research he was contemplating, especially since he did not know where he would find the financial support and the collaborators he needed to carry it out. And try as he might to dismiss such thoughts, he could not help feeling that Alva's eagerness to begin a chapter of her life that would take her farther away from him than ever represented a form of abandonment. His letters to her grew more plaintive week by week.

Gunnar's dark moods frightened Alva, she wrote him after a visit in August to the Abano mud baths in Italy, where he was taking a cure for his stiff hip. She was convinced that the moods would pass, but urged him not to diet so strenuously until he felt better, and tried to reassure him in every way she knew. Meanwhile she was preparing to move to India and wrote of her own uncertainties in taking up so many tasks that were new to her, as well as of her eagerness to have him join her there for a first visit in January. Why should they not be able to reestablish their companionate marriage, now that they were going to be childless again? Of one thing she had been certain all along: if she were going to accept Gunnar back, it would be on her own terms. She would have to feel entirely free to have a career of her own, never again risk being solely a wife. But she wondered. How could she be sure that these conditions would hold?

Alva did not discuss these particular problems with me during the months before my marriage, in part because she could not make any decisions until later that year. Instead she shared with me the sense of the new adventure about to begin—the great joy of being able to return to India, which she had come to love during her first visit, and the great wonder that she, unlike so many women in their fifties at the time, had no reason to fret at the thought that life was largely over when her children left home.

"Life is a dance of death on burning high wires," I wrote in my diary, then flew to America. In Paris, Alva prepared her move to India. And because we both faced such vast changes, my wedding was not darkened, as hers had been, by guilt feelings concerning the mother who would be left at home. I *left* no mother. We were both about to start a journey, begin a new life.

Gunnar with Jan, around 1935

Alva, Sissela, and Kaj in Long Island, 1939

Alva, June 1940, after her wartime return to Sweden from the U.S.

The family house in Äppelviken, soon after its construction

Sissela, Kaj, and Gunnar's mother during the winter of 1941–1942

Karin Anger, late 1940's

Alva, Gunnar, and Sissela, 1947 (photo: Sallstedts Bildbyrå)

Kaj, Sissela, and Alva, 1941

Kaj, Alva, and Sissela, 1954

Alva and Pierre Mendès-France at the wedding of Sissela and Derek Bok, in May 1955

Sissela and Derek

Alva with Nehru, around 1957

Sissela and Alva in Cambridge, Massachusetts, 1980 (photo: Georgia Litwack)

Alva receiving the Albert Einstein Peace Prize in 1980.
Her grandson Tomas hands her the crystal bowl.

Alva and Alfonso Garcia Robles during the Nobel Peace
Prize ceremonies in 1982 (photo: Arbeiterbladet, Oslo)

13

India

❖ ❖ ❖ ❖

Gunnar, here I am on the way to India—to what in my youth was a dreamland of pearls and turbans, of rajas, of mogul history and Gandhi, Tagore, and Buddha. . . . Gunnar, just put this back in the context of our childhood, with its hunger for learning and its upstart insecurity. We who met on a fence and who found that we wanted to do so much, can now come together in houses all readied for us in this continent of wonders and with human contacts that shut us out from no one.

Alva was writing to Gunnar on November 30, 1955, from the plane taking her to Karachi and then on to New Delhi. She wanted to share her amazement that she was finally on her way. But she hoped she could also relieve his anxiety over her departure—his sense of the discrepancy between her expanding new world and his own bleak self-doubts the preceding fall—while reminding him of his part in the sacrifices that they had come to take for granted:

This, we have both agreed, is going to be the last, great, ambitious excursion in that world which endures and functions far beyond our personal fates. When we are together, to be sure, our sacrifice of nearly all forms of private life and personal happiness feels especially painful. . . we live as if intoxicated by work, for the sake of our employers, for the sake of honest workmanship, for the sake of those larger ideals that of course in reality drove us into this work in the first place, even though the work has now become an end in itself and the ideals in the international context are mentioned with only bitter nostalgia. But on this first page in the book of the great adventure, I must also say that, right now, I feel gripped by the uniqueness and the grandeur of the task.

Alva's midnight arrival at the Delhi airport took her by surprise. Dazed after the journey and expecting no one to meet her save, perhaps, a sleepy emissary or two from the Swedish embassy, she found herself in an "ovation-like whirl of women, garlands, and press photographers." Her friends in the women's movement had seized the occasion, she wrote to Gunnar; and as always when she encountered such shows of affection and support, they truly lifted her.

The welcome at the Swedish embassy the next morning, however, was decidedly more lukewarm. Bo Siegbahn, the first secretary who had substituted for her until she arrived, let her know in subtle ways just how inexperienced he found her. And she herself felt that the intricacies of the diplomatic world were new to her—the gossip, the jockeying for position, the overt and unspoken rivalries and resentments, the shadings of interpretation accorded even seemingly trivial events. That she was a woman in the male world of diplomacy did not make matters easier. All in the embassy expressed willingness to give her any help she might ask for, but quietly continued working much as they had before her arrival. Alva confessed to Gunnar that she felt marginalized.

Nevertheless, merely being in India overshadowed all else. The first weeks brought shock waves of conflicting reactions. Yes, she felt once again so much of what had drawn her during her first, brief visit in 1952: she relished the mild December sun, the drenched colors, the morning mists over Delhi, meeting so many deeply cultured, engaged, often brilliant individuals, and seeing a society in a state of creative ferment the like of which she had never encountered. She never ceased admiring the vividness and beauty of Indians and their sense for color and for decoration even in the midst of poverty. But she also felt overpowered, more so than earlier, by the "cacophony of problems, problems, problems." She saw, once again, the street sweepers with withered faces, the emaciated women doing the heaviest labor on farms and at construction projects, the hunger in children's eyes—and everywhere the signs of just how much India's relentless population growth aggravated every other problem. Like most others, she felt herself developing a protective shield in the face of so much mute suffering. Without some way of focusing on the tasks at hand rather than on the vastness of human need, she would be immobilized.

Alva did not doubt, at the time, that India would find a way out of its severest problems. It had led the world in the postwar struggle for independence and had achieved a democratic form of government only eight years before. The nation's momentum and its leaders' immense hopes for the future were nearly tangible. They were the hopes voiced by Jawaharlal Nehru at the midnight meeting of India's Constituent Assembly, which had been called in August 1947 to mark her independence:

> At the stroke of the midnight hour, when the world sleeps, India will awaken to life and freedom. A moment comes, which comes but rarely in history, when we step out from the old to the new, when an age ends, and when the soul of a nation long suppressed finds utterance.

The years of dismal harvests and mounting corruption and the despair at seeing so many advances negated by the growing number of mouths to feed had not yet eroded those high hopes. Within a few years, Nehru himself would be discouraged enough to consider resigning as prime minister. But at the time his ambition for India to become the egalitarian and progressive society that so many had envisaged during the struggle for independence still seemed within reach.

It was to be part of the efforts to move in that direction, not just in India but in Ceylon and Burma, where she had also been named ambassador, that Alva had given up her UNESCO position. Here she would represent Sweden, another neutral nation that had, not many decades ago, lifted itself out of poverty by the same combination of democratic reform, education, and cooperative measures that Nehru and other leaders advocated for India. She was convinced that she would be able to convey something of what that earlier experience had required. And she saw in Nehru a leader singularly gifted for bringing about a transformation: someone of unique moral force, dedicated to the service of the same ideals of social justice and economic development that she had held since childhood.

She awoke with a special feeling of solemnity on the Monday morning after her arrival: later that day she was to pay an official call on Nehru to present her ambassadorial credentials. She was accompanied "of all things," as she later ruefully noted, by her dour first secretary.

It was a catastrophe. Many have recounted something similar: Nehru at his large desk and with his rose in the buttonhole, so painfully uninterested. I went home frightened that I would probably never attain the personal contact that I had expected after our meeting the last time. I knew, from his greeting, that he remembered me. Was it the presence of Siegbahn?

Alva would see Nehru in such moods again and again during the years to come. At times he would grow silent when receiving or paying official calls—as with the young Congressman John F. Kennedy, for example—tapping his feet and looking at the ceiling. Alva, too, had to suffer through such responses when she brought visitors to see Nehru; she learned to hesitate long and hard before doing so. At most other times, however, and especially in less formal settings, she, like so many others, found him a man of warmth, humor, and immense charm.

As soon as Alva went to her first dinner in Nehru's residence, Teen Murti, she had a chance to renew her friendship with him. She also met his timid widowed daughter, Indira Gandhi, who lived in his household with her sons, Sanjay and Rajiv. In a letter to Gunnar, Alva wrote that she had again seen that Nehru of whom I—we—have been so deeply fond: high-spirited, playful, naturally playing an authoritative, not to say world-historical role without the slightest tendency to Caesarism. Isn't it true that he is perhaps the only person we have seen reach a high and powerful position without taking on new self-importance?

Shortly before Alva arrived, a revolt had broken out in Goa, one of three small remaining Portuguese holdings on India's west coast, against Portugal's obsolete imperial rule. Nehru had urged, ever since independence, that it be reunited with the rest of India. But even though diplomatic methods seemed to get nowhere, he was unwilling to intervene militarily on behalf of the Goans, however much he sympathized with their plight. This reluctance allowed the Portuguese to reestablish their rule for several more years and decimated the number of resisters. It was only when the Goans rebelled once again, in 1961, that Nehru sent in troops to help free them.

Because diplomatic relations between Portugal and India had been severed over this conflict by the time Alva arrived, the Portuguese ambassador's residence on Hardinge Avenue in New Delhi stood empty. She was delighted to take it over for the time being until she could move into the new combined residence and embassy that the Swedish government had promised to build. Known as the White House, the residence had vast, airy rooms and a garden with banana trees and exotic flowers that Alva described glowingly in her letters to relatives back in wintry Sweden.

As always, she turned the actual move into a vast and complex undertaking. Furniture was shipped from Geneva and Paris and ordered from Sweden in complicated routing patterns that only she fully understood. She wanted her new home to be representative of the best in modern Swedish design and drew up reams of drawings and plans to spell out where everything should be placed. Meanwhile, she had left the details to Gunnar about how to dispose of the Paris apartment: he was to start the process in early December, while visiting Jan and his second wife Maj, whom they had invited to live in the apartment until a new tenant could be found.

It was when Gunnar was spending his last night in the apartment that he began a disconsolate letter to Alva. It grew to be eleven pages long, pages in which he poured out all the grief and bitterness and fear he felt in the face of the changes in their lives. Alva had asked him to send the huge old oak trunk in which they stored all their papers either to Geneva for safekeeping or to India, as he saw fit. Because of Gunnar's bad hip, the concierge brought batches of the papers up from the basement for him in sackfuls, emptying each one in front of the couch where he sat.

Instead of merely packing up all the papers, as he had planned, Gunnar fell to reading them. Old letters, Alva's diaries, yellowed newspaper clippings, even household accounts from every year of their lives—all lay in front of him. Suddenly he came face to face with his own youth and with the past that he had shared with Alva. And he wept as he read. He wept over the loss of all that had gone before, over all that he and Alva had jettisoned from that past experience, and over what had become of his life. From time to time he paused to write something of what he felt to Alva. Not a word in this first letter to her in India asks how she was experiencing her new life; yet the entire letter is, in a sense, about her and about his despair at having squandered the love she had lavished on him for so many years in their youth.

> My own little wonderful Alva from so long ago: do you exist? Do I exist? Where are we headed? I weep when I begin to write about it. . . . Dearest, I am so heartbroken; what do I have to offer you now? The hip smashed, my sight darkened, two teeth lost and two more that sit there rattling. And no future. I don't even want to become anything. It was not to one like me that you wrote as you wrote then. I am so alone and so despairing and see no path to choose and to take.

It was he who had thrown it all away, Gunnar wrote. He could now see how his single-minded ambition and his infidelities had first wounded her, then cut her off, and finally made her strike out on her own: "Now you have learned to live happily and successfully alone." He himself felt as if he were rotting away, decrepit, old, and lame. He feared death, but had nothing to live for. He feared solitude, yet had lost all close human contacts. There was only one hope left: to start all over again with her as they once were, just the two of them, without encumbrances, in a small apartment somewhere. Then they might just be able to find themselves, find meaning in life again, rediscover their old happiness. Yet why should she consent to that, seeing all that he had done and what he had now shrunk into? He was saddened, he wrote, to the very roots of his being.

The letter arrived in the midst of Alva's absorbing new existence like a bombshell. She had known that he had had periods of dark depression during the fall and that he felt uncertain about his role in their future, but nothing like this. She knew that she could not, did not want to give everything up to start again with him on his new terms. Nor did she think that doing so would in fact bring back the old bliss. In answering, she made no such promises. Rather, she wrote of her feeling for him: "I see with you from within—suffer with you, agonize with you, *ache* with you." She wanted him to know that he still had every reason for self-confidence: in her eyes, he was still as creative and brilliant and worthy of self-esteem as ever. But he was also now more reachable, she suggested. This terrifying period of despair might even presage the birth of something new—if only they knew what! And she longed for him to come so that they could talk. What they most needed, she insisted, was to find a formula for living jointly—one that was proud, exhilarating, joyful about the future. "Darling, you will get your confidence back. And your beloved you have. There is *much* left. Gunnar—do you hear me?"

When I first read Gunnar's long letter and Alva's response, left in a special file after their deaths, I was astounded. He, who seemed to me so self-confident at the time, so filled with plans for the future, with such deep interest in what was happening all around the globe—could the same person have written this letter? A letter to me written the same day he mailed his letter to Alva speaks in a voice of cheer and optimism about his plans with her,

the fine house she was renting in New Delhi, the art books from
Venice he was sending me for Christmas. But he himself saw the
contrast between his outward demeanor and what he felt inwardly
and revealed to Alva alone. His letter to her points out that while
he felt "as nearly finished as I have ever been," he still functioned
well at work, could run the ECE, write letters, give excellent
speeches. "The shadow of my person acts—I myself am
rotting. . . ."

When Gunnar arrived in Delhi some weeks later for his first
month-long visit with Alva, she was on tenterhooks. She went
out of her way to accommodate his wishes, furnishing a comfortable study for him apart from all the packing cases still standing unopened. Knowing how little he enjoyed official functions,
she turned down as many of the invitations meant to welcome
her as a new ambassador as she could. Instead she brought him
together with people she knew would interest him and discussed
how he might approach the great new project about Asia that he
had worked toward for years but that now seemed so tenuous in
his mind.

She never enjoyed a situation, she told him in a later letter,
in which one of them seemed pitiable and somehow not equal to
the other. She wanted him strong and independent. From the
beginning, she had admired the way in which he gloried in being
what he was. When he had first urged her to seek a position in
India and she had accepted the offer of the ambassadorship, she
had no concern that he would not be able to take in stride being
an "ambassador's spouse"—something that other husbands might
have found bewildering or even demeaning. And yet now, with
Gunnar so unsure of himself and his future, she knew that she
had to exert all her talents at understanding and diplomacy, at
home even more than in public.

Kaj arrived shortly after Gunnar, in January 1956. That she
arrived at all was something of a triumph. She had had little desire
to come back home again, especially since "home" was shifting
under her feet and taking her away from her friend Horst. It was
only when it became possible for him to go to India as well, to

write a doctoral dissertation on Indian red laterite soils, that Kaj decided to join Alva as soon as she could find passage on a ship.

Kaj could see Alva's efforts to accommodate Gunnar during that visit while also responding to all that was new in her own life. And slowly, his worries seemed to lift. He thrived on the warmth and enthusiasm of so many in Delhi who heard about his plans to study South Asia—among them the engaging, brilliant economist Tarlok Singh, who had led India's first planning commission and who became a lifelong friend. Once again, Gunnar's project came into focus for him, expanding as his interest in everything in India—that "quite abnormal curiosity" that he said had driven him since childhood—took over. It became possible for him to envisage how Alva and he might rearrange their lives, with Alva joining him in Europe each summer and he visiting her for shorter periods in Delhi until his planned departure from the ECE a little over a year later.

When Gunnar returned to Geneva in February, Alva could devote herself more completely to the work of representing Sweden and sending her observations and analyses back to Stockholm. During the spring she took Kaj along on an extended tour through southern India and Ceylon. As she would throughout her stay, she visited villages and cities, farms and schools, factories and development projects, stopping wherever she went to see the work of Swedish missionaries, merchants, scholars, and others working in these countries.

The contrast between the arid harshness of life in India and the comparative ease of living in Ceylon's abundantly fertile though shaky economy astounded Alva. Seeing people's relaxed enjoyment of life in one village after another, without anyone appearing to worry overmuch about the morrow, also made her more conscious of the contrast with her own life. She thought about her striving, her orientation to the future, the value she placed on self-sacrifice, qualities she shared with Gunnar and that had taken hold so completely of his life. In the letter she had written to him from the plane on the way to India, she had touched on the ways in which their intense dedication to these values had meant giving up a degree of privacy and of personal happiness. And even though she knew that few contemporary societies could long afford to do without a measure of these values, she could relish the more intensely the attractions of doing so in villages where time seemed to stand dreamily still. Although Ceylon was already importing most of what it needed, including—absurdly, as she pointed out to Kaj—the fruit and other produce that grew so abundantly at home, commerce and industry were at least functioning in much of the society. The barbaric civil war that was to wreak havoc at every level of its society was yet to come. At the time, Ceylon's stability and well-being justified the appellation "the Switzerland of the Far East," much as Lebanon was once known as "the Switzerland of the Middle East."

Kaj remembers Alva as sparkling, on this trip as throughout her years in India, taking in with fascination every new experience. Alva herself looked back at those years as having offered "the very finest memories." To her, the most interesting aspect of her work, she wrote me, was

> all this learning, this opportunity to grow, as it were, into a world of new problems, and in particular a world of problems that will be even more dominant for our grandchildren than for us. I am expansively happy to be here.

It soon became clear that Alva was a spectacular success as an ambassador. It helped that Sweden and India had no conflicts and that both their governments were dedicated to a nonaligned but energetic foreign policy and to the democratic pursuit of egalitarian ideals. She used to say that she almost took more seriously the need to help Sweden discover India than the reverse. She immersed herself in the study of Indian history and cultural traditions, and the subtle analyses of conditions in India that she submitted to the Foreign Office in Sweden came to be regarded as small works of art. Instead of having to undertake tense negotiations or feeling reduced to engaging primarily in entertaining and other diplomatic formalities, Alva could play a different and unconventional ambassadorial role: one of active engagement in the reforms and educational activities under way in India. She noted in an interview that she did not think that many ambassadors had traveled as much:

> Of course, I promoted the image of Sweden—that was my job, but that image which I was eager to paint in my speeches was one of democracy and of wide popular participation in civic affairs, and of education being very advanced—ideals and goals which coincide with the Indian ones. So, I think I served both countries as a matter of fact.

The role of education, in particular, was one she stressed wherever she went. She could see how the problems of democracy multiplied in a country where the great masses of voters were illiterate, poor, and held back by barriers of language and caste, and where massacres and wars had left an immobilizing legacy of suspicion between Hindus and Moslems. This situation was utterly different from that of Sweden, where literacy had long been almost universal and where the industrial revolution had already taken place by the time voting rights were extended to all citizens. Some argued that only an authoritarian government could overcome India's vast social problems; she admired Nehru the more for insisting on pursuing the double aim for India of full democracy and economic and social development.

Both aims required an unprecedented educational effort at every level of society. It was one in which women had to play their full part. Throughout her stay, Alva worked closely with different women's groups to help bring about greater access to schools and universities for young girls. And she formed close friendships with women such as Kamala Devi, one of the founders of the women's movement in India, who had worked with Gandhi and been instrumental in inducing him to bring women on his long Salt March to the seacoast in 1930. Wherever she spoke, Alva would elaborate on mottoes such as that "an uneducated woman is a dangerous woman for society," taking issue with those who insisted that ignorance suited the gentleness and motherliness of women and was dangerous only in men. The thought of opening schools to girls was anomalous to those who were used to the idea that only the boys in the family went to school. Nothing could be worse for the nation, she insisted, than relying on a narrow male elite, the more so since uneducated mothers often served as a force of reaction.

Were there any special advantages in being the only woman ambassador to India? Extremely few, she would tartly answer the journalists who asked that question. The one advantage she could think of was purely social. Being the only woman of ambassadorial rank, she was often seated next to Nehru or to the guest of honor at official dinners. And at smaller lunches or dinners with just a few guests, Nehru often turned to her as a single woman to round out his list of invitees when he had visits from, for example, Tito, U Thant, Prince Philip, or Lady Mountbatten.

For Nehru, Alva's admiration only continued to grow. She used to say that three world leaders had impressed her above all others as possessing a rare combination of profound intellect and great moral force: Willy Brandt, with whom she had worked since he was a young German refugee in Scandinavia during the war; Pierre Mendès-France, whom she had come to know during her Paris years; and Jawaharlal Nehru most of all.

Nehru had an extraordinary ability to inspire affection among those who knew him. Reminiscing about his years with Nehru, the former foreign secretary Jagat Mehta has written that "Gandhi we worshiped but Nehru we loved" because of his courage and his nobility of purpose in the quest for India's freedom. That courage and nobility of purpose were apparent to Alva from the beginning. Nehru embraced the ideals he stood for with a single-mindedness, dedication, enthusiasm, and emotion she had never witnessed before: together, these traits constituted the moral force that gave his leadership such power. Among statesmen she had seen, she said in an interview, Nehru's charisma was enormous, "like a radiance around him."

Nehru would often ask Alva to travel with him, by helicopter or plane, to some village project or agricultural development he was visiting. And when she traveled on her own, he wanted to hear her impressions. She later characterized their warm mutual

rapport as "an affectionate relationship that never became a relationship." In a letter to me in 1964 she wrote of Nehru as

> "The light man in my life," as I often say. (I hope that you
> know what the quotation marks point to: the fortune-tellers'
> eternal talk of "a light man and a dark man.") Gunnar doesn't
> even get annoyed when I tell him that he is neither the one
> nor the other figure of destiny, but—if he should ask: "What
> [am I] in that case?" . . . The eternal companion.

In an essay written late in life, she related how they first met
in 1952 and described her discouraging first official interview with
him in 1955. She went on to convey her sense of his view of
foreign policy—one that combined, she felt, the idealist's vision
and the realist's capacity to get things done. To observe him in
action in the midst of extraordinary difficulties and opportunities
was for her to witness the most creative aspects of leadership.

In foreign relations, Alva saw Nehru as dealing with a "three-
body problem" in which India was affected, as in a magnetic field,
by three large foreign bodies of immense power: the combined
English-American force field, the Soviet Union, and China. Nehru
aimed quite consciously, she felt, to balance the three powers,
their struggles so foreign in one sense to India and to his concern
for neutrality, in order to elicit what was best and most creative
from each, not only for India but for the world. But at the same
time he insisted on the importance of retaining full independence
with respect to all three. In this he influenced Alva strongly. She,
who had been so outspokenly pro-American before and during
the war, now increasingly stressed the need for nations to speak
out freely about the world's problems without being locked into
the rigid cold war positions of the three large power blocs. Her
advocacy of what she called Sweden's "active neutrality" gained
a new perspective during her years in India.

Of the three power blocs, China, in Nehru's opinion, posed
the greatest threat to India. Alva agreed; but while she admired
his efforts to counter this threat with pacts, exchanges, and a
stress on mutual friendship, there were times she thought he was

too hesitant in opposing the escalating Chinese provocations that would lead, ultimately, to war between India and China in 1962. Likewise, while she had admired Nehru's reluctance to use force in Goa when she first arrived in 1955, she later doubted the wisdom of his caution. It allowed the situation to fester until 1961, when he finally felt forced to intervene.

Alva was also troubled by Nehru's reliance on V. K. Krishna Menon, his brilliant, querulous ally in the independence struggle and minister without portfolio in his government, later minister of defense. She found him not only unprincipled and manipulative, but also doctrinaire and given to temperamental outbursts on subjects such as Kashmir. She could see how often Nehru refused to act on Menon's advice: but in that case, why did he listen to him so assiduously? Alva finally concluded that Nehru knew Menon's shortcomings but kept listening to him because of his brilliance. Menon was the only genuine intellectual foil Nehru had in the government.

It was increasingly clear to Alva how much Menon could hurt India's reputation through his speeches and actions. When the Soviet Union invaded Hungary, for example, in October 1956, Menon abstained on India's behalf from a vote condemning its action in the United Nations. Nehru expressed his unhappiness with this vote in private but felt obliged to stand by Menon in public. This position, in turn, compromised Nehru, especially since he had been severe in his condemnation of the French-British-Israeli attack on Egypt shortly before the Soviet action. To Alva, Menon was much more of a liability for Nehru than he himself seemed to acknowledge.

Alva's fascination with all that she was seeing and doing in India permeates her letters to me. They show her work as fulfilling, not only intellectually and emotionally, but also in bringing into play her interest in the arts. She filled her house with writers, sculptors, dancers, and others whenever delegations from Sweden came on visits. And planning for the new embassy brought into play her concern for architecture, color, and design. Even her love for beautiful clothing—the "original sin" that she shared with her mother and her sister Rut—found new outlets. She could have

silks and cottons in glorious, subtle shadings made into suits and
dresses for astonishingly little money as compared to what had
been possible for her in Geneva and Paris.

I could also sense in her letters her desire to stay in close
touch by trying to enter, in her imagination, into all that I must
be experiencing. Already the previous summer, as soon as I flew
to America to begin my married life there, she had sent me a
series of letters filled with affection, discreet encouragement, advice, and details about family and friends. Always, I could feel
her reaching out to understand. And she spoke directly—as if we
were sitting facing one another over a cup of tea. In a series of
letters written in June and July 1955 she wrote, among much else,
as follows:

> *Darling, darling Sissela,*
> Just got your letter this morning, your first American letter.
> Had wondered so much. Then heard from Gunnar that you
> had arrived and were happy. . . . Darling, feel truly fine—
> experience the joy of being free—free from worries and free
> from strivings. And use all your dear wealth of inventiveness
> to make Derek happy—then you will also receive tenderness
> in return.

> *Darling Sissela,*
> It is Friday evening. I sit in bed and have just "slaughtered"
> *Elle* [a French women's magazine]. And then there steals over
> me such despair: that you will never more come over from
> your room. If only you could look in and we could chatter a
> little. For instance that I plan to steal your pink orlon
> dress. . . .

> *My darling Sissela,*
> It was so far away and so disquieting not to have an address
> for you. I had wanted to write you almost every day in order
> to maintain a thread, as it were, from me to you, from us to
> you both, from the old home to the new. . . . Right now, I am
> sitting in a conference hall listening to boring debates about
> amendments, etc. Therefore it will be a bit hard to write in as

heartfelt a manner as I would really like. For it truly has to do with the heart—it feels as if a bit of it had been torn away when you disappeared. But enough about that: for I don't want to burden you with any thought about the emptiness that has arisen within me. Let me instead take care of a few practical matters. . . .

Angel child,
It was so wonderful to receive your little letter. So now I know that you have arrived happily. But I know far too little about the journey itself [by car from New York to California]. I wanted to hear about Georgia O'Keeffe and about others you have met. And about the Indians in New Mexico—does one not feel what an extraordinarily rich culture the US actually has, like a treasure underground? Too little used in depth, too much in its external, ornamental details. . . .

Gunnar also began writing to me most warmly. His efforts that summer to show himself more attuned to Alva and to human relationships in general made him focus on us children as well. In my case, this desire was enhanced by the fact that I had, to his amazement, married someone whom he admired and whom he wanted to help and advise—and, not least, someone whose judgment and editorial expertise he had already enlisted for his own writings.

"Here comes the first immigrant letter!" I answered from America. Throughout the summer I wrote home as a wide-eyed European about arriving in the midst of a grueling East Coast heat wave and about all my adventures in traveling across the country with Derek. I described the openhearted welcome I had received from two new sets of relatives in Philadelphia and Los Angeles as well as their intricate relationships and tribulations, feeling a little as if I had stepped between the covers of several interlocking and absorbing family novels. And I peppered Alva and Gunnar with questions about the doings of family and friends. But when it came to inquiring about their own lives and plans for the future, my letters seem, as I reread them now, friendly but curiously remote.

It was not until Derek asked me, in September, how it could be that I was still not fully on close terms with my mother, whom he found so fascinating and so warmly concerned for us both, that something seemed to burst within me. I suddenly realized that I had not done or said nearly enough before I left Paris. I saw that I had not taken her own concerns into account, confronted as she was with so many changes in her life. Nor had I acknowledged the love and support that I had always been able to count on from her. True, she was abroad, once again, when I left, but I knew I could have sought her out before then. I sat down right away to write, in a letter with IMPORTANT written in large letters in the margin:

A great feeling of shame has suddenly come over me when I think of all that you have always done for me and mostly understood over the years, and how little I have ever dared express my gratitude. Perhaps it was some kind of pride or need for independence, but now I am truly sorry to think how little I have used every opportunity for showing how much it all meant for me. Perhaps I did not even feel it as much then; therefore I am doubly sorry now.

From that moment on, our correspondence stretched over nearly three decades. As I reread Alva's letters, I see how anchored they were in daily existence—but an existence intensely experienced with all its sources of joy, beauty, problems, and sorrow—while at the same time she had her eyes open to larger developments in the world. Vignettes abound in so many of her letters:

[November 1957, about a garden party for four hundred persons that Alva gave to mark the Swedish king's seventy-fifth birthday]
The best thing was that Nehru came, which he almost never does. And I had hit on the idea of inviting the children in the Swedish colony. No one does this—in the persistent false belief that these are cocktail parties, whereas in reality they are the most innocent fruit-juice occasions. And who, more than the children, can better enjoy the fancy sandwiches that I have

finally prevailed on the caterers here to make, the festively dressed guests, the light streaming from a huge illuminated royal crown, the two rows of yellow and blue lamps around the top of the house, the floodlighting of all the banana trees and other large, exotic trees, some of which convey the impression of a giant cupola above the guests. And when they were then photographed with a truly beatifically smiling Nehru, they have a memory for life. That he himself seems to have appreciated this unconventional touch was, so to speak, an extra plus.

[January 1958]
We've had an entangled New Year, with Czech Prime Minister, Indonesian President, and English Prime Minister almost stumbling across one another in the palace entryways. It is probably politically very important. At least, one senses how different the atmosphere around them is. The above-mentioned order can also serve as a measure of the warmth in their reception, from very lukewarm to almost warm.

[February 1958]
What more could there be to tell? Perhaps just for fun that Saturday night I "made a little history" by being the first woman ever to pass the threshold of one of the main dining halls of the University. Of course, it was a small barricade to storm, but it has nonetheless been considered as a bit of pioneering. It only goes to show how faithfully Oxonian the academic republic here can be.

Just now I looked out of the window here in the library and saw two baby monkeys climbing in the bamboo sun screens that hang in front of the veranda.

Alva's work called on her to convey back to Sweden as complete an understanding as possible about India, Burma, Ceylon, and Nepal and their relations with other nations. But much of her time was also taken up with the various personal problems for which people sought her help. What to do, for example, to assist a Swedish sailor who, ten years before, had had a child with

a woman in Bombay and wanted to look her up to see his child—
did Alva know how he might go about searching for them?

About her travels, often with Gunnar or with Kaj and Horst,
she wrote often, and never more than when it came to visiting
jungles in different parts of India. She described her amazement—
in part that of a Scandinavian who could never quite believe she
had the fortune to come to places so utterly unlike those of her
childhood home:

[January 1958]
One of the greater experiences was the silent journeying in the
jungle itself. First, in the chilly morning, when the animals are
still awake and out, when the jeep moves across tufts and
rocks with trees that whip one in the face. Then on elephant
backs during the long, sun-gorged day, when one equally silently sails, swings along, peers after birds, deer, porcupines,
etc. Peering, swinging, enjoying the whole time. These long
elephant rides—4–5 hours each day for five days—when absolute silence must reign, even though four of us are sitting
on a little upside-down bed on the elephant's broad back
(while the mahout sits astride its neck)—yes, it is inconceivable
how anything can be so captivating, so unforgettable, so con-
ducive to yearning. It was the true, deep rest!

And in March 1957, Alva wrote me a long letter about her
"greatest diplomatic triumph so far": she had had to rescue Arne
Sucksdorff, a Swedish filmmaker specializing in anthropological
and wildlife subject matter—not from wild animals, but from the
jaws of the rigid Indian bureaucracy. He had already started a
documentary film about the Muria people in the Bastar District,
in central India, when it was learned that he had filmed a woman
with one breast bared. The Ministry of Information threatened to
withdraw his license. All work on the project came to a halt.
Already on location, with over fifty persons hired for the film and
a great many animals assembled, Sucksdorff could not conceive
of stopping for good, nor afford to do so. He turned to Alva in
despair, and she agreed to visit the ministry with him. She ex-

plained to the Minister of Information that it would not be right to judge artists by bureaucratic standards and invited him, instead, to send photographers to take part in the filming. Sucksdorff promptly received his license. In return, he asked Alva to visit the village where he and his wife, Astrid, were shooting the documentary:

> I came straight into a gang of warmhearted, simple people. They lived in a rest house on the edge of the jungle and in a village belonging to people of the primitive Muria tribe. These small, beautiful beings, who live a true Rousseau idyll, were utterly enchanting, since Sucksdorff had gained their trust. I, too, received a tribal name: Laharo, and was looked over and then wreathed by them.
>
> But just a few hours after our arrival, a youth came wandering down from another village higher up in the jungle in order to tell memsahib that a [man-eating] tiger had come around and taken a cow. "Then I have to go," said Astrid, the sweet young wife with eyes like stars. My Second Secretary, Roos, got to go with her in the jeep. The men of the village had already prepared a *machan,* that is a small "veranda" in a tree above the cow cadaver that the tiger had not finished eating. The two sat there silently for two hours. When the tiger came, Roos was astounded, first to see a live one, then to see Astrid fell it with one single well-aimed shot without spilling blood or ruining its hide.
>
> Then they blew a horn to signal to the men in the village that it was safe to come forward to carry down the beast. When they arrived with it in the jeep, it was discovered that it was the tiger's somewhat less dangerous mate who had been shot. As a result, Astrid knew that she would soon have to go up again. This was her ninth tiger that year, not for purposes of hunting, but simply to respond to the villagers' pleas for help. Not fewer than 60 people had been eaten by tigers that year. So she is almost a saint in that region. And I was there the next day when a man came walking twenty miles to tell Arne and Astrid that two of his little girls had been missing since Wednesday. Now he hoped that they would look in their camera to see where the girls were!

I could write page up and page down about this: especially the Muria people. Forgot to say that the boy, like all the men, goes naked and walks around with bow and arrow! Elwin has written about them. Not only because they seem to be the sunniest and happiest of primitive peoples but also because they have a *ghotul system,* in which boys and girls sleep in common dormitories, dance, and have a pleasant time until they marry. There are books about that, too. But of course it is a revelation to *see* it.

Enough now. I must return to Delhi and the ordinary reality. I enclose a clipping about Gunnar so that you will see that he begins to have a role here, not just as the ambassador's wife, which almost became a problem. He is immensely appreciated. Nehru [speaks of] what a great economist he is and how "he can advise us." . . . Elections and much else are at hand. All of which I relish more than I can really describe.

In May 1957 Alva flew to the United States, where she visited Derek and me in our first real home, a one-bedroom garden apartment in Alexandria, Virginia. In our eyes it was paradise on earth, and many letters had already gone back and forth between Alva and us about its beauties. We had worried whether we would be able to receive her there since Derek's military service had taken him, some months earlier, from the Judge Advocate General's Office in the Pentagon to basic training in Fort Benning, Georgia, and then to Charlottesville, Virginia. I had interrupted my studies at George Washington University to go with him. A letter from Alva arrived as a beacon of familiar light one day when Derek, sick with dysentery, returned from what seemed interminable hours of crawling on maneuver through the Georgia swamps. To our joy, she announced that she had decided to visit us wherever and whenever it would be most convenient for us. Earlier, she had written to Derek's mother that she was undertaking the journey in part because the change after I left Paris had been too cruel:

first to have a daughter going in and out of your house day after day, knowing where she is, what she wears, with whom

she is, what she thinks—and so another day she is beyond
reach. I have just come around to telling myself that I cannot
stand it much longer, and so I have planned to return to
Europe via the States this summer. Then I will go and find
them wherever they are.

She later told me that the suddenness of this breach, to be
repeated when Kaj married a few years later, brought a lasting
sense of great loss, the more so as we both turned out to live so
far away. She wished that she had taken more time to savor and,
as it were, store up the experience of being with us when we were
at home, now that she knew how brief that period would be. The
experience of simply being together, of reaching into and sharing
one another's lives as fully as possible, was what she sought on
her first visit as on all later ones—though with tact, so as not to
burden us with feelings of guilt for having left.

We were delighted to welcome her to our beloved Alexandria
home when she arrived, toward the end of May. Somehow, her
visiting us in our first home mattered to me more than I had
realized; it was as if much rode on my being able to demonstrate
to her that Derek and I had managed to create a life of our own
that she would think a good one and, more than that, recognize
as a happy one. In so doing, she would reaffirm its reality, and in
turn, my living an adult life of my own.

After her visit with us, Alva flew on to Sweden to meet Nehru
and to accompany him on his first state visit there. She had
suggested this journey and helped plan it in every detail. Traveling
around the country by train, car, and helicopter, he charmed
everyone, from the business leaders whose thinking he hoped to
challenge to the villagers with whom he danced around the may-
pole on Midsummer's Night. When Nehru continued on his way
to Finland, Alva joined Gunnar for a month of work and relax-
ation in Europe before returning to her post in India and readying
the house for his move there in October.

Gunnar had already done much preparatory work for the
study of South Asia that would end up taking fifteen years of his
life: *Asian Drama: An Inquiry into the Poverty of Nations.* He

had made extensive trips throughout the Third World and discussed the problems of poverty and development in such works as *An International Economy: Problems and Prospects* and *Rich Lands and Poor: The Road to World Prosperity.*

Much as he had done in working on *An American Dilemma* twenty years earlier, he had begun assembling a team of scholars—the economists Ester and Mogens Boserup, his former colleagues at the ECE, being the first to join him—who would assist him in the massive work of gathering and interpreting data. And just as he had set forth the principles of the American Creed as explicit value premises in the earlier study, so he chose economic and social development as the basic value premise to be stressed in the present one. He would write in *Asian Drama* that he saw the South Asian nations as awakening, like Rip Van Winkle, from the sleep of centuries. Without extraordinarily energetic efforts at development, they faced stagnation and in the end calamity, given the unstable world situation and their rapidly increasing populations.

As he had in *An American Dilemma*, Gunnar also aimed to help find ways to resolve the problems he was studying rather than merely to describe them. With respect to both sets of problems, he opted for what he called an institutionalist approach that took into account the "cumulative causation" through which factors such as education, employment, housing, and population density affected one another. These could in turn be guided by careful planning, "the intellectual matrix of the entire modernization ideology." He felt that his years of international research and writing had prepared him more thoroughly for this new task than for writing *An American Dilemma*; but he was also aware of the nearly insuperable difficulties inherent in such an effort.

Alva was elated to see Gunnar with a great task before him once again. She was convinced that she could be of more substantive help to him than when he was working on *An American Dilemma,* given her experience in the region and her years of steeping herself in the study of its history and cultures. Gunnar had asked her to do the research needed for the section dealing with education. This time they would be working side by side, with the same set of problems in mind but with different activities, something that might well be preferable to collaborating directly on the book. Already, she wrote to him in August 1957, she was planning how she could best help him truly visualize and understand the various Asian societies. She longed for him to come so that they could discuss these plans and so much more: "Nothing is as pleasurable as talking with you. I *suffer* when the intellectual nourishment is lacking."

At the same time, Alva was cautious about this more permanent common life on which they were now embarking. She wanted true equality, she wrote him, with neither of them having the upper hand. She did not want him to seem in any sense forlorn or piteous; but neither did she want him "trumpeting so that I disappear like a bit of dust into a corner." And she recognized, she wrote in a letter dated October 9, 1957, that sensuality was unlikely to be part of their togetherness. There is oblique wistfulness in the various references in her letters, ever since their move to Geneva in 1947, to this distance between them. It was as if she had set her expectations of Gunnar on another plane. She hoped, she added, that the two of them could enjoy a wholehearted collaboration, a full appreciation of one another, and a warm sense of belonging. India itself offered a dimension of sensuality and a sense of the importance not only of doing but of being— precisely what she felt she and Gunnar had never been good at in the past and what she had come to regard as more important than anything else.

"I experience everything so deeply," she wrote a few days later. "Little Rock, Sputnik, everything. So it is turning out, then, that life's conditions are changing in our time. And so exciting, so blissfully challenging, if only human beings could trust one another!" But trust, precisely, was of course glaringly absent within nations as among them.

> It may have been a misfortune of global dimensions that it was Marx (rather than Gandhi) and industrial workers (rather than the people of the soil) who led the revolt, set the tune for the future.

Alva's sense of expansive fulfillment during this period was evident in all she did. The personal conflicts that had tormented her in the past and that would recur late in her life—between her work and her family and between her individual needs and those of Gunnar—were quiescent or suppressed. Her work was all-absorbing, yet she had no sense of guilt regarding us children. We were no longer in her charge. And she felt our family, which had at times been so split apart, geographically and emotionally, coming together. With me, her relations were closer than they had been in years. And Kaj, who had moved away from home so early, had joined Alva in India at nineteen. She was flourishing, fascinated by all things Indian, and had close friends at the university. After taking a B.A. with honors, she was pursuing a master's degree at the Delhi School of Social Work. She was planning to marry Horst, who was completing his dissertation on Indian soils. And though she was hurt by Gunnar's inability to accept this relationship and to reach out to Horst, she enjoyed ever more fully the grown-up friendship that had developed between her and Alva during those years.

Even the relationship with Jan seemed good. Already Jan had come to stay for long periods in the Geneva house and the Paris apartment. Alva and Gunnar kept in close contact with his two ex-wives (Jan having divorced Maj in 1957) and their two children—Janken, Jan's son with Nadja, and Eva, his daughter with Maj. And while they were still providing him with financial support, he was increasingly able to make his way as a writer. Alva wrote to tell me about the trip he was planning to take, and then write about,

> in a Citroën that he has received in part as an advertisement, through Yugoslavia, Greece, Turkey, Iran, Central Asia (Russia), Afghanistan, and here, toward the end of the year. Together with his new girl [Gun Kessle], a divorced painter. . . . Yes, I have nothing to do other than to receive the confidences and then wish them happiness! Write he really can. And politics seems almost out of the picture, now that things are beginning to go so well for him.

After Jan and Gun arrived in India they stayed with Alva and Gunnar for long stretches of time, in between returning to Afghanistan and traveling to Burma, Nepal, and China. Alva enjoyed their company enormously, finding the dialogue with them invigorating and relishing the chance to have a family nearby once again. To be sure there were tensions, but they reflected stresses within an existing family, not one that had broken apart, as before. And because we children were now adults, with independent lives and on terms of equality with her and with Gunnar, we were no longer his rivals for her attention in the same way as when we had been younger. Even apart from the family, Alva felt an improvement in her relationship with Gunnar. The two could live together, yet she was not forced, as in Geneva, to stifle her own interests. She enjoyed being part of another vast and extraordinarily important project. She could help, collaborate, yet need not fear being swallowed up.

Alva has left a note sketching a plan for memoirs that I believe dates from this fulfilled, creative period of her life. It was to be entitled *Memoirs of the Surviving*. In three parts, it would deal with her strivings to be of use in the world, the dilemma of family and work, and an "intimate journal of a marriage." She planned to write the last part first, her note explained, since the memory of it was so fresh, beginning by bringing out what she most prized: the nature of her discussions with Gunnar, their comparisons of all that they read—"every minute exhilarating."

Under this heading Alva also entered the cryptic expression "consort battleships." Since the 1940's, she had used this metaphor for her relationship with Gunnar to evoke the image of the two of them criss-crossing the world, each fully capable of maneuvering alone but strengthening the other whenever they joined forces—"sister ships," as Gunnar would sometimes say, sending one another signals no matter how far apart they might be. The image was a far cry from Alva's original vision of the two of them blending together in full unison, as in the novel *Stella* that had captivated her at fifteen. It differed, too, from the image of intertwining branches in the letters AGM that decorated so many of their household goods—towels, ashtrays. It represented, rather, two individualities operating separately, strong and even fortified, ready for action, in touch with one another and mutually supportive but fully self-sustaining.

These different metaphors are variations on Alva's lifelong exploration of what she called, late in life, "the problem of twosomeness: one that is perhaps eternal and omnipresent, always 'solved' at best through compromises." This problem arises each time two persons join their lives together: to what extent does each one then remain a separate person, while also becoming part of the other's existence? It is a problem that arises regardless of whether one or both parties work outside the home and is indeed often ameliorated when both have such an outlet. As a result, it is not simply identical with the conflict between family life and work that Viola Klein and Alva had discussed in *Women's Two Roles.* Rather, the degree to which the problem of twosomeness makes itself felt influences the ways in which women as well as men respond to those conflicts. In her own case, Alva noted, it had of course been especially difficult.

The metaphor of the two battleships strikes me as reflecting her desire to be both united with Gunnar and separate, even protected, from him. Being in part defensive, this metaphor would increasingly jar with Gunnar's tormented stress on the two of them being one and the same person. His insistence on this oneness stemmed, in part, from his long-standing horror at the thought of old age and the possibility of death. It had intensified with his distraught discovery, when Alva left for India, of how much he needed her. He was reverting, in a sense, to her earliest vision of the two of them as one person; but she, who had once been willing to burn her writings in order to blend the more harmoniously with him, was now guarding her individuality even with respect to him.

Gunnar's insistence on his and Alva's oneness would, over time, make him reach for greater and greater control over her activities. She in turn would remain adamant about certain formalities of separateness, such as a bank account of her own, that she might otherwise have thought less necessary. The question "How do I become myself?" would no longer, as when she had pondered it in her teens, only concern finding her own identity and becoming all that she was capable of becoming; it was now, also, a matter of preserving that identity while at the same time fully recognizing all that bound her to Gunnar. But the period beginning with the years in India and continuing for over a decade was still one in which she felt most at ease in balancing this equation.

During the fall and winter after Gunnar's arrival, in 1957, they saw India's economic situation grow ever more desperate. In August Alva had written me that she was "living intensely with India's travails." She was unable to think of a single thing that had gone well for the country of late. "The strains on this country are almost inhuman." The year that followed brought no improvement. Unprecedented floods and droughts continued. A crisis in foreign exchange brought a greater need for loans and economic aid. The country's production of grain was shrinking even as its population rose inexorably. Scarcity of even the most indispensable supplies led to higher prices and in turn to greater levels of profiteering and corruption. Many believed that the economy was nearing a breakdown.

Alva and Gunnar had admired India's efforts to establish five-year plans; the more so because, unlike those of the USSR, these plans were set forth within a democratic framework. They had both come of age, intellectually, in the belief that rational planning and government intervention were needed to shake nations out of their doldrums and to cut back on poverty and suffering. Coming from a small, still homogeneous nation like Sweden, with its long history of independence, community cooperation, and democracy, its widespread literacy and its work ethic, its scrupulous standards for public officials as well as its watchdog mechanisms for uncovering any misuse of public funds, they may have been unprepared for the problems that large-scale planning would pose in a vast new heterogeneous democracy such as India. By 1958, however, it was clear for all to see that India's plans were not working well; many argued that they were making the situation worse.

It was in this atmosphere that Nehru asked Gunnar to address the two chambers of Parliament on April 22, 1958, at a meeting that Nehru would himself chair. Gunnar had long resisted many requests for advice, saying that he was in India as a student rather than as a teacher. But now he decided that he would, for once, speak out about the severity of the situation as he saw it.

In his speech, Gunnar brought out the related themes that he would later develop in his book *Asian Drama*. He spoke of the need to overcome the narrow nationalism and sectarianism so common in India and among her neighbors; and he warned against the exaggerated optimism about the future that stood in the way of a realistic assessment of the country's difficulties. Pointing to the bleak prospects for traditional exports such as tea, rubber, jute, and cotton, he decried the tragic squandering of resources, in both India and Pakistan, on military machines and munitions. And he stressed the desperate need to look to the human factor in order to understand the two main development problems that he saw in India: how to bring about full employment and how to raise labor efficiency. These problems could not be resolved without unsparing attention to the difficulties presented by the low status of women, by the scorn for manual labor on the part of so many aspiring to a middle-class existence, and by poor health, insufficient nourishment, rigid social inequalities, illiteracy, and inadequate family planning.

Recognizing the special challenge posed by a country trying, for the first time, to bring about successful development while stressing the principle of universal suffrage, Gunnar suggested that these efforts might well fail unless pressed more forcefully than at present. Addressing Nehru and the assembled parliamentarians, he concluded:

> It is for the political leaders to turn this tremendously explosive power of adult suffrage, realized for the first time in history in an underdeveloped country, into a concerted and constructive effort towards rapid economic development of an ever more integrated nation. To proceed slowly in this situation would for a democracy be suicidal. Of this I am deeply convinced.

Gunnar wrote me that he felt he had never had an audience so receptive, so fully *with* him, in spite of the seriousness of the message he had to convey. Alva added that Nehru, increasingly troubled by the severity of India's difficulties during the past year, had been greatly taken with the speech, using it to focus on what could be done right away to avert the risks of which it warned.

In May of that year, Alva and Gunnar saw Nehru agonizing about whether or not to resign. His faith in himself as capable of offering the right kind of leadership was wavering. He felt, as we would now say, burned out, with little chance to do the reading and writing and thinking on which he had drawn in the past. His faith in India's future, likewise, was shaken. It was not just that the plans were failing and that harvests were poor and misery great. He also saw the destructive influence of feudal boss rule in the provinces and of greed and corruption among many of his fellow members of the Congress party.

When Nehru announced that he was thinking of resigning, a storm of protest arose. From abroad, President Eisenhower and Nikita Khrushchev both urged him to remain in office. Alva remembered, in an interview, how she had seen him torn apart by this decision:

> Listening to the tone of his voice and seeing the tremendous sorrow he was showing at that time I understood that he wanted to resign because he was disappointed, and how deep it went into him. I think he was never the same after that. He never had that same burgeoning enthusiasm any longer. . . .
> He went to Manali in the Kulu valley to ponder over these problems. One reason I know a little bit more than some others of how he felt is that he recommended it to us. So we had that Manali Rest House for a period after him. . . . To me, Nehru became a tragic figure after that.

Alva and Gunnar spent the summer of 1958 in Delhi. The heat was blistering. It was next to impossible for them to go outdoors for any length of time. Gunnar labored, more slowly than usual, on his book in the midst of the heat. Alva, who had grown more used to the climate, carried on with her duties while also planning Kaj's wedding to Horst, which would take place on August 23. It would be a simple affair, she wrote to me—"all I can do is to get the puritanical youngsters to dress up and to accept gifts." In July, however, Alva began to have attacks of fever, accompanied by a swelling in her throat and difficulty swallowing. Her doctor prescribed one regimen after another, but to no avail. She grew weaker every day. By early August, the nerves in her throat were no longer functioning and her lungs were inflamed, causing "horrible pains and convulsions for hours," according to Gunnar.

Many advised Alva to fly back to Sweden for help, but she could not bring herself to leave. She did not want to show a lack of confidence in her doctors, nor seem to flee her beloved India for medical reasons. At the very least, she was determined to stay put until she had seen Kaj through the wedding. She used the little strength she had left to assert a stubborn will not to leave.

Kaj finally took the initiative to insist that Alva return to Sweden. Perhaps for the first time in her life, she put up blunt face-to-face opposition to her mother. This confrontation was hard for her, but a physician friend from Goa, whom she had asked to examine Alva, had told her of the seriousness of the situation. It was irresponsible just to lie there in bed, Kaj argued, getting worse with each day that went by.

A few days later, Alva wrote me that she was in Sweden. As soon as Kaj had spoken, "Gunnar woke up and, in a flash, saw the dangers, and here we are!" By then she had also lost all sensation in her hands and feet. It took weeks of tube-feeding and misery, with intervals of lying in near-coma, and innumerable tests before the Swedish doctors finally concluded that her illness had begun as diphtheria but then attacked her entire nervous system. Only then could the correct therapy begin. She could easily have suffocated had she not returned in time; even so it took a year before she had regained full sensation in her hands and feet.

Gunnar stayed with Alva until he knew she was out of danger. "He has been extraordinary this whole time," Alva wrote from her hospital bed. "All in all, this must have been one of the great experiences." He had even found a place in Stockholm where they could live after Alva's term in India was over. After her close brush with death, she was more convinced than ever that they should return to their home country as a base from which to continue their traveling and foreign assignments; and Gunnar had accepted the offer of a professorship in international economics at the University of Stockholm. They would be living in a building that Gunnar had bought on a narrow lane in the heart of Stockholm, its medieval Old City, located on an island. Once the building had been refurbished, they planned to let the present tenants continue to rent the bottom three apartments and then turn the top three floors into a spacious, sunny home.

While convalescing, Alva invited Rut to stay with her at a seaside hotel for ten days. Rut, at fifty-four, suffering from extremely high blood pressure and a worn-out heart, had been warned by doctors that the end might come suddenly. But together for what turned out to be the last time, the two sisters had an utterly blissful visit, with no responsibilities save to rest and try to recover, enjoying the leisure to read to their hearts' content and, most of all, to talk as uninhibitedly as they only could with one another. When one of Rut's daughters came by she found them giggling and joking like two little girls; at times, Rut dressed up in Alva's bed jacket while Alva hovered in the role of the visiting sister as their meals were brought in.

In New Delhi, meanwhile, Kaj and Horst disinvited most of the wedding guests and scaled down the festivities that Alva had originally planned. Then they proceeded to marry in a garden ceremony, according to the Indian Civil Marriage Act, garlanded with flowers and with the traditional red marks on their foreheads. The only one of Alva's arrangements that they were unable to cancel in time was her order for a huge three-tiered wedding cake. They ate it for weeks as newlyweds.

By the time Alva returned to Delhi in mid-November she had regained part of her strength. For months she worked mornings between 8:00 A.M. and 1:30 P.M., then took care of household matters, sat in the sunshine, read the newspapers, and relaxed. The new Swedish embassy was taking form in a a suburb of Delhi, set aside as a diplomatic compound, where desert jackals still howled at night. Alva had worked with the architects, Jöran Curman and Sune Lindström, to plan a low-lying building, spare and elegant in style. They built with the climate in mind so as to require as little air conditioning as possible during the hot months while allowing easy contact with gardens and terraces whenever the weather permitted. And they designed the building to allow for large receptions while also facilitating the work of the staff and providing model living quarters for everyone connected with the embassy, from the ambassador's family to the maintenance crews.

Rebelling against the ornate extravagance of many embassies, Alva wrote me that she wanted everything in the embassy to reflect the best in Swedish taste. It should be "not only comfortable (i.e. no uncomfortable antiques) but at the same time also both elegant and democratic (i.e. cheap)." She aimed for coolness and airiness throughout in order to counteract the sense of claustrophobia that so easily overcame people feeling housebound during the hot season.

> The airiness we got by, for example, not having walls in certain places. White "skies" from very transparent draperies. Large, airy chandeliers (crystal or modern so-called Orrefors lamps). Pale walls. Light colors elsewhere, especially turquoise blue and gold. "Thin" pieces of furniture even if they are large. "Airy" placement—furniture along the walls and then rather sparse groupings.

Throughout her stay in India, Alva had also devoted evening hours and other free moments to research for the chapters on education that were to form the concluding part of Gunnar's book. This involved studying the history and the prospects for education on every level not only in India but throughout South Asia, from the Indian subcontinent all the way to the Philippines. Researched in India, then largely written by Alva in the early 1960s and finally gone over by Gunnar, the chapters offer a thorough survey of past and present educational methods in South

Asia, of differing achievements and ideals, and of the obstacles standing in their way—all interpreted in the light of the urgent educational needs of any society intent on development. Foremost are the needs that Alva and Gunnar advocated even in their earliest writings: for rationality, for emancipation from dogma, and for critical questioning. If the South Asian nations are to succeed in bringing about social and economic development, these abilities will have to be developed on a much vaster scale than in the past, through education aimed at all children and at every level, from the earliest years on up.

The educational efforts by Catholic colonizers in South Asia receive comparatively high marks, as do those by the Americans who followed the Spanish in the Philippines. Both groups were concerned to spread literacy as broadly as possible, unlike the traditional elitist and obscurantist schooling too common in Asia through the centuries and unlike the policies of British and Dutch colonizers who, for long, did little or nothing to further mass education.

Widespread ignorance was, for both Alva and Gunnar, the most severe handicap facing the new nations emerging from colonial rule. They had no sympathy for those sentimentalists who endorsed illiteracy as somehow more natural or in tune with reality. The population explosion, generating ever more numerous cohorts of children, made it difficult even to maintain the already desperately inadequate educational status quo. And the vast inequalities of gender, caste, and occupation, often religiously based and made more dangerous still by superstition, helped to keep large segments of the population in a state of debilitating ignorance. Combating the interlocking evils of superstition, exploitation, and ignorance would require not only far more education but eliminating widespread miseducation and the astounding waste of educational resources.

From 1958 on, Alva's reports to Stockholm increasingly concerned India's deteriorating relations with her neighbors in addition to almost catastrophic domestic difficulties. Once again, India's always precarious relations with Pakistan worsened over Kashmir—then as now, a source of never-ending recrimination and suspicion. At the same time, China was putting greater pressure on India's frontiers by publishing maps that differed from Indian maps in showing large areas in northern India as Chinese territory. The Chinese government expressed its dissatisfaction with Nehru for giving asylum to the Dalai Lama, who had fled to India from Tibet in March of that year. War had not yet broken out, but tensions were high; they were even reflected at home, where the crisis occasioned stormy arguments with Jan and Gun, who sided with the Chinese.

In December 1959, Prime Minister Tage Erlander of Sweden arrived to inaugurate the new embassy and to travel around the country with his wife and their entourage. Alva had prepared the visit in meticulous detail and planned to travel along as a guide. And then she received a telegram that shattered everything. On Christmas Day, she wrote to me from the Summer Palace in Mysore: "I am on an intensive journey with Prime Minister Erlander. And something horrible has happened. Rut has died." Her pen slipped across the page. "This, my pen did not want to write. The shock came an hour before I was to leave for the airport to meet the Erlanders. All would be so different if despair did not come crashing through at times. And the gruesome nights."

All at once the old anguish arose, this time with greater pain than ever, about the sheer physical inability for her or anyone else to be in two places at the same time, however desperately one wants to and knows it is one's duty to be in both. It was impossible for her to abandon her post for the funeral during Erlander's state visit. She did not even feel able to give in fully to her grief during the days she was showing the Erlanders around. Only at night could she do so. Each time the sorrow exploded within her.

Talking with Rut's daughters later confirmed what Kaj and I only slowly came fully to understand: the intimate and utterly uncomplicated friendship that Rut and Alva had kept up, beginning in childhood when they had to share a bed and join in the hard farm work. It appears to have been a friendship without tensions, like the safest of life buoys. Rut, a true farmer's wife, and Alva, the high-level diplomat and world traveler, always found each other, as if nothing could disturb what they had felt for one another from the beginning. No one could ever take Rut's place for Alva: for her Rut's death, she wrote a month later, "severed the last true link with childhood and youth."

The year that followed was Alva's last in India. Gunnar had already shifted his research operations to Europe, where he moved between Oxford and Stockholm depending on the needs of his project. In the fall of 1960 he delivered his inaugural lecture at the University of Stockholm. Alva was preparing to join him in April 1961, after a trip that would take her, among other places, to lecture at Vassar College in Poughkeepsie, New York, and to visit Derek and me in Belmont, Massachusetts.

In a speech given at the end of her stay, Alva described her wistfulness at the thought of leaving her coworkers, her life in an embassy of such exquisite beauty, and above all India itself, with its compelling problems and its extraordinary people:

> And personally? I can only note the joy at having been able to work among people in a land where more or less romantically isolated villages remain to be visited—under the palms of Kerala or in the valleys streaming with Himalaya's melted snows—but where so many people are also so deeply cultured, and often quite simply brilliant. . . . I often say: If one has, among one's acquaintances, Indian state secretaries and editors in chief, then one has access to some of the most superlative contacts for stimulating exchange.
>
> Nehru? Yes, it is of course especially satisfying to have come to know India during the epoch characterized by his achievement. When one thinks of Asia's history and of the social forces gathering there, Nehru's profile becomes even more marked, not to say unique. It is hard to believe that we shall ever see another leader who combines his wide-ranging knowledge—profound learning—about the problems of our time with such uncommonly high moral standards in his strivings to improve society and with an utterly sensitive, charming personality, full of wit even in small things.

14

Act II

❖ ❖ ❖ ❖

*W*hen *Alva returned to Sweden* in April 1961, she was fifty-nine years old. She had no idea that she was about to begin more than two decades of the most absorbing and difficult struggle of her life, centering on disarmament. Although she had plans for a book drawing on her experiences in India, she saw no clear career path ahead. Rather, she hoped to be able to round out her period of public service in whatever capacity her colleagues in the government thought most needed. Three years earlier she had already written to Gunnar from India about their "learning to grow old by and by" while working at projects they valued. And she longed to be closer, once again, to family—including, by now, five grandchildren—and friends.

The beautiful apartment in Stockholm's Old City seemed the perfect setting for this new phase of their lives. Having planned the interiors from India and spent the previous summer overseeing the transformation of the top three apartments into one free-flowing environment, Alva could now bring into it furnishings from each period of their lives. In the living room, over a wall-long Indian couch upholstered in pale orange linen, clustered the paintings acquired in the thirties. The walls of the ultramodern kitchen were in green and blue mosaic—the colors of the peacock's neck, which always reminded Alva of India. In their book-lined study upstairs, two birch desks faced one another as always. Across the hall, grandchildren who came to stay in the "student chamber"—a monastically narrow room under the eaves with a robin's egg blue ceiling to remind guests of the sky above—could look over the roofs and gables and copper turrets of the Old City and wake up to eight sets of church bells pealing at intervals in the background.

And yet, now that the time had come at last for Alva to enjoy this more settled existence, neither she nor Gunnar was ready for the process of learning to grow old together harmoniously that she had hoped for. Gunnar was consumed by his work on *Asian Drama: An Inquiry into the Poverty of Nations.* Having begun with the intention of spending a few years writing a "facile but . . . still respectable book on the main development problems of South Asia," he was entering on the fifth year of hard work with no end in sight. When the 2,284-page work finally appeared in 1968, complete with sixteen appendixes, he would apologize for its "abominable length," explaining that the study

> became to me personally a destiny, the course of which I had not foreseen or planned at the beginning. I sincerely believe that at the present stage an important contribution to the advance of knowledge about these countries is the negative act of destroying constructs that we have rapidly put together and exposing to criticism masses of more or less worthless statistics collected within the framework of these constructs, which we are using all too confidently.

Alva admired Gunnar's struggle to overcome the biases and simplistic constructs and fallacious statistics that skewed social science and its applications. But she also saw the effort as devouring him. In a letter to Derek, who had written her of his own "rather restless desire to find some subject in my field that matters enough to enlist my complete enthusiasm," she answered that he had "hit all of life's problem nails on the head" by stating that the main thing was to find a subject that enlists one's complete enthusiasm. "At least for the four of us [herself and Gunnar as

well as Derek and me] who want to give that extra something."
She described that kind of engagement in her own life, thinking
and dreaming about a project, turning all possibilities around in
her head, absorbed yet not becoming obsessed. And then she
touched—ever so obliquely—on what she most feared about Gunnar: "I think we will never become inhuman through work enthusiasm—at least not three of us!"

But while Alva was aware of the dangers of becoming de-
humanized through utter obsession with a project, she saw even
greater risks for herself in having no absorbing project at all. With
her energy stored up and experience gathered over the decades, it
was as if she were poised to engage in some great task. Already
the summer before, when Derek and I were in Stockholm, we had
seen her restless as never before. Yes, she was planning for the
new apartment, and yes, she had much to do before winding up
her work in India. But she did not see how she might continue to
be of service after her return. And no one had offered her a
position allowing her to do so in more than a piecemeal fashion.
As soon as she had moved back to Sweden she was appointed
ambassador-at-large and given one brief assignment after another
by the foreign minister, Östen Undén.

Alva thus had time for initiatives of her own. She had been
looking back at her years in India as she prepared two lectures
that appeared as a short book in August: *Vårt ansvar för de
fattiga folken: Utvecklingsproblem i social närbild* (*Our Responsibility for the Poor Peoples: A Social Close-up of Development
Problems*). The "social close-up" she meant to offer was one of
the human reality of mass poverty in the year 1961, when world
population was passing the three billion mark. Alva wanted to
shock her fellow Swedes out of their cozy insularity and to question their easy rhetoric about equality and human rights and
international cooperation. To what extent were they actually willing to apply those terms beyond their own frontiers?

Alva seized every opportunity to travel around the country
and to speak to audiences large and small in order to bring home
her message: that the world itself was not poor, that its miseries

were mostly brought about by human beings, and that cooper-
ating to bring about a reversal was only as hard as peoples and
their leaders made it. Without massive development efforts, the
world confronted a catastrophe that was "fateful even for our
own peace and our well-being, but which, in its most direct human
terms, simply means that many millions will die of *hunger*." Her
persistent advocacy forced the issues of poverty and hunger
abroad and of Swedish foreign aid to the top of the political
agenda. She helped to create an unprecedented public groundswell, pressing the Swedish government to give a higher share of
the country's GNP to foreign aid than the amount—already high
by comparison with that of other nations—it was spending for
that purpose.

In May 1961 the foreign minister asked Alva to undertake
yet another assignment: to prepare a report on possible disarmament proposals that he might make on Sweden's behalf in his
farewell speech to the UN General Assembly later that year. She
was taken aback at first, aware that she had no special expertise
in arms policy and disarmament. Having worked abroad since
1947, she had not entered into the heated domestic debate about
whether or not Sweden should develop nuclear weapons. Internationally, she had based her work on the assumption, as she
later wrote in *The Game of Disarmament*, that the historical
mission of the postwar era was to build a better world. This "left
me as rather an idle bystander when atomic weapons first came
onto the agenda of the United Nations." It was no wonder she
doubted her capacity to carry out the task set her by Undén:

> The task seemed so awesome that I asked him not to announce
> the assignment for a couple of weeks while I explored the
> possibilities to render service in a field of specialization so new
> to me. My apprentice work started by plunging me into the
> great flood of debate material and academic writings which
> were coming out at just about that time. To make the tale
> brief: once I had begun, I was never able to stop the search
> for the why's and how's of something so senseless as the arms
> race.

It is easier to see a pattern in looking back at one's life, "to make the tale brief," as Alva said. At the time she had no idea that Undén's request would set her on a path that would build on all she had done before. When she submitted draft proposals for his speech, in late July, she thanked him in a diplomatically understated tone for giving her the opportunity to study the disarmament issue, "in which I now have the greatest interest."

Here was a subject that could enlist Alva's complete enthusiasm—that sense of whole-hearted commitment she had described in her letter to Derek. It would clearly have to be a long-term commitment: she knew she had barely begun to penetrate the hardest questions about disarmament. And even as she was preparing the final draft of her proposals, she witnessed the cold war and the arms race accelerating. During the past year, Soviet premier Nikita Khrushchev had been stepping up his military pressure on West Berlin. In April 1961, the Bay of Pigs fiasco had exacerbated his distrust of President John F. Kennedy. Two months later, the Vienna summit meeting between the two closed without progress on disarmament. Their heated exchanges showed none of the "spirit of Camp David" that had been proclaimed two years earlier after the summit between Khrushchev and President Eisenhower. In August, the world was shocked by the erection of the Berlin Wall to stem the flow of East German refugees. Later that month the Soviet Union announced it would break the existing informal moratorium on nuclear weapons testing that it had observed, along with England and the United States, for three years. The United States followed suit the following month and accelerated its military buildup.

Everywhere, the fear of nuclear war mounted. With testing resumed by the two superpowers, public concern about the dangers of fallout surged once again and the debate over bomb shelters took on new immediacy. In a letter to Alva in August, only weeks before I expected the birth of my second child, I wrote of my sense of the insanity of the Berlin Wall, while still doubting that anyone would seriously want a war over Berlin. But there was much talk in America of calling up the reserves, I added, and a greater sense of crisis than at any time since Korea:

We have even begun to wonder which room in the basement would be best as a bomb shelter and what measures we ought to take, and it is so horrible to think of all that can happen if there were to be a war. Especially when one has small children.

Alva's immersion in nuclear weapons issues gave her an even darker perspective on these events. The assignments she had been given, she wrote me in August, were causing her to lie awake at night thinking about the world's misery. "Berlin—*why?* as they say in the death announcements. Why shouldn't K. have allowed the East Germans better conditions? Arranged with them to *choose* whether to stay or leave?"

And "why?" she asked again, on September 19, about the enigmas surrounding UN Secretary General Dag Hammarskjöld's death the day before in an airplane crash over the Congo. She and Gunnar had known him since their student days. Seven years younger than Gunnar, he too had studied law and economics and taught at the University of Stockholm before going into public service. Hammarskjöld had been an ally in working to reform Sweden's social policies and later a fellow internationalist whose goals Gunnar and Alva shared, however much they could at times differ about the means. And now he had died a violent death while on a mission of peace, as had their compatriots before him, Raoul Wallenberg and Count Folke Bernadotte. But why? He had been warned not to fly the particular route that he nevertheless chose. Had he been assassinated? Even gone out of his way to invite such a fate, perhaps longing for self-immolation as a way out of seemingly insuperable obstacles to peace? Could another pilot, another plane, another route have avoided the tragedy? Or did it simply result from a series of unfortunate coincidences?

Alva could hardly think, she wrote, so weighed down did she feel by the news. She could muster but a few conventional words of cheer in response to a telegram from Derek about the birth— also on September 18—of our daughter Victoria. For Alva, who had empathized with family pregnancies from beginning to end, jubilant at the birth of every new grandchild, this reaction was utterly uncharacteristic. She, who had traveled all the way from

India to see our newborn first daughter, Hilary, and who had written me only three weeks earlier of how she shared my longing for this new baby to arrive, how she thought of me from moment to moment and worried that I might have trouble breathing during the hot summer nights—now she had no feelings to spare.

Even that earlier letter had hinted at "more or less desperate thoughts" too hard to convey in writing. Although it was still a year before the Cuban missile crisis would put the world at its greatest risk of devastation ever, she sensed fear wherever she went. Irrationality and inhumanity seemed to govern not only the arms race but so many regional conflicts. The very lives of those who, like Hammarskjöld, led the search for peaceful solutions could be snuffed out in an instant.

One year after his death, Alva spoke at a memorial service for him at UN headquarters in New York. She recalled him as a brilliant young student with a strong sense of mission, "of relent- less struggle to change man-made chaos into a cosmos of peace and progress." This sense of mission was a faith that human beings are capable of organizing a better world—a faith that was being sorely tested, but that needed stressing above all else "for the sake of us, the survivors":

> Without that rock-bottom of optimism, his dedication to duty could not be understood. This faith in an ultimate victory for reason, good sense, neighbourliness, cooperation, gives us guidance as to how we should strive to carry on his work, namely with an indomitable will for victory for these very forces.

This was the Enlightenment faith that Alva and Gunnar had shared for so long: not that human beings necessarily would, but that they could achieve such a victory. But the Enlightenment thinkers had never known the present vast and impersonal threats to survival. Now Alva voiced the faith almost as an incantation, as if to draw strength from the example of Hammarskjöld at a time when her own doubts about such a victory were growing. An unaccustomed mood of powerlessness and doubt came over her as she contemplated the risks of an ever-escalating arms race. Why should she or anyone else imagine that anything they did could help reverse the tide? But if she could not, then how much meaning could she attach to any of her efforts to improve living conditions at home and abroad?

Alva's doubts were not rooted in the conviction so common in the nineteenth century that despair was inevitable unless one could believe in a divine purpose for human existence; nor did she share the sense of the vanity of "all things under the sun" expressed by the Preacher in *Ecclesiastes*. To be sure, she could feel the power of his asking "What profit hath a man of all his labor which he taketh under the sun?" But his reason—that everything has been done before and shall be done again in the future over and over without end as each generation succeeds the next—that reason was not hers.

Quite to the contrary, her fear was precisely that generations might no longer succeed one another in the nuclear age as they always had in the past. The atomic bombs over Hiroshima and Nagasaki *had* been grotesquely new under the sun, their blinding fire scorching and killing on a scale never aspired to by human beings before. The devastation recalled, rather, that wrought by Phaeton in Greek mythology: the sun-god's young son who drove his father's golden chariot across the sky and careened too close to the earth, setting it aflame and turning to ashes all who lived and all that grew within his range of destruction.

After 1945 there could be no easy assurance that generations would always follow one another as regularly as the seasons. This fact became fully real to Alva only when she immersed herself in the study of nuclear weapons, by then vastly more powerful and numerous than the bombs first deployed against Japan. And while her own country had become as vulnerable to annihilation as the superpowers, it had little say in helping to stem their escalating arms race. The meaning of human life and all the aims she had fought for seemed to Alva newly precarious.

This crisis in her life arose at a time when she had unusually little outside support. In India her work and the human contacts that it made possible had given structure and meaning to her life.

Now her activities were more scattered. She had as yet no close colleagues with whom she could share her most personal doubts, nor an official position from which to speak out as forcefully as she wished. She could do no more than hint at these concerns in her letters to us. Her sister Rut was dead. And Gunnar, to whom she might have turned for support, was of less help than usual, so great and so single-minded was his effort to bring his book project to a conclusion. He used to say that, deep down, Alva knew that human beings never mattered as much to him as his books—not even she. This was never more true than during his long years of toiling over *Asian Drama*. And the increasingly dark view of human affairs that informed his writing of that book only served to corroborate rather than challenge her own doubts.

Alva therefore had to seek some new balance on her own between these doubts and her sense of the desperate urgency of human needs the world over. In what new ways could she continue her efforts, however modest, to address these needs while working for the reduction in armaments without which they would be beside the point? Early in November 1961 she wrote me that she had been elected to the Swedish Parliament as part of a Social Democratic slate. This position would give her a forum without being as time-consuming a post as in many other nations. Her letter added that she had "delivered the ammunition" for Foreign Minister Undén's proposal for a "non-atom club"—the so-called Undén plan, stressing the role of nonnuclear nations in the disarmament debate—in his farewell speech at the UN General Assembly. Since all nations were equally vulnerable to destruction through nuclear war, he argued, all should have equal access to the debate about how to reduce the chances of such a war. The nuclear powers' continued inability to agree on arms limitations or on a nuclear test ban should not silence all debate. Rather, the Undén plan called on nations free of nuclear weapons to set an example for the others by agreeing not to produce or harbor such weapons and by jointly urging a halt to all nuclear testing. Working at such tasks and others, Alva wrote, "fills one's life and begins, even, to give it meaning."

A radio talk on Bertolt Brecht's play *Galileo* in November

1961 conveyed still more fully her questioning of the meaning of existence. Asked to discuss one play of her choice in a radio series entitled "My Drama," she had chosen Brecht's *Galileo,* thinking it a timely choice because of its protest against the atomic bomb— "the worst betrayal of humanity that politics has been able to wrest from science." While rewriting *Galileo* with Charles Laughton in 1945, Brecht had been struck, she noted, by the harsh new light the bombing of Hiroshima cast on Galileo's conflicts with the powers-that-be of his time.

> Galileo has a long, powerful soliloquy, in which he speaks of the struggle over the uses of knowledge. He sees, as in a vision, how science, which was going to help human beings to a better life, might also come to be twisted to serve altogether different purposes. And then a day could come, he prophesies, when some new discovery would be met by a cry of horror from all humanity—a vision that is of course hair-raisingly actual.

Alva began by speaking of Brecht as one of the masters for those who, like her, went to the theater as others might go to church—to seek enlightenment, self-examination, and a way to expand the bounds of personal experience. His *Galileo* was great drama because it offered such an experience in concentrated form. To her, its central theme was that of one individual's struggle to reach deeper truths than those acceptable in his time, and of the sacrifice that he was then forced to make. Few plays, she said, dealt specifically with this agony of truth-seeking and of the courage and the personal sacrifices that were often extracted before the simplest truths could be publicly accepted.

In the end, Galileo betrayed his science and himself in bowing to the Inquisition and recanting what he knew was true—that the earth revolved around the sun, as Copernicus had claimed, rather than the other way around, as the church still insisted. Brecht portrayed him as doing so, not only because he was attached to life with all its pleasures, but also because of his passion to press his inquiries further. He was possessed, Alva suggested, as all creative persons are possessed, by the sheer passion to think.

Although he recanted in public, he never gave up his right to think for himself, or his capacity to see through hypocrisy and lies. But because he explored his own motives with equal clarity, he refused all attempts to whitewash his actions. He ended his life in what Alva referred to as "the valley of darkness known as self-contempt."

As with Galileo and the Inquisition, so, Alva suggested, with Brecht and the East German government. Having fled the Nazis to go first to Sweden, then to California, Brecht returned to settle in East Germany after the war. Once there, he too gave in to authority, betrayed his own integrity, sacrificed on the altar of conformity, and was granted commensurate privileges. In so doing he surely knew that he had renounced all claims to heroism. Yet just as Galileo's works outlived his recantation, so Brecht's play would continue to carry forth his message: that by whatever means they choose, all human beings can and must struggle to resist propaganda and falsehoods; and that this resistance is never more important than for those who have thought and language as their professions. It is their singular temptation to become yea-sayers instead of risking their lives as the critics who alone can restore society's health.

Alva stressed Galileo's denial, in the play, that truth would somehow make its own way: "No, no, no. It goes forward only as far as we allow it to go forward; reason's victory can only be that of advocates of reason." It was the belief in authority, and its stupefying and demoralizing influence, she argued, that rendered us human beings defenseless. The only protection lay in thinking for oneself, in keeping skepticism alive even in the face of the most loudly proclaimed certainties. "The greatness in being human lies in not giving up, in not accepting one's own limitation."

With these words, I believe that Alva was striving to answer her own questions about the meaning of existence and the worth of human efforts as they arise not just for great thinkers such as Galileo but for all human beings, including herself. Shortly before writing this essay, she had spoken to a convention of women's groups in Stockholm's Concert Hall on the subject of disarmament. It was unrealistic, she had pointed out, to envisage an end to the arms race in the near future given the failure of the super-powers to take serious steps toward such a goal. But it would be equally unrealistic for citizens in other nations to give in to despair. The Undén plan represented just one of the ways nonnuclear nations could begin to press more actively for deescalation. There was so much more, likewise, that individuals could begin doing to decrease the threat of conflict and war in their own regions of the world. Human dignity required that they not give up, no matter how great the danger to survival:

> I know only two things for certain. One is that we gain nothing by walking around the difficulties and merely indulging in wishful thinking. The other is that there is always something one can do oneself. In the most modest form, this means: to study, to try to sort out different proposals and weigh the effect of the proposed solutions—even if they are only partial solutions. Otherwise there would be nothing left but to give up. And it is not worthy of human beings to give up. This wonderful planet that we have been given . . . should we not be capable of preserving it, guarding its peace, developing its resources to share in justice with our fellow humans?

The draft of Alva's essay on Galileo refers to him throughout as "G." As she speaks of G.'s being possessed by his passion to explore knowledge, of his courage in daring to challenge dogma and superstition, and of his brazen delight in shocking the right-thinking, it is hard not to think of Gunnar, to whom she often referred as "G." in letters and notes. And I wonder, in rereading the essay, whether it does not also reflect her effort to come to terms with Gunnar's obsession with work by honoring the passion in his effort to pursue knowledge, even if it blinded him to her own concerns just when she needed him most.

The deepest question the play raised, Alva suggested, had to do with the price of free thinking. It applied as personally to Gunnar as to herself: Do not all societies, even the freest ones, require some kind of sacrifice on the part of those who choose to exercise their freedom to think and to speak out about unpopular conclusions? In Sweden, the unseen shackles traditionally imposed in its tightly knit and conformist communities held back the outspoken. And the nation's otherwise laudable stress on adopting policies only after thorough debate and the achievement of consensus, rather than by dictum from above, added to the pressures on nonconformists.

Alva and Gunnar responded differently to these pressures and had, as a result, to make different kinds of sacrifice once they chose to settle in Sweden rather than live abroad as expatriates. To the end of his life, Gunnar would refuse to accommodate himself to social or political requirements that he regarded as confining. He had long claimed that progress in social science was best furthered through sharp, unsparing controversy. Now that he held no office that required him to be diplomatic, his chosen role would increasingly be that of the outspoken, often highly critical scholar rather than that of the conciliator—"an angry old man," as he used to say. The price paid was that many of his criticisms or suggestions for reform would be politely ignored or else attacked on grounds he considered trivial.

Alva was less willing and less temperamentally suited than Gunnar to be the bull in the china shop, the irritating truth-teller. She wanted to be effective within the political debate and to help Sweden play a more constructive role internationally in both development and disarmament. She saw these issues as inextricably linked: governments, including those in the poorest nations, were squandering resources on armaments and preparations for war that should be going for social and economic development. Rechanneling these resources would alleviate some of the most virulent factors contributing to regional conflicts—conflicts that in turn risked sparking war and destruction so vast as to undermine all hope of development.

But time pressed. The problems were urgent; she herself was almost sixty years old, and the Social Democratic government was then as hidebound as the opposition parties when it came to entrusting high positions to women. If she was going to play a role in public life, she would have to create that role herself. She would capitalize on her gift for drawing public attention to a problem in order to buttress her effectiveness in dealing with it as an insider, both as a public official and as a delegate to international meetings. But in her effort to shape such a double role, she too would pay a price. From this period onward she spoke often of the personal sacrifices asked of many in public life: not the exalted, almost Christlike sacrifice alluded to by Dag Hammarskjöld in his book *Markings* so much as the everyday limits on self-expression and personal relations when they conflicted with one's public role.

This was not just a matter of living up to the standards expected of public officials. Alva had always been scrupulous in observing even the most inconsequential laws and regulations—never bringing home office stationery for personal use, obeying every parking and traffic rule, leaning over backward not to take advantage of the slightest tax loophole. During her years in India her government role had called for more attention to secrecy than she had been used to before. She knew that she had sometimes irritated both Jan and Gunnar by refusing to speak to them about confidential government matters. And now, in studying military affairs, there was so much more to be kept secret.

But Alva's sense of sacrifice went beyond such routine requirements. She came to fashion a public self seemingly more assured, omnicompetent, and invulnerable than her private self. Her sense for drama influenced this public role, even as it contributed to the sacrifice of her freedom to be fully herself. She had always dramatized and even personalized debates on social issues while trying to keep her private life out of the spotlight. Increasingly, she planned her own role in these debates and all other public appearances in advance, down to the smallest details. Always immaculate, her striking appearance created a space around her, a discreetly conveyed air of privacy and distance. It served to protect her against prying, but it also isolated her.

There was an element of staging in these appearances, as in the photographs of her accompanying the interviews she was increasingly asked to give. Whether she was portrayed in a crimson taffeta gown greeting King Gustaf Adolf or wearing a black wool suit with a silver necklace, seated on her pale orange couch in front of a wall full of contemporary art, or walking with Gunnar down a medieval lane in the Old City dressed in a turquoise shirtdress vivid against the gray stones, there is no mistaking her awareness of composition and color.

This impeccable staging contributed to the myths that sprang up about her infallible competence, her inexhaustible energy, her perfect marriage—especially since Gunnar could always be counted on to support these interpretations with gusto. Alva's own reticence prevented her from commenting on personal matters one way or another. Thus the myths were reinforced by default, making it ever harder to break away from them. They undoubtedly facilitated her work, preventing others from dismissing her because she was a woman or nearing retirement age. But in the end she would feel trapped, more than she had foreseen, within a stifling public mask.

The metaphors of drama, of conflict, and of unfolding destinies came often to mind for Alva and Gunnar during the years he was working on the book that he had named, from the very outset, *Asian Drama*. Gunnar always remembered his labor on that book as the hardest test he had ever set himself:

> I used to wake in the middle of the night and think with horror and fear: What in hell am I doing and when will it ever be ready? Writing a book like that is like standing in the trenches of the First World War up to your knees in mud.

The book would finally be published in 1968 and become as much of a classic as *An American Dilemma,* after a chilly initial reception in Asia due to its sharp critique of failed reforms and corrupt ruling elites. In the prologue Gunnar sets forth the economic and social conflicts in South Asia, pitting people's highest aspirations against the bitter experience of everyday reality as a vast drama played out on the world stage and speeding toward a climax. Its leading figures are the peoples of South Asia; outsiders such as himself, who are attempting to study the conflicts or to offer aid or advice, form a relatively unimportant sideshow. Gunnar sees little room for optimism about the outcome of this drama. But because it is being played out in life rather than onstage, human beings still have the power, if they have the will, to change the course of events: "And the drama thus conceived is not necessarily tragedy."

In the Personal Note at the outset of *The Game of Disarmament,* Alva likewise uses the language of drama in referring to the period before and after the spring of 1962, when she was appointed to head the Swedish delegation to the newly formed eighteen-nation Geneva Disarmament Committee:

> What I have so far described is like the first act of my involvement with disarmament issues. The second act was played out during twelve long years of yeoman service to the cause of disarmament in the United Nations and various UN-related disarmament committees. Here another process gradually began to operate: my initial optimism began to look—to myself—more and more like naiveté. . . .
>
> The third act is, as yet [in 1976], unwritten. It has not even begun. We are in a strange interlude of no-motion on all disarmament issues. . . . The stage has not as yet been set for a serious and concerted effort by all actors, as I would still hope, to win victory over the arms race, so senseless and cruel, and to bar a complete militarization of the whole world.

The second act of this drama opened in Geneva, a stone's throw away from Les Feuillantines. Behind the high, moss-covered walls and through the branches of the trees in the park inside, Alva could see glimpses of the house where she had once felt so restive and so close to defeat. Now it was March 1962, and she couldn't wait for the Eighteen-Nation Disarmament Committee to begin its deliberations. As she walked through the gates of the palace of the United Nations, past the peacocks strolling on the lawn and into the great hall where she had listened to so many debates in the past, she felt elated. In part because of the Swedish initiative that she had helped shape, eight nonaligned nations—who, after all, had as much to fear from nuclear war as the superpowers—had been asked, for the first time, to join such a committee: Brazil, Burma, Egypt, Ethiopia, India, Mexico, Nigeria, and Sweden.

Alva wrote me that she had never felt so uplifted by any task. The stakes were high, but the problems ought to be manageable since everyone's survival was equally at stake. Unlike many other human problems, she contended, those of disarmament had a crystal-clear straightforwardness that made them especially captivating. In principle, they were as simple as algebra. One could offer one equation after another that clearly benefited both sides, working toward a solution by taking one sensible step after the next. But so far, she added, such straightforwardness existed in principle only. In practice, nothing turned out to work. The great powers had become the prisoners of their own public opinion; reasons of prestige kept them from taking serious steps to guard their own long-term security as well as world peace. "*Only* the will to press the political button is missing. This '*only*' that is so politically inexplicable."

I wrote back that Derek and I felt more intensely as if we were participants with her in this effort than in any other she had undertaken. But I could not help adding that I found it hard to visualize the crystal-clear straightforwardness of which she wrote, given the difficulties of verifying arms accords and the additional, uncharted risks posed by bacteriological and other forms of warfare.

During her twelve years of serving as a delegate to disarmament meetings, Alva claimed gradually to have understood that the superpowers would take no forceful steps to reverse the arms race, however evident its suicidal irrationality. Instead she came to see the two enemy camps as allied in at least one respect: their interlocking desire to pursue the arms race on their own terms, without interference from "outsiders." And in this pursuit, she concluded, they succeeded with a vengeance. When the committee began meeting, in 1962, there were five hundred intercontinental missiles in the world; a decade later, there were over twenty-six hundred.

At the time, however, there did seem to be room for maneuvering. Both the Soviet Union and the United States offered lofty though vague new versions of their earlier proposals for complete disarmament to take place over the coming decade. The most promising avenue for quick action appeared to be that of instituting a permanent test ban. Such a ban had first been proposed by Nehru after the casualties to Japanese fishermen from the U.S. test of a hydrogen bomb at Bikini Atoll in the Pacific Ocean in 1954. As the risks posed by radioactive fallout from such tests became more widely known, public outcry intensified, supported by protests from scientists and public figures the world over. Massive demonstrations took place to protest the resumption of testing in 1961 by the Soviet Union and the United States. And scientific testimony at the time demonstrated that existing mechanisms of inspection could replace the elaborate and hugely expensive ones previously thought necessary to guard against one nation's violating a test ban unbeknownst to the others.

By April 1962, Alva had initiated a proposal for such a ban on behalf of the eight nonaligned nations at Geneva. The negotiations continued off and on during the summer in Geneva and at the United Nations that fall. Alva worked harder than ever both during the various meetings and informally. She spoke in a letter of feeling stretched, as the Swedes say, "like a leather strap along the ground," hurrying from meeting to meeting, meticulously preparing each speech and each effort at negotiation, hoping to nudge the superpowers closer to the accord that was so clearly in their own and humanity's urgent interest.

After the shock of barely averting nuclear war during the Cuban missile crisis in October of that year, the United States and the Soviet Union seemed newly determined to decrease the risks of another such confrontation and well on the way to completing a test ban agreement. All that remained, at least on paper, was to iron out the number of annual on-site inspections a nation had to accept when it was accused of violating the ban. The Soviet government, secretive and suspicious of inspections by foreign powers, had consented to two or three inspections; the Americans had agreed to be satisfied with seven. A negotiated compromise seemed imminent, but neither side made a further move in that direction. And when the Soviet delegates withdrew their offer to have any obligatory inspections whatsoever on Soviet soil, everything had to be started from scratch once again.

The meetings resumed in Geneva in 1963. As always, then and during UN sessions in the years to come, Alva moved into the room she came to regard as her own at the Hôtel Beau Rivage, with a balcony overlooking Lake Geneva, its sparkling water jet seeming to reach higher than the mountains in the distance. It was the very balcony, she would tell visitors, where a princess had once been shot to death by a Prussian duke. She was grateful to be able to concentrate on the disarmament talks alone without, as when she was back in Stockholm, having so many competing official duties. But her letters to Gunnar repeatedly stress that even though she found her work absorbing, she did not want to continue such a hectic existence with its endless traveling, often feeling overtired; she missed her day-to-day life with him at home. She was forever projecting a different, calmer existence for the two of them together, yet forever agreeing to take on still more far-flung responsibilities.

In Geneva, negotiations for a test ban stalled. After the United States and the Soviet Union announced that they would hold bilateral talks in Moscow that summer, Alva, along with many others, rejoiced when the two nations agreed to ban nuclear tests in the atmosphere—those that had caused the greatest public outcry. She took the two governments at their word when they said that this partial ban would be a first step to a general test ban. Over the years of continued meetings and negotiations concerning such a ban, however, she realized that there was no end in sight for the underground tests. And public opinion, which had been such a great force on the issue of atmospheric testing and its attendant health hazards, was for many years less unified regarding underground tests. The danger from radioactive fallout in atmospheric tests was immediate, whereas the risks from continued underground testing seemed more indirect and harder to envisage at the time:

> The public was too easily satisfied with the ostrichlike solution
> of driving the tests underground—which had no effect on the

major objective, to hamper and curtail nuclear weapons development.

Alva saw the debates about this issue as about so many others of war and peace as crippled by the lack of reliable information. Slogans that neither side believed too often took the place of informed debate, grass-roots political action, and serious negotiations. It was to provide a solid basis of trustworthy research on the world's military arsenals, arms expenditures, and conflicts that she conceived of an independent research institute. She convinced her colleagues in the government that such an organization should be publicly funded and located in Stockholm to mark Sweden's 150 years of uninterrupted peace. In December 1964 she was asked to head a planning group for what would become, a year later, the Stockholm International Peace Research Institute (SIPRI). Situated in a neutral nation and free from any ongoing conflict, it could keep its research independent, without risk that its data might be skewed by official pressure or bound by secrecy requirements, as was the work of existing research institutes.

Alva thought up the idea for SIPRI and chaired it during its first year. In 1967, when she joined the Swedish cabinet and could no longer serve, Gunnar, at last through with his book, took over as chair. SIPRI turned out to be as much a collaborative project as any book they had ever written together. During this decade, Alva spoke more and more often about their joint role as "consort battleships" in struggling for the causes of peace and development. She operated from within the government, he as a scholar. In her work, disarmament was the central preoccupation, with international development a close second; for Gunnar the reverse was true. Both were convinced that an informed debate would help speed the end of long-standing conflicts such as those in South Africa and Vietnam and of the arms race. And each such shift would allow the transfer of resources—what we now call a "peace dividend"—from destructive aims to pressing human needs, not least in the so-called Third World.

Alva's and Gunnar's shared conviction that such changes were possible drew once again on one of their most fundamental

Enlightenment premises: that evil, though it plays a large part in human affairs, still takes second place to ignorance. Evil succeeds as often and as long as it does because of human ignorance, whether it be due to sheer stupidity, imposed by repression and censorship, or self-inflicted through passivity, bias, shortsightedness, and superstition. Although careful analysis and accurate information can do little to remedy stupidity, it can greatly reduce the various forms of self-inflicted ignorance and in turn provide weapons in the battle against repression and censorship. Both Alva and Gunnar had long since abandoned any Enlightenment optimism about the inevitability of human progress. But unlike fatalists of various persuasions, they never gave up the underlying premise allowing for its possibility. This belief inclined them to focus less on blaming those who exploit the ignorance of others than on the institutional reforms and personal efforts that could stop such exploitation and prevent its resurgence in the future.

In founding SIPRI and in traveling around the country to speak on issues of disarmament and development and foreign aid, Alva helped to bring these issues to unprecedented visibility among Swedish voters. Once again, as during the campaigns of the thirties and forties, she turned out to be an extraordinarily gifted speaker, capable of moving her audience as few others could. She could feel the public's response and did not hesitate to draw on it to press the issues ahead. As she remarked in a letter to me in November 1964: "Of course I use the popularity in order to goad the government. On questions like foreign aid and Swedish trade policy. Am *enjoying* this." She knew that she used strong language and once admitted to an interviewer that, yes, she could be aggressive, but only about issues, never about people. It was as if she transferred her anger from individuals to ideas.

As international issues became major concerns of the Swedish people, Alva became an indispensable political asset for the Social Democratic party. When the party won a continued mandate in the 1966 elections, she was appointed minister for disarmament—the first and only such post in the world. She planned to take full advantage of her new visibility to press for greater international cooperation in turning back the arms race.

By the time she took office, in January 1967, she was about to turn sixty-five. In response to an interviewer, she noted that she became a cabinet minister twenty-five years after Gunnar did. "There's not twenty-five years' difference in our ages, only four. Add twenty for the handicap of being a woman." Her cabinet position encompassed three domains. The first two corresponded to her priorities at the time: disarmament and foreign aid. She linked them by speaking of the negative and the positive meanings of the word *disarmament*: the negative meaning pointing to the reduction of weapons of war, the positive one to the transfer of resources to economic and social research and development. She had already played a leading role in working out Sweden's decision not to develop nuclear weapons of its own; now she would also argue within the government against the laxity with which it supervised the thriving Swedish arms sales abroad.

The third of Alva's domains as minister was added a few years later and came as a surprise: she was named minister of church affairs. In one sense, her combination of duties was not inappropriate: beginning in the 1960s, the churches in many countries had become increasingly engaged in disarmament and foreign aid. A year later she was asked to head a commission to consider the separation between the church and the government. Sweden, Lutheran since the Reformation but by now quite secularized, with only around 5 percent of citizens attending church on a regular basis, was, paradoxically, one of the few remaining nations with an established state church.

Alva agreed with the purposes of the commission. Church and state held one another in an unhealthy grip. The Church of Sweden was stagnating, with most citizens only nominal members; but because it was still partially administered by the state, its clergy felt needlessly entangled in a distasteful bureaucratic web. It was high time, moreover, to place other faiths on a more equitable footing with the Church of Sweden. But no sooner was the commission's grand design for disestablishment and greater interfaith equality ready, than it was already in trouble. Although many in the clergy agreed that change was needed, the proposals seemed too bold to many decision-making councils in the parishes and to Alva's own government. In the end, the main proposals were rejected. But they had set in motion a reform process that still continues, and it was agreed that other religious groups should henceforth receive state subsidies in proportion to the number of their members. Without being declared equal to the dominant state church, they had at least gained official recognition.

The theme of equality, between faiths, between believers and nonbelievers, and—still fiercely contested by a minority within the church—between men and women priests, had been in the background of the commission's debates from the beginning. As Alva looked back at her own childhood, she saw that the Sweden of the late 1960s was astoundingly different from the point of view of equality. There were no longer separate school systems for rich and poor. Women had access to education and to work as never before. Health care was a right for all citizens. Pensions protected every old person, regardless of previous work history. And poverty had been just about wiped out. Although most Swedes her age remembered economic hardship in their childhood, only a small proportion of young people reported having had that experience.

Both Alva and Gunnar observed ruefully, however, that the higher standard of living and the new freedoms had not brought the fellow-feeling and imaginative concern for others that reformers had hoped for. Alva, especially, had started out with great faith that if only people were freed, spiritually and materially, from the shackles that held them down, then they would be able to devote themselves to better parenting, more productive contributions to society, and more fulfilling human relationships. While she and Gunnar saw nothing but sentimentality in the view that the poverty, malnutrition, and injustices of the past gave greater scope for meaningful human lives, they were disturbed to witness the level of greed, materialism, and petty, self-promoting dishonesty that seemed to be rising, in Sweden as in other industrialized nations, during the sixties and seventies. In addition, they could see that some of the most urgent reforms had brought about unexpected new disparities.

Alva suggested, in response, that the time was ripe for a

careful look at where Swedish society stood in achieving the goal of equality. How far had it come? What costs had been incurred? And what remained to be done? When a government study group was formed in response to this proposal, she was, not unexpectedly, asked to head it. She was eager to do so, but she also knew that she would be treading on sensitive ground. Her own party was not always willing to press ahead with egalitarian reforms as imaginatively as she hoped, whereas conservatives challenged the steps already taken as "leveling" measures that threatened to bring a deadening uniformity to Swedish society. Was it right, still others asked, to extrapolate from equality within a community to that in a family or at the workplace? Or among nations? Did citizens really want to live in a more egalitarian society, anyway?

The members of the study group seemed to Alva as congenial as any she had ever worked with. They knew that they had a remarkable opportunity. It may have been the first time that a group of public servants ever sat down to brainstorm about all the possible steps toward greater equality in a society already as egalitarian as Sweden's, knowing that much of what they proposed had a reasonable chance of being put before the voters and ultimately implemented.

The resulting report, *Towards Equality,* turned out to be a headier exercise in social engineering than anything Alva had helped prepare up to then. In the name of equality, it addresses a vigorous redistribution of income, of social and cultural advantages, of educational opportunities, and of working conditions. It even recommends measures to alleviate unintended new forms of inequality that have sprung up in the wake of past reforms and other social changes. The extension of compulsory nine-year schooling to all children in Sweden, for example, which was carried out in the name of equal access to education, has brought about a troubling chasm within families—between those who have grown up in such a system and their parents, most of whom received only six years of frequently inadequate schooling. The remedy proposed is to direct part of an improved system of adult education specifically to those who have had least schooling. With greater numbers of women working has come a new need to ensure that children are well cared for, with society and both parents sharing the burden. Higher family allowances for each child are among the measures recommended, as well as paid parental leave after the birth of a child, to be divided between mothers and fathers as they see fit.

Alva did not foresee just how much opposition there would be from her own colleagues in the government when they saw an early draft of the report in the spring of 1969. Some of them disagreed with the direction Alva's group had suggested, others worried about costs, still others about the upcoming election campaign. In a letter to Gunnar written May 31, 1969, Alva told of a confrontation between the cabinet and her study group. A few, including Olof Palme, were on her side. The prime minister, Tage Erlander, maintained a cryptic silence. But a number of ministers attacked the report sharply. One of them proposed a rewritten version of the chapter on international equality that she characterized as "pure aspirin." She would be prepared to resign, she wrote, rather than stand for a watered-down report.

When the report finally appeared that summer, it could hardly be said to have been watered down. And a new edition, published three years later, concluded with a section listing a series of reforms that resulted in new tax laws, educational planning, housing, and revisions in criminal law. First among these measures was a decision to press for higher salaries for those earning least. Greater equality would gradually be achieved not by lowering high salaries but by lifting the lowest ones.

Even as the new edition was being prepared, however, the salary initiative was running into heavy weather. The government had chosen to raise the salaries of primary school teachers while leaving those of teachers in secondary and higher education untouched. The union representing academics and academically trained civil servants (including judges, officers in the armed services, the clergy, and many civil servants), reacted by asking key personnel to go on strike. The government responded with a lockout that idled all teachers, army officers, Foreign Office personnel, and many others. Sweden entered a period of crisis "at the top," as Alva wrote. She was deeply disturbed that people would go out on strike, not because their own salaries had been cut, but simply because salaries were going up for those lowest on the wage scale and most in need of support. After partial retreat by both sides, the crisis was resolved, but much bitterness remained. Alva found herself on the defensive in the press and in some Social Democratic circles. She wrote to me of her failure to predict the crisis:

> Both about raising primarily the lowest salaries in the nego-tiations and about equality in general, we who are *rationalists and moralists* have perhaps underestimated the political diffi-culties: that is, quite simply, people's irrational egoism.

Olof Palme, who had been named prime minister in 1969, was strongly supportive of Alva on this issue; he also impressed her by his political astuteness in timing the presentation of the various remaining proposals concerning equality so as to increase their chances. Boyish-looking at forty-two, with lively, shining eyes and sharp features, he was young enough to be her son. She knew that conservatives regarded him as a maverick for having joined the Social Democratic party in spite of his origins in a venerable Swedish banking family. And she had witnessed the anger that his quick-witted, cutting sarcasms could inspire among adversaries. But she found him an invigorating presence in the government, not least because of his idealism and his broad-gauged interest in world affairs.

It was natural for her to stand by him during the late sixties and early seventies, when his outspoken criticism of the war in Vietnam precipitated a crisis in Sweden's relations with the United States. Public horror over the war's brutality had proved nearly as divisive in Sweden and many European nations as in the United States, pitting young people against older generations, rocking even the stablest institutions. Gunnar, as chairman of the Swedish citizens' committee against the war, insisted, as did Alva and Palme, that he was against President Nixon's war policy, not in any sense against the American people, who, he knew, were increasingly opposed to the war themselves. But there is no doubt that in Sweden, as elsewhere, many others fell for a mindless form of anti-Americanism. At times, mass marches and demonstrations outside the U.S. embassy turned to violence. Palme's willingness to shelter U.S. deserters strained relations between the two countries further. Ambassadors were mutually withdrawn between the fall of 1972 and the spring of 1974.

America's preoccupation with Vietnam, along with the Soviet retrenchment at home and its defense of the invasion of Czechoslovakia in 1968 as consonant with the Brezhnev doctrine, made for an especially arid period in international efforts toward disarmament and human rights. The most that could be hoped for was that a policy of détente between the superpowers might reduce the chances of war, at least temporarily, and that the Strategic Arms Limitation Talks (SALT) between the Soviet Union and the United States might limit the quantity of new missiles produced, though not the increased destructiveness of each one. Because these talks excluded all but the two great powers, they offered little relief to the vulnerability felt by many other nations.

In 1973, Alva came to the reluctant conclusion that she should retire from the government and thus also from her post as chief Swedish delegate to the negotiations. Her physician had first recommended that she resign in 1969, warning that the heart condition that she had inherited from her parents was exacerbated by the stress of her work and especially her travels. When she finally stepped down, she knew that the time had come. She was seventy-one years old and nearing the close of what she called the "second act" of her involvement with disarmament issues.

As she looked back on the twelve years she had devoted to those issues, she was struck by the contrast between the many successes she had helped bring about in domestic Swedish policies and her sense of failure internationally to nudge governments toward a reversal of the arms race:

> In Sweden we were successful; I became accustomed to see our plans, my dreams being victorious. However, in a later

period, that has changed. The great exception to my habit of winning through, at last, has been the shocking experience of failure in the field of disarmament.

Alva also felt a sharp disparity between this painful failure to bring about meaningful steps toward disarmament and the honors that were increasingly bestowed on her for her work in this very arena of disarmament. As early as 1950 she had received her first honorary degree, from Mount Holyoke College in Massachusetts; many more were to follow. In 1970 she and Gunnar had jointly won the prestigious German Book Publishers' Peace Prize, which had gone, in earlier years to Albert Schweitzer, Martin Buber, and Sarvepalli Radhakrishnan, among others. The German citation praised them for working, through scientific research and personal engagement, for peace wherever it was endangered: "Thus they fulfill their own call for individuals in our time to be both dreamers and realists." But Alva felt keenly the gulf between such exalted words and the little that was actually being accomplished.

Alva's farewell speech at the UN Disarmament Commission reflected her sense of this discrepancy. All day long she had listened to one delegate after another commend her for her efforts to bring disarmament issues to the foreground. When the Japanese delegate, Mr. Masahiro Nishibori, praised her as "the conscience of the disarmament movement," many others seconded him. In responding, Alva called, one last time in that great hall, for freezing the development of new weapons. And once again she chided the superpowers for the deadlock so apparent at all levels of negotiations. She explained that she would happily forgo all the generous praise that her colleagues had lavished on her if the slightest move could be made, instead, to break the deadlock:

> May I end this last official statement of mine by asking my colleagues: "When is some action for disarmament to start in earnest?"

15

Disarmament

❖ ❖ ❖ ❖

There exists a necessary sort
of madness: to believe that precisely you
can change the world.
Madness that borders
on genius
and that is also the simplest
everyday wisdom. . . .

Bernt Rosengren*

Peace, Alva had concluded, was much too grand a word for her. In setting out to write *The Game of Disarmament,* she had no desire to add to the innumerable vacuous writings on the benefits of peace or the evils of war. Lasting peace might be a distant goal, but what mattered right away was to bring about more urgent results: to limit the role of war and above all to reduce the threat of a nuclear conflagration. Having taken a strong anti-Nazi stance during the Second World War and supported Finland's effort to defend itself against the Soviet invasion in 1939, she did not write from an absolute pacifist perspective: she took for granted that nations needed military means of deterrence and, in case of attack, the capacity for self-defense. It might not even be possible ever to eliminate nuclear weapons altogether, she suggested; it would be fruitless to try to recreate the state of "nuclear innocence."

Rather, Alva wanted her book to sound a sharp alarm about

---

*Verse 2 of a poem by Bernt Rosengren read at Alva Myrdal's memorial service, February 16, 1986: "*Bara genom att inte blunda*" ("Only by not shutting your eyes").

the vast, needless, and ruinous arms race and about the precarious "balance of terror" that placed all of humanity at risk. The note of alarm was needed, she felt, because of the almost-complete paralysis of the superpowers with respect to serious effort at reversing course.

She herself had been taken in at first by their rhetoric about disarmament, only to realize that what to her was a genuine drama with the fate of the planet at stake seemed little more than a game to them. It was an infinitely complex game, to be sure, the more absorbing because it was so mystifying to outsiders, but a game nonetheless. Insofar as government leaders and their advisers dealt with that drama as merely a game, it was the more likely to have a tragic ending.

As for the delegates traveling to and from innumerable disarmament sessions, writing their myriads of position papers, haggling endlessly over the minutest points without knowing, any more than she had, that it was all simply a game—what of them? Perhaps, she concluded, their work could most charitably be described as occupational therapy.

Alva was the more eager to get started, therefore, on exploring all that had contributed to stalling serious disarmament measures and proposing an agenda for regaining momentum. She and Gunnar were planning to divide their time between periods of work in Sweden and the United States: she on her new book, and Gunnar on a book that he intended to call *An American Dilemma Revisited,* in which he would update his earlier study in the light of events since its publication in 1944.

As they had so many times in the past, they were once more arriving at the end of one segment of their lives only to embark on another. They had kept moving from continent to continent and from one series of problems to another, always drawing on their combined past experience to help structure and enrich the new project.

I found the zest with which Alva and Gunnar undertook each such change inspiriting, no matter how familiar I was with the ruptures and anxieties—at times terrors—that came in its wake. There was grandeur and a sense of high adventure, even exaltation, each time they set forth to explore a new set of problems and to propose a blueprint for combating them. It was impossible not to be caught up in this spirit, seeing the future as thus open rather than plodding resignedly along one set course throughout life. New projects were always waiting; still others might be around the bend.

As the decades passed, I could see how they undertook each new venture more defiantly, aware that the odds were shifting. They could hardly count on living to complete the tasks they had set themselves, much less witness societies change in the ways they recommended. Yet stopping was out of the question. It had turned out to be impossible for them to stay home and simply "learn to grow old together," as Alva had suggested in a letter to Gunnar from India in 1957. They would rather take the risk of foundering.

The two were working in New York during the fall of 1974 when Gunnar received the news that he had been awarded the Nobel Prize in economics, which had been added five years earlier to the existing prizes for the sciences, literature, and peace. Gunnar and the arch-conservative Austrian economist Friedrich von Hayek shared the award for their separate, pioneering studies of monetary theory and their analyses of the links between economic, social, and institutional conditions. In Gunnar's award, special mention was made of his books *The Political Element in the Development of Economic Theory, An American Dilemma,* and *Asian Drama.*

Sharing the prize in this way was probably as much of a cold shower for von Hayek as for Gunnar. The two were polar opposites from a political point of view. Neither they nor anyone else could avoid thinking that the prize was the result of an ideological balancing act. Many among their colleagues even surmised that the choice reflected a condescending joke on the part of members of the Swedish economics establishment. Although they could hardly avoid giving their brilliant but cosmopolitan and flamboyantly un-Swedish compatriot a prize, they had it within their power to do so in a way that prevented him from relishing the honor or feeling truly recognized in his home country. Already, many criticized the Nobel prizes for literature and for peace as motivated too often by ideological considerations. From then on Gunnar would level the same charge against the economics prize, arguing that it might be best to abolish prizes in which politics played such an intrusive role.

Derek happened to be in New York when the announcement came. He brought Gunnar a bottle of fine wine to toast him along with Alva, only to find him sarcastic and downplaying the event. True, not receiving the prize at all would have been troubling to Gunnar, now seventy-six, since a number of those to whom it had already gone had been younger colleagues of his. Yet being awarded the prize in this manner clearly gave him little sense of recognition for his life's work.

Morosely, Gunnar urged us not to travel to Stockholm for the ceremony itself. When it took place he went through it with stoic dignity. A photograph shows him sitting next to Aleksandr Solzhenitsyn, who had received the Nobel Prize for literature four years earlier but could accept it in person only after he had been forced to leave the Soviet Union in 1974. Both men look out at the festivities with somber, questioning eyes.

In Gunnar's Nobel lecture, entitled "The Equality Issue in World Development," he contrasted the embarrassingly naive rhetoric, in the UN and elsewhere, about the right to be "free from hunger" with the realities in poor nations and detailed the stark failures of the richer nations to address these realities in a serious manner. He delineated, once again, the growing gap between rich and poor nations—an idea that many still regarded as unduly pessimistic but that would eventually become a commonplace, as was already the case with many of the words he had coined, such as *stagflation* and *underclass*. His pessimism about the prospect for the poorest nations would deepen further in the decades to come, and he would increasingly insist that financial assistance to poorer nations would be squandered so long as they did not take drastic steps against corruption, mismanagement, and political oppression.

In order to prepare his Nobel lecture, Gunnar had had to interrupt his work on *An American Dilemma Revisited*. He would set aside the work on this book again and again during the years to come in order to assist Alva with her book or to work on intervening projects of his own. Above all, however, his work on the *Dilemma* was delayed by illness and by advancing age. He had suffered a mild heart attack in 1970, and his lifelong heavy smoking made it increasingly difficult for him to breathe freely. His deafness troubled him, and as he neared eighty his eyesight was gradually giving way. Walking, too, had gradually become more laborious for him, but the doctors were still misdiagnosing what turned out to be symptoms of Parkinson's disease, attributing them to the hip injury from his car accident in 1952.

When an operation to replace his left hip in 1975 only incapacitated him further, he became deeply despondent. He spent months, Alva wrote, without any strength or desire to work and with pains and cramps that left him limp. She ached with pity for him, the more so because she knew how he had feared such decrepitude since his accident so long ago. "It is so diabolically hard on him," she wrote. Yet to the rest of us he would acknowledge no such feelings. Rather, he discoursed with almost-scientific precision and seeming ease on each and every symptom, while maintaining that all his problems "stopped below the neck" and that his scholarly work would therefore not be affected in the long run.

The only thing that Gunnar feared more than his own deterioration was the possibility of Alva's dying before him. His concern intensified during the 1970's as she grew visibly more frail, slowed down by angina and by greater fatigue than in the past. She had to take medication to counteract high blood pressure and to use nitroglycerine tablets when her pain from angina grew too severe. Both her parents and her sister Rut had died of heart disease long before they reached Alva's age, and her two younger brothers, Folke and Stig, suffered from it as well. When Gunnar and Alva came to visit us in Cambridge, Massachusetts, in the spring of 1975, I noted in my diary how nearly transparent Alva's pallor was and how Gunnar hovered over her like a solicitous thundercloud. He recited her symptoms over and over again like a litany, gloomily warning her not to overdo and taking her pulse many times each day.

She seemed half understanding, half rebellious at his efforts to monitor her health. If opportunities arose for independent travel, she would seize them; but not for long, since she knew that he, too, needed help more than in the past. She wrote me that she feared illness and death more for him than for her, just as he did for her. Caring for one another's needs, they now lived together in a more fragile but at a times closer symbiosis than ever before. Friends who visited them saw different sides of this symbiosis: the concern and tenderness they showed one another, their unfailing fascination with one another's views on political as on all other matters, but also Gunnar's incessant demands for Alva's attention and for her services, at times his brusqueness and her silent withdrawal. After so many decades together, it was as impossible as ever to pigeonhole their relationship.

When it came to Alva's work on her book, both of them agreed that it should have priority, given the ominous world situation, and that it should move ahead as energetically as possible. She found his advice indispensable, even though his suggestions for revising and correcting the different chapters added greatly to her labors. He set aside all other work during the summer of 1975 in order to go over her manuscript as carefully as if it were his own. In a letter written on September 1 of that year, she declared:

I am *enormously* grateful. I have also had to learn to sit—like him—like a slave at the desk, not go out, not prepare food, not give in to any extracurricular activities. Not even sit in the sun on our new balcony. One thing is certain—never again a thick book. Especially since there is reason to hurry with this one—one never knows how long one lives. And the material, reality, changes so fast. But the book will probably turn out *well*. I am happy about it and am therefore glad to work so hard. But it isn't my rhythm. And of course I am also used to having more assistance, which also allows for interruptions, respite.

This was an explanation. But also useful for me as a way of summing up and thinking through the situation.

During the summer of 1976 Alva labored still more intensely on correcting and updating the galley proofs of the book. The work was doubly hard since she was going through the Swedish and the English versions simultaneously. Gunnar was at her side, pressing her continually for greater rigor and clarity. Toward the end she was bone tired. Her only thought was that once it was over, she and Gunnar would be on their way to the small, idyllic house they owned in the little town of Mariefred, an hour's drive from Stockholm. Two weeks later she wrote me:

> A year of veritable galley slavery lay behind me on August 3 when I mailed the last proofs at 11 and we left at 12 for an utterly free, sunny holiday in Mariefred. And the following afternoon I collapsed!

She would never forget the horror of what happened—later diagnosed as a combined heart attack and brain seizure. She had been going down the narrow stairs to the garden when she was hit by a shattering headache and paralysis. She stood, her hands as if frozen to the railing, inwardly shrieking but unable to make the slightest sound. Gunnar found it hard at first to understand why she simply stood there, halfway down the stairs, clinging mutely to the railing, her eyes terror-struck, but he finally called an ambulance. On her way to the hospital she heard what those who were leaning over her were saying but was still unable to utter a single word.

Within a few days Alva recovered her ability to move and to speak, but she remained weak and exhausted throughout the fall. Over the years that followed, similar attacks would strike when she least expected them. Most of them were milder and did not leave her paralyzed or entirely mute. Some lasted for hours, others whole days. Her doctors prescribed medication that helped only moderately; what she needed more than anything, they suggested, was to relax at home and to give up some of her most demanding activities—above all her extensive traveling and lecturing. But she was loath to do so, especially during that fall, when her book was about to appear.

Instead she traveled to New York, Washington, and Boston in order to launch the book. I met her in New York and went with her when she testified before a Senate committee in Washington at the request of Senator Stuart Symington. Calling the book "the best summary of the growing danger to the world of nuclear proliferation that I have ever seen," he wanted his colleagues to hear her speak. And she was eager, after putting in so much work on a subject about which she felt so strongly, to have its message reach as many people in decision-making positions as possible. By electing to forgo all royalties for the book, she was able to have copies sent to members of Congress as well as to government officials in the United States and a number of other countries, and to insist that it be sold at the lowest possible price so that it would be more accessible to students and other potential readers.

She brought us copies of both the Swedish and the American editions, which had appeared almost simultaneously. The American jacket showed two sets of missiles, grayish and near-black, ominously facing one another against a dirty gray sky. The Swedish cover featured a sculpture she had long admired by Johan Peter Molin of two muscular Viking *bältespännare,* or "belt strainers." Bound together with a large belt, each brandishing a knife, the two men have no recourse but to fight on until one or both die.

While Alva found that the first image made the arms race appear too simplemindedly mechanical, as if driven more by weapons than by human choice, she did not wish to go so far as to imply that the balance of terror between the two superpowers was as personal and hopeless as in the second. Both images were needed. Nuclear weapons had made the East-West contest, unlike the struggles of past duelers and belt strainers, endanger even the most innocent and uninvolved of bystanders. But human choice could still bring about a reversal before it was too late. The arms race had become "the major intellectual and moral dilemma of our time. Having been created solely by man, it lies in our power to solve it."

The book opens with a personal account of the road Alva had traveled, arriving at near-despair about the increasingly dangerous inaction of the superpowers on disarmament. The history of disarmament efforts, she argues, is one of a long sequence of lost opportunities, with each side stalling whenever the other showed the slightest signs of movement. She warns of the progressive and accelerating militarization of the Third World, which both East and West encourage through their far-flung alliances and their arms trade, and of the irrational laxity of measures ostensibly meant to prevent the spread of nuclear weapons, even to the most unstable of regimes.

This dismal series of lost opportunities has been driven along, Alva suggests, by a gross miscalculation on the part of policy analysts and leaders in successive governments East and West. Each side has tried to keep up with the other, past all reasonable needs for deterrence, out of fear that the other is somehow "getting ahead" and tipping the "balance of terror." Yet "the military capabilities do not need to be 'equal' or 'balanced' when the limits for effective threats of terror devastation are long since overreached." Persistent miscalculation, stemming from a twisted concept of equality and driven along by vested interests in both camps, has pressed nations to buy ever greater insecurity at higher and higher costs—while desperately needed social programs go unmet because of the ruinous drain on resources.

And the miscalculation, reenacted year in and year out, has in turn resulted in an equally gross misallocation—human, financial, and material—of national and global resources:

What kind of thinking lies behind the fact that 400,000 scientists, at least 40% of the world's best brains, or in terms of money half of all resources for research are devoted to improve still further the weapons technology which is already incredibly efficient for mass death?

What kind of calculation lies behind the amassing of nuclear weapons such that the two superpowers now have in their hands what corresponds to a million Hiroshimas?

Precisely because the superpowers have become so overinsured militarily, Alva argues, and because even minimal foresight should warn them of the long-term domestic consequences of squandering desperately scarce resources, they have ample incentives to take brave new steps, even unilaterally, so as to initiate a mutual chain reaction of deescalation. They have everything to gain by shifting gears so as to lead the way in disarmament rather than to continue to collaborate in stalling all progress.

Rereading the book in 1991, with significant new arms reduction agreements being negotiated, it is hard to recall how, at the time it was published and for over a decade afterward, officials and experts recited in unison all the reasons why such steps were impossible even to contemplate. And it is sobering to see her conclusions about what the feeble limits set on chemical warfare and nuclear proliferation may portend. If nations fail to enforce a ban not only on using but on producing or exporting means of chemical warfare, she argues, and if the superpowers do not set the highest standards for their own conduct in this respect, the time will come when poison gas and a multitude of chemical weapons will serve as the poor nations' nuclear weapons, capable of wiping out indigenous populations deemed expendable or of being launched against external enemies. And if a nonproliferation treaty "with teeth" is not signed and implemented for nuclear weapons and all related technology, there will be no way to keep them from spreading, even to unstable, possibly fanatical governments embroiled in fierce regional conflicts.

The second part of *The Game of Disarmament* is devoted to detailed step-by-step suggestions for moving toward such treaties and, more generally, for gradual measures to cut back existing armaments, both nuclear and conventional. These measures would culminate in an agreement on a "minimum nuclear deterrent," leaving some few and carefully controlled nuclear weapons in the hands of the great powers.

Alva's perspective, throughout, takes into account the many peoples the world over who see their survival endangered because of conflicts in which they have no part. They are the pawns in a game that they never wanted to play. So are those young people and future generations whose lives may be blighted long after the present conflicts had been overtaken by yet others. She sees the peoples of Europe as running a special risk of being sacrificed as pawns in any East-West nuclear confrontation. They are not about to go to war once again with one another, yet they are poised in high military preparedness for a war not of their making. For persons living in Europe, all abstract talk of a "limited war"—a war limited to Europe, if at all possible—that could prevent the conflict reaching either Soviet or U.S. territory concerns a nearly unthinkable reality: "nothing less than utter devastation, mass killings, and, most probably, annihilation."

Although she directs such criticism to both superpowers jointly, Alva makes clear that she does not regard their political systems as equivalent. Her allegiance to a democratic form of government was well known. Yet potential victims of nuclear war would suffer the same devastation no matter which side started a nuclear war. She takes for granted that calls for deescalation have to be addressed to both sides alike, since both are entrapped in the spiraling arms race, seemingly unable or unwilling to reverse gears.

With the book to publicize and lectures to give, Alva's visit to the United States had been exhausting. When she returned to Sweden in November 1976, she wrote me that the doctors had asked her to enter the hospital for a complete rest cure, having concluded that she was apparently unable to follow their orders about curtailing her travel.

For a few more years, Alva and Gunnar would continue their old life-style, living now in the United States, now in Sweden, moving between continents and nations for speeches and awards and study trips. But by the late 1970s I knew that I could not expect them to come to stay with us in Cambridge as regularly as before; I tried instead to visit them in Sweden as often as I could, as did Kaj and our various children. Each time we came we saw them struggling to keep working in spite of obstacles that would have brought most people to their knees.

I began to visualize that struggle as the breaking of waves rolling onto a beach diagonally from two different directions. From one direction I could see the vitality, the habits, and the ambitions of a lifetime impelling them always onward, with new projects overtaking those that were receding and still others only half formed in the background. Yet from the other direction moved toward them so many of the impairments and illnesses and periods of fatigue that old age can bring. Both Alva and Gunnar kept going as long as they could and longer than most. But where the contending waves met and broke, they were battered into a loss of initiative, a slowing down, a sense of dejection at times and deep fear—how would it all end?

After an especially grueling transatlantic flight in the spring of 1977, during which Gunnar had slept on the airplane's floor so that Alva might stretch out as best she could on their combined seats, they learned, on arriving in Stockholm, that both of Alva's brothers had died—Stig, her youngest brother of a heart attack just before they had embarked on their flight and Folke ten days earlier. Neither letters nor a telegram had reached them in New York, and the shock on hearing the news so suddenly was immense. Now she, the oldest of five siblings, was the only one left. For over a year she suffered from moods of bleak despondency that came and went. Medication could only partly help, she wrote me in 1978: "it can of course not alter reality—that life will soon end. My anxiety is not so much about death itself as about a long torment of dying."

Adding to her despondency was the relentless escalation of the arms race during the years that followed. At the time she wrote her book there had been talk of détente; since then, the rhetoric of hatred and aggression had grown commonplace. No major arms control agreements had been signed, and the brutality of the Soviet attack on Afghanistan had helped bring about the collapse of the SALT II negotiations, modest though that agreement would have been. At about the same time the NATO governments decided, in response to the Soviet Union's deployment of ss-20 missiles in Eastern Europe, to install new Pershing II and cruise missiles in Europe that would be capable of pinpointing targets inside the Soviet Union with great accuracy. The Soviets, sensing an escalated threat, spoke of matching these Western missiles when they were deployed.

In an updated edition of her book in 1982, Alva describes how the pace of threat and counterthreat, fear and counterfear, grows in such an arms dynamic. With hawks in both camps in the ascendancy, advocates of "war-fighting" strategies were bringing the world closer to military confrontation by "turning to scenarios that demand the need to successfully fight wars, not just deter them."

During the spring of 1980, as Alva watched superpower relations deteriorate still further and as Ronald Reagan thundered against what he would, as President, call the "evil empire" and Soviet leaders replied in kind, she received a surprise message. She had been selected as the first recipient of the Albert Einstein Peace Prize, designed to honor each year "the person who has contributed most significantly to the prevention of nuclear war and to the strengthening of international peace." Alva was about to enter the hospital for a hip operation, having fallen and broken a bone shortly before. Nevertheless, she wrote me that she was sure she would be strong enough to travel to New York for the ceremony by May. She had met and admired Einstein in Princeton during the war, and as she planned her acceptance speech she referred to his decision after Hiroshima and Nagasaki to take as his highest priority the struggle against nuclear war:

> How much more seriously should all of us others then not take that issue—As we do not. Yes, I mean it: right in the face of the stupendous risks of our time, *public opinion is asleep.* . . . With every move upwards in the arms spiral, *peace is betrayed.* And, worst of all, youth is betrayed. . . . We are actively involved in *teaching* the young to accept brutality, aggressiveness, hawkish nationalism and unconcern for human rights as a way of life. But it should not have to be *their* way of life.

Many friends and family members were in New York to be with Alva when she received the award on May 31, 1980. A photo shows Gunnar, pride illuminating his pale, drawn face as from within, seated with Derek and me as we watched her receive the award. Our son, Tomas, then eleven, had been asked to hand her the crystal bowl commemorating the occasion and to say a few words about her if he so chose. Reluctant to do so, he concluded his part in the ceremony with a hug and a kiss instead.

In her address, Alva spoke of the need to shape much stronger public resistance against war and incitement to aggression. "We must create a resistance movement of public opinion against the war propaganda—the whole ongoing militarization of our culture." World public opinion could, if mobilized, once again exert a powerful force, as it had against nuclear testing in the atmosphere or against the war in Vietnam, and as it was beginning to do against the war in Afghanistan. Now it was time for widespread action at the grass-roots level.

In a press conference after the ceremony, Alva added that she saw such an opinion growing, especially in Europe, in the face of heightened fear that its territory might become the battleground for a war between two outside powers. As she wrote in a new conclusion for the reissue of the book:

> Europe has without its own volition been chosen by a kind of mutual, albeit usually tacit, agreement between the two superpowers to become the battlefield in a potential war of their own making. It is a battlefield now vastly oversaturated with their military threats and preparations. And the situation is deteriorating rapidly.

By then, citizens in many European nations had grown restive about the possibility that a nuclear war might be unleashed on their territory. In Europe as in the United States, peace movements were making themselves heard. Physicians, theologians, scientists, and other professionals were joining together in order to combat ignorance about the consequences of nuclear war. Labor unions, student associations, church groups, youth organizations, and political parties were organizing huge meetings and taking a stand against the increased militarization of Europe. Peace research institutes such as SIPRI contributed statistical and other information not previously available. To Alva, these developments represented renewed hope. Just as, in her youth, pressures from the labor movement, the cooperative movement, the temperance movement, and the women's movement had helped to mobilize the reforms that had transformed Sweden, so now, she hoped, world public opinion could help overcome the paralysis among leaders with respect to serious arms control.

She herself had decided in the late seventies that she wanted to devote her remaining years to promoting such citizen involvement in activities resisting war. In 1978, she and Gunnar had formed and endowed the Myrdal Foundation to support broadly based citizens' groups and to make information on issues of international security and disarmament more easily accessible, beginning with the earliest school years. In order to aid in coordinating groups working for peace in Sweden, Alva also helped found a Peace Forum (*Fredsforum*) and became its chairman in 1981. It was organized with the help of the Swedish labor movement—in part, as Alva indicated in a letter to me, to thwart communist efforts to take over or infiltrate so many peace organizations. At the same time she founded Women for Peace, a movement that spread throughout communities across Europe.

Although Alva could not attend all the meetings of the various peace groups, she spoke at a number of rallies, and her calls to action were read aloud at the start of many others. Many women, young and old, identified with Alva as she continued into her eighties taking such a strong stance. She in turn did everything she could to encourage more women to join in the antiwar debate. But she also cautioned them against falling for the illusion that they were somehow uniquely suited to excel as "peacemakers." Already she sensed a renewed cult of motherhood among a minority of peace activists, even what she called a "uterine mystique," or *livmodersmystik* (the literal meaning of *livmoder,* the Swedish for "uterus," is "life-mother").

Alva herself never laid claim to special expertise in matters of war and peace on the ground of being a woman. She had long rejected all efforts to stereotype women, whether by men or by women themselves. Idealization isolates and weakens those idealized, she used to argue, and

> the more you exaggerate so-called femininity, the more completely you deprive men of the tender, considerate, gentle role for which they, too, have the natural prerequisites.

In raising this issue, Alva renewed a dialogue about the role of women that, for her, had begun when she first read the works of Ellen Key. Key had adopted ancient stereotypes about masculinity and femininity in order to promote the liberation of women from second-class citizenship; but in so doing, she had forged new shackles for them out of the maternal instincts she saw as governing all they did. Now Alva was reaching out to those younger women who claimed that maternal instincts guaranteed special status in the fight against war. She saw them struggling, as she once had, to combine family concerns with an active working and political life. But active motherhood comes to an end, she reminded them, and not all women want to be mothers. Anatomy was not destiny, in the peace struggle any more than elsewhere. And to the extent that women aim to monopolize the nurturant role, they shut men out from that domain. In the antiwar movement it was more important than ever to reach out to men, given what she saw as "their traditional militaristic legacy."

What the peace movement needed from men and women alike, Alva insisted, was that they buttress passionate concern for the future of humanity with clear analysis based on careful, at times brutally honest study of the facts. Emphasis on concern alone led too easily to unpersuasive sentimentality, whereas analysis by itself could peter out in the game playing she had witnessed so often in disarmament negotiations. There was no need to place masculine and feminine labels on such characteristics, and indeed there was great risk in doing so.

When the reissue of *The Game of Disarmament* appeared in the fall of 1982 it had a new preface, "An American Update—1982: 'So Much Worse,'" along with a last chapter entitled "Europe and Disarmament: 1982." Since the book was first published six years earlier, Alva argues, the arms race has intensified to the point that she now sees the superpowers as on a catastrophic collision course. And while a new and deeper understanding of the mounting threat is evident in an avalanche of scientific and popular literature, this understanding has, so far, led to no breakthroughs. If one chooses not to despair but rather to hope, the conditions for hope to be reasonable must be clearly set forth: above all, the two superpowers must be brought to *want* disarmament. Popular opinion movements, decision makers in each nation, weapons producers—all must come together to press, as first steps, for a pledge of no first use of nuclear weapons, a freeze on their production and deployment, and the coordinated conversion from military to civilian production.

> The ruin of the planet is there for all to contemplate. But so, too, is its potential richness if we learn to cooperate. We still have a choice. But we must act now as never before.

16

Displacements

❖ ❖ ❖ ❖

Those who reach high often lose, I fear,
contact with reality and with humanity.
Did this happen with Alva? With Gunnar?
There is a power sphere . . . where abstractions begin to form lethal ice crystals
on the plane flying up there so high.

OLOF LAGERCRANTZ, PERSONAL LETTER, 1986

The danger described by Lagercrantz was one that Alva knew and feared. She had observed many in high public office isolated and encrusted in the manner he described. Even Indira Gandhi, the shy young widow whom Alva had come to know in Nehru's household during her years in India, seemed to change completely after becoming prime minister of India in 1966. When Mrs. Gandhi attempted quasi-dictatorial rule in 1975, Alva wrote me that such an abuse of everything that Mrs. Gandhi and her father, Nehru, had stood for could be explained only as a personality transformation brought about by "the isolation of power and the panic of suspicion."

Alva had often seen these dangerous changes in less extreme form: how human bonds could freeze and grow brittle for ambassadors, ministers, and high international officials as they shuttled from one continent to another, their minds always on some new crisis or vast long-range scheme. Her awareness of these risks in the rarefied air of high public office made her all the more determined to maintain close, fully responsive relationships in her own life, no matter how demanding and at times confining her public obligations.

As I think back on Alva's struggle to do so in the last decades of her life, I have to take seriously the danger of distancing and loss of contact to which Lagercrantz points. How did her ties to each of us in the family fare during the 1960s and afterward, when she was increasingly admired as a model public figure, given vast responsibilities at work, and presented with one honor and international prize after another? Did she feel more remote from us, distanced, as Lagercrantz wrote? And we—did any of us feel overshadowed, frozen out, perhaps "displaced" by her in this new, more public phase of her life?

By the 1960s, Alva had long enjoyed the freedom that comes when children grow up and move away from home. Even as adults, none of us had lived at home with her and Gunnar since the years in India. Although she kept in close touch with us all, her day-by-day child-rearing responsibilities were over. Her life seemed an exultant vindication of the thesis she had advanced in *Women's Two Roles:* that the period of active parenting, however strenuous it might be, leaves a number of decades free for most women to devote to work outside the home. In speaking to women's groups, she repeatedly stressed the need for them to look beyond the years of child care. They ought not to restrict their own life plans by forcing their parenting role on their children for life. "Once a mother, always a mother" should not be overdone: rather, the independence of one's grown children called for respect at the very least, and preferably for the close friendship that she herself so desired.

That closeness had never been fully possible in her relationship with Gunnar's parents any more than with her own. By the time she and Gunnar returned from India in 1961, they found his eighty-four-year-old mother Sofie in declining health. Along with Gunnar's brother and sisters, they had provided financial support for her since she was widowed, in 1934. By 1963, she moved from Dalecarlia to Stockholm where she could share an apartment with Gunnar's sister Mela and be near her three other children. Alva and Gunnar kept up with her and invited her to stay with them at intervals until her death two years later. But as her deafness and confusion increased, Gunnar gave up all efforts at communication with her during these visits, leaving Alva to see to her needs as best she could.

Alva wrote me about her pain in seeing Sofie become more and more dependent on others, and about her fear of what would happen to her and Gunnar if they became similarly debilitated. Gunnar pushed all such thoughts aside every time she raised them, but Alva grew more certain than ever that she would not wish to live on beyond a certain point of incapacitation. She joined an organization advocating the right to die and signed a Living Will specifying the conditions under which she wished no further medical intervention to keep her alive. She also began to speak out in public about what she saw as the right to leave life voluntarily. Late in life she wrote that she did not agree with the conventional taboo against all suicide and found it disturbing that people sorely pressed by illness should have to feel guilty about having such thoughts:

> I frightened the French when a TV interview with me ended with an explanation about the right to end life freely as a "human right."
> . . . If one is not afraid of dying, then one can postpone the decision on the basis of this sense of freedom from day to day, and enjoy each day that soon becomes months and, why not, years, as a *gain*. "On Borrowed Time" is the name of a fine play I have read.

Alva's attitude to aging, disability, and death had an additional, more instinctive component. The older she grew, the more she preferred the company of younger people. By middle age, most people seemed to her to have settled too placidly into their routines, unwilling to take chances or to ask the most troubling questions. They could be guppies in an aquarium for all they cared about the larger world. And yet the security of that world was anything but assured, even for the generations of their own children and grandchildren, let alone those not yet born. It was their fate that concerned Alva most—the generations that risked being cheated by the rapaciousness and belligerence of so many of their elders and the indifference of still more. To be sure, many younger people exhibited the same closure of spirit she saw among her contemporaries, but with them there was at least still hope for change.

This preference for those younger than herself was clear not only in Alva's dealings with colleagues at work and when she lectured or spoke at political rallies, but also in the family, especially after she had lost her sister and closest friend Rut in 1959. Apart from Gunnar, it was to her children and grandchildren that she directed her affection most abundantly. With all of us, Alva kept up the same lively, down-to-earth correspondence that she had carried on from India, reaching out to take part in our lives and keeping us in touch with one another's doings. She kept separate hempen baskets by her bedside for clippings to send to each of us concerning our different interests. And even though we lived continents apart, she arranged her travels so as to have as many visits with each of us as possible, indulging her gift as a photographer to capture her observations of each family and to send them around to everyone else in the family.

Alva would try to squeeze in visits with Kaj and her family in Göttingen, West Germany, on her way by night train from Stockholm to UN meetings in Geneva. Because the trip itself took several days, she could never stop for long and tried the harder to make every minute count. Kaj remembers these visits as lightning-quick efforts at intensive contact that were rarely relaxed and "normal." They spent time together with the children, went to the theater, talked about books and about plans for the future— and then Alva was gone, like the wind, as fast as she had arrived. Kaj often felt torn between admiration for Alva and fear of not being able to convey enough of her own life and activities fast enough for such brief visits, especially in the turbulence caused by Alva's intent focusing on the doings of her three lively children and on Horst's research and travels. Genuine dialogue was difficult, she remembers with regret in looking back at that period when Alva would "dive in like a rocket surrounded by air from the whole world."

Alva's visits with Derek and me and our children in Belmont,

Massachusetts, where we had lived since 1959, were more relaxed. Beginning in 1961 and for over a decade her UN work frequently took her to New York. It was easy for her to come for weekends with us or join us for short vacations by the seashore. Having been so far apart from her during her years in India—unlike Kaj, who had lived with her there before her marriage—I now felt in closer contact with her than at any time I could remember.

If I close my eyes, I can see her arriving all over again. She would step off the plane or train, vibrant with anticipation, casually elegant with her matching hat, coat, and luggage, several leather camera bags slung over her shoulder, scanning the crowd for our faces, ready with a swooping hug for the grandchildren first of all. She came as an old-time world traveler with tales to tell from all the exotic corners of the earth that she had visited since we last met, but at the same time intent on entering our more intimate, family-centered, slower-paced lives as fully as she could. We marveled at her ability to detach her mind so completely from her meetings, speeches, memoranda, and resolutions. The minute she sat down with the children she would focus all her attention on them—playing card games, telling stories, listening intently, taking each one seriously as an individual with unique yet open-ended potential.

Once the children were off playing or in bed she would then turn, with the same engagement, to what she used to call our "talk-fests" as we celebrated her visit with lobster, blueberry muffins, and other American foods that she especially loved. We could feel her relief at being able to throw her diplomatic, carefully restrained public self to the winds and talk uninhibitedly, exchanging views with us about every subject that came to mind, from the often theatrical unfolding of world affairs to the bizarre, at times comical, doings of public personalities. We could hardly feel distanced or frozen out by her far-flung professional activities since they brought her in our direction so often.

With Gunnar we had few such exchanges; when he came he would talk at us rather than with us about what he was doing and thinking. This could be a heady experience, given the vast scope of his concerns, but there was not much chance for two-way communication. Unlike Alva, he took little interest in the details of human lives—what William Blake called "the holiness of minute particulars." Consequently, the ice crystals of abstraction to which Lagercrantz referred risked isolating him more and more.

Gradually we ceased trying to break through what we realized was also his shield against close contact, while guarding ourselves against his habit of making wounding or dismissive remarks. We simply allowed the flow of his thoughts to continue, learning much in the process from watching his mind at play but not engaging ourselves as fully as we could have in a more mutual exchange of ideas. I had practiced this guarded stance since childhood and Derek slipped into it out of politeness. In retrospect, I wish we had challenged this pattern, bluntly if need be. When I finally did, during Gunnar's last years, we could at times break through to what we truly needed to tell one another; but at the time, a blend of deference and of self-protection kept both Derek and me from trying.

It was to Alva, therefore, that we would turn to discuss our plans for the future. Derek had been asked to teach at the Harvard Law School in 1958, after his military service was over. He was awed by the job itself and glad to have the opportunities for research and public service that it led to within a very few years. Early on, he also began to receive offers for administrative positions from universities across the country. Gunnar, perhaps reflecting his own relief at having shifted from administrative to scholarly work in 1957, repeatedly urged Derek to turn down all such offers, each time pointedly citing the old adage about administrators being nothing but failed scholars. What Derek had already written, Gunnar wrote me in 1962, proved that he had been meant for an important scholarly contribution rather than for finding an escape by becoming a dean.

Alva saw no reason why administrative work should represent a flight from scholarship, any more than it had for Gunnar during the years he headed the Economic Commission for Europe. When Derek became dean of the Harvard Law School, in 1968, she thought back to her own managerial experience in running the Seminar for Social Pedagogy for preschool teachers in the 1930s and evoked the sheer intellectual joy of trying to ferret out creative solutions to seemingly intractable educational tasks and human entanglements. And as Derek took her on walks around the campus, she shared, as few others could, his pleasure in improving the law school's physical environment—renovating the buildings, choosing beautiful furnishings for offices and common rooms, and looking at every barren nook and cranny around the campus grounds to see what plantings would thrive where.

Derek, who had felt close to Alva from the outset, came to think of her as both a mentor and an ideal mother-in-law. She combined affectionate respect for our independence with a lavishing of ideas and suggestions about everything in our lives, from our most distant career hopes down to advice about children's books and flower arrangements and floor plans. We could relish her affection and trust her advice without the slightest feeling that we would hurt her by going our own way.

When Derek was asked, as a fledgling law professor in 1960, to give a talk to a group of law students' wives, it was natural for him to turn to Alva's *Women's Two Roles*. In his talk he conveyed what he thought was a noncontroversial message: encouraging his listeners to consider preparing as soon as possible for their future careers if they had not already done so, given the disappointments in store for those who waited too long. To his amazement, this mild message was received as practically a declaration of war on motherhood itself. I wrote to Alva about having been in the audience, where so many were pregnant that I could almost imagine myself at a fertility cult, and about the vehemence I could hear in the voices of those who responded to his talk. How could he so downgrade their family responsibilities? Didn't he think it had already been hard enough for those among them who had had to work to put their husbands through law school? Did he want their children to turn into juvenile delinquents? Betty Friedan's *The Feminine Mystique* had not yet appeared, but the mystique itself was nearly palpable that evening at the Harvard Law School.

Even though Kaj and I had been inoculated against any such

mystique from our childhood on, we were far from clear about just what to study or what career to pursue. Here, too, Alva was of unobtrusive help. In letters and in person she had long served as a counselor, never ordering, never insisting, but eager to point to the variety of paths open to us and to what she saw as educational pitfalls and blind alleys. She often told us of her wistfulness at seeing so many young women opt for university studies that prepared them for little in the way of employment, so that they had to settle for lackluster jobs or none at all after graduating.

Alva had had little difficulty in persuading us that whatever we studied should be capable of being put to practical use, not acquired purely for our own intellectual pleasure or self-enrichment. "See to it that you find a niche of your own in life, where you are needed, and do that well." She often said that all those who had been fortunate enough to receive an education owed it to society to give something of themselves in return—women no less than men. As a reminder, she suggested, we might all imagine ourselves wearing an eye-catching pendant indelibly inscribed with the figure of the amount society had invested in our studies.

Kaj, who was thought to be the most practical one in the family, took these ideals to heart in her own way. She left for Sweden to study agriculture in her teens, in part as a protest against Alva and Gunnar's cosmopolitan existence. When she went to live with them in India, at eighteen, she worked toward an M.A. in sociology and social work, continuing with a Swedish degree some years later. After moving to Germany with her husband, Horst Fölster, she encountered obstacles to working, both as a foreigner and as a mother. Her own childhood experience had convinced her that she wanted to stay close to her children when they were small. But while they were still young she went back to the University of Göttingen to study for a third degree, then gradually took on full-time responsibilities in politics and public management.

At forty-nine, Kaj was selected for a public post dealing with questions of women and equality in the city of Darmstadt. She moved on, a few years later, to a high position in GTZ, the German Agency for International Cooperation and Development, with additional responsibility for the office dealing with women's issues in social and economic development. Now it was she who traveled the world over.

As for me, Alva had asked as early as 1953, why concentrate on studying something as abstract as philosophy right away, as I had thought of doing, unless I knew I wanted to go into teaching? Why not anthropology instead, like Margaret Mead? Or as Gunnar had long hoped, economics? Or, best of all, psychology, the subject she had never had the chance fully to pursue in her own abbreviated university career? The study of any one of these fields, she insisted, would not only be fascinating but would equip me to be of use in the world.

Swayed by her enthusiasm, I settled on psychology. It was a thriving field at the Sorbonne at the time with close links to philosophy, not least because of the stimulus of Jean Piaget's regular visits from Geneva. I hoped to put my training to use by working as a clinical psychologist taking care of disturbed children and had no doubt that this approach would leave plenty of scope for my interest in philosophy. But by the time I had finished my M.A. in clinical psychology at George Washington University, Alva's advice no longer seemed so clearly right for me. Not only did the psychologists whose works I studied clash about the very fundamentals of what helps or hinders human development; they also struck me as relying in an oddly uncritical way on murky and by no means self-evident assumptions of a philosophical nature—much as philosophers often seemed to labor with naive presuppositions about the workings of the human mind. How could I hope to be of genuine help in my chosen field before addressing these problems at the juncture of theory and practice? I was already pregnant with our first child, moreover, and half relieved, given my doubts, at being unable to find part-time work in clinical psychology.

After our daughter Hilary was born, in 1959, and then Victoria two years later, my life focused on children in a more intimate and concrete way than during my years of studying psychology. Having gone through so many separations as a child and witnessed Alva's struggles to combine home life and work, I knew in my bones, as did Kaj, that the family would play an entirely different role for me. I knew, too, that my role would be much easier on account of Derek's participation and support, so utterly different from Gunnar's desire to monopolize attention and to shut us children out. I felt fortunate in being able to be at home with the children while they were little and fiercely certain that I did not want to travel away from them as Alva had from us. But I also realized, for all the reasons that she had outlined in *Women's Two Roles* and that Derek had repeated to the Harvard Law wives, I had better set in motion any plans I had for further study as soon as possible.

My decision to go back to graduate studies in philosophy represented a shift from Alva's earlier advice. I was eager to combine these studies with my interest in the psychological aspects of human conduct, both in order to challenge the theoretical shortcuts in both domains and to consider practical moral problems that arise in everyday life. In that way, I could still hope to put my studies to practical use.

On this score, I later learned that Alva had voiced doubts to Gunnar. Would I not risk being drawn into studies so abstract as to serve no practical purpose at all? Here it was he who came to my defense. He reassured Alva and wrote to me of his delight that I was taking up ethics. He had been convinced, he said, from the time when he first struggled to resolve the problem of the influence of values on scholarly work, that moral philosophy was central to all efforts to understand the world; and even as he worked on *Asian Drama,* he was striving to specify its role further.

A year after I finished my doctorate, Derek was named president of Harvard University. In a flurry of letters, Alva pondered how our lives might change as a result of Derek's more public position, our move to a new, larger house in Cambridge, and the children's new schools. Our son Tomas, born two years earlier, in 1968, helped to provide a focus and sense of rootedness for the family during this move.

With such a young child at home along with the older two, and with plans for writing and part-time teaching, I knew that I would not be able to devote myself to the teas and other social functions traditionally thought to go along with being a university president's wife. I felt deeply attached to Harvard and knew it well, both from the perspective of my years spent there as a graduate student and through Derek and many friends. As a result, I greatly enjoyed taking part in its activities, so long as I did not have to neglect either my family or my work. When Derek was first approached about the presidency he explained that since I wanted to pursue the career for which I had prepared myself, I could not be expected to play the traditional role, and this position had met with no resistance among those who appointed him.

Alva wrote to suggest that I "give" Derek a year in order to organize our move to Cambridge and help the family settle smoothly into our new lives. Exactly when I began working full-time was far less important, she thought, than that I have an independent existence ready about ten years later. Then Tomas would be as far along as Kaj was when she took her first real job at the UN in Lake Success. She added that a flaw in her own plan had of course been that her job was located so far from home: "But that was my personal problem; I have never held it forth as worth imitating."

Insofar as I could contribute to the public debate about the role of women, she also suggested that it would be important to support the search for imaginative alternatives to the rigid "either/or" of family versus profession for men as much as for women. Such alternatives are needed not only, or even primarily, as a sheer matter of justice for women, "but for the children—and because life becomes fuller and happier then." Women needed to agitate, she later pointed out in an interview, for a chance to unfold their personalities and to lead a richer life, while at the same time moving the family and society, men and women alike, "into a new climate, a softer climate where feelings and togetherness can find more room."

The close contact that Alva kept up over the decades with Kaj and with me was one she hoped would come even more easily with Jan and Gun, once the two of them and she and Gunnar were all living in Sweden after their years abroad. While Jan and Gun were in China, doing interviews for what was to become

Chinese Village, Alva found a house for them on a lake in the little town of Mariefred, an hour's ride from Stockholm, where she and Gunnar had also bought a small apartment for country weekends. Both wrote to me in the early 1960s about Jan's growing recognition as a writer and Gun's successes as an artist and photographer. Within a few years, Jan was earning enough through his writing so that their financial support became unnecessary.

But it was impossible not to notice the mounting friction, both personal and political, whenever the four got together. Personally, Jan still felt wounded, as when he was younger, by Gunnar's inability to keep from aiming belittling remarks at him; only now Gunnar's attacks seemed to him more crude and brutal, as if Gunnar, advancing in age, was losing whatever inhibitions he had once had in that respect. Meanwhile, the political strains also grew stronger each year, especially after Alva became a cabinet member in January 1967. Jan, a passionate defender of Mao Tse-tung and of the Chinese Cultural Revolution, attacked the Swedish Social Democrats, in newspapers and in a magazine that he helped found, as at best hopelessly bland in their reformist approach and often willfully corrupt.

As a result, many meetings of the four turned into angry exchanges, especially between Jan and Gunnar. At such times, Alva was usually silent. She thought heated arguments unlikely to resolve matters and did not want to supply Jan with ammunition, inadvertently, for further writings attacking government policies. She felt increasingly beleaguered. It seemed to her that Jan wanted to cross-examine her more and more often about why the government had taken positions he disagreed with; and for reasons of confidentiality she could not always be as forthcoming as might otherwise have been the case. "I was always having to defend myself. And I said that we had to find a way of seeing one another on a personal level without involving our—divergent—political views." Jan, for his part, has written that she told him she had political reasons for not wishing to meet with him. He felt shunted aside on grounds of political expediency.

It was during this same period in the mid-1960s that Alva

and Gunnar decided to write a will that would, in effect, disinherit us children. They had already financed our education and provided additional support when we or our children needed it. Now they wanted to do more for others whose need was greater. While they were alive they would continue to give away substantial portions of their combined income to organizations representing the blind, the retarded, and other needy groups; to scholarly institutions, as when Gunnar donated the sum the University of Stockholm used to finance the Institute for International Economics where he taught; to writers and artists in need of financial assistance; and to peace research. After their deaths, they wanted their money to go to a "universal heir" designated in their will: a foundation that they had set up to assist young artists and writers.

Gunnar sent me a copy of the will, dated September 16, 1966, with a note at the top in his handwriting: "With our heartfelt greetings. This is what we have decided." How much of this decision was Gunnar's and how much Alva's I shall never know. I never asked, nor, so far as I know, did Jan or Kaj. When his own father died, Gunnar had pressed his brother and sisters to abstain from part of what came to them in their father's will in order to provide more for their mother; likewise, when Alva's parents died, he had urged her to insist that their will required her siblings to repay loans their parents had made to them.

Alva herself had long been opposed to inherited wealth as an undesirable privilege, and her work on the Swedish Equality Report only reinforced that position. Moreover, her insistence that active parenting should take up only part of life, leaving parents free thereafter, may have played a role in designing the will. Here, she may have said, was yet one more way in which she could benefit society financially by going against the traditional understanding of family obligations.

Whatever their reasons, it seemed to Derek and me that Alva and Gunnar had every right to use their money as they wished. We knew the pleasure they already took in providing support for artists and writers through their foundation. It did not occur to us to write to Jan or Kaj to ask how they felt about the decision—

indeed, we were extremely uncomfortable at thinking about our parents dying and about money in that context. They, in turn, may well have reasoned that our relationship with them was surely mature enough not to depend on any financial expectations after their deaths. Perhaps they even meant, like King Lear, to test that relationship: if we did not measure up, then we would not have deserved to inherit in the first place.

It was perhaps predictable that this will, in appearance so eminently rational and matter-of-fact, would precipitate far less matter-of-fact emotions once the time came for it to take effect after Alva's death in February 1986 and Gunnar's in May 1987. Its detailed accounting of what each of us had received for support and university studies did not square with everyone's memory. And Alva and Gunnar had not fully thought through what it meant to will their physical belongings to a legal abstraction such as a "universal heir" rather than to ordinary flesh and blood relatives: in particular, they may not have foreseen the effect on us of learning that this faceless heir would receive not only their money but also everything else that they left, including their books, photo albums, household goods, artworks and other objects—all that we had grown up with as part of our childhood world. When, after Gunnar's death, we asked whether we could be allowed to go over these belongings to select a few items that our children and we would be grateful to keep, the representatives for the heir graciously acceded; it was nevertheless dismaying even to have to ask for such permission.

Shortly before Christmas 1967 occurred what was to be the final breach between Jan and our parents, lasting until their deaths. They recalled the breach differently from Jan. As Alva wrote in a letter to him ten years later, begging him to resume at least minimal relations, she thought that a real misunderstanding had arisen when she and Gunnar flew in from America to the Arlanda airport near Stockholm. As soon as they arrived, Gunnar had telephoned Jan to exchange news and to see about getting together. They had not seen the morning papers and so did not know that Jan had taken part in a demonstration against the war in Vietnam and been arrested in a scuffle with the police:

There was therefore no heartlessness toward you: had we known, we would naturally have been on your side. (I had been at the UN and therefore not taken part in any decision about a police action against the demonstration.)

To Jan, however, Gunnar's matter-of-fact call following his arrest seemed in line with the other forms of rejection and belittlement on their part. It was Alva's government, after all, that had agreed to prohibit the demonstration and thus precipitated the actions leading to his forcible arrest: indeed, Gunnar remembered Jan as shouting accusations against "Alva's damned government" before hanging up on him. Jan has written, rather, that what precipitated the final rupture at this moment was his shock, at a time when he feared he might be facing up to four years in prison, at Gunnar's callousness. Instead of offering to hire the finest defense lawyer in the country, a response Jan thought would have been more appropriate, Gunnar urged him, as Jan remembers it, to go to Vietnam and die for what he believed in rather than stay home and protest the Swedish government's policies. Jan felt, he wrote, that he had to draw the line then and there. He answered that Gunnar and Alva could have Sunday dinners with Prime Minister Erlander rather than with him and Gun from then on.

Alva and Gunnar did not call Jan back, even when they understood what had happened the day before. "That I have kept silent, as about everything else, depends, of course, on my being proud when I am wounded," Alva explained in her letter in 1977. She had taken for granted, at first, that the breach would be temporary. Jan had often come and gone in their lives in the past. Perhaps she experienced the same sense of mingled grief and relief that she had known after Jan's leaving home as an adolescent. At least she would no longer have to sit through the searing exchanges over Swedish politics. Her term of office could not last many years, given her age. Sooner or later, there would be time enough to pick up the personal threads once again.

Such a reconciliation never took place. Jan replied to Alva's letter that while there had been periods when he had found it possible to meet with her and Gunnar, he could never feel sure of them. All of a sudden Gunnar would get the idea of beginning his "teasing" or have a fit of anger, or else she might find it politically or socially inappropriate to show herself with him. As the years passed, Jan wrote, he had become ever less inclined to be exposed to such treatment.

And so a split began that was never healed. The three never met together again. Yet eerily, they could frequently see one another "live" on TV giving talks and interviews. Where many family members and friends who break off relationships begin to envisage one another, over time, in an ever-dimmer half-light, Jan saw Alva and Gunnar, and they him, only in an equally distorting glare of publicity. Olof Lagercrantz's remark about the power sphere where icy abstractions begin to form takes on intensified meaning when the struggle for power, both political and familial, so distances individuals once intimately linked that they perceive one another most directly as images on a screen.

Of the three, only Alva sought to renew contact through letters, birthday gifts, invitations, and reminders of all that they had shared in the past. She took the permanence of the breach increasingly hard as the years went by. Unlike Jan and Gunnar, however, she always refused to discuss it publicly. She made it clear to the reporters who sought her out for interviews that although she would be glad to talk with them, she did not want to bring her family into the discussion. From adolescence on, Kaj and I had been grateful to be left out of the publicity surrounding our parents, and we recognized how especially difficult it would be for someone as instinctively private as she to discuss her differences with Jan in public. Yet it led to the oddity that accounts of her life could present her views about children and child rearing at length while passing over her own children almost in silence.

The silence about Alva's family life was especially striking in an exhibition devoted to her life and work that was mounted in Stockholm in 1976. Entitled "It's a Matter of Our Life," it was meant to illustrate the links between one woman's life and the larger theme of the struggles, during the previous half-century, for equality and greater solidarity. The exhibition presented her life's work through photographs and excerpts from her writings, many

illustrated with wall-long paintings. Including testimony from colleagues in many arenas, it documented the ways in which she had
tried to influence how people lived, comparing apartments, play-
grounds, schools, and factories in the thirties and four decades
later and depicting changes in relationships between parents and
children, men and women. But there was no reference to her own
family and how they lived.

Even so, Alva found this focus on social issues through the
lens of her life story cloying. She told the organizers, for whom
she had great regard, that she felt nearly traumatized by the very
idea; she had only gone along with it in order to help disseminate
the ideas she had worked for. "Ideas are like manure. If you don't
spread them they don't do any good." Still, she would have
preferred to see the ideas themselves taken up directly rather than
"personalized." Only after the exhibition was over did she send
us, somewhat apologetically, its flamboyant ruby-colored cata-
logue in case we wanted to see the photographs it contained.

What made her most uncomfortable was the image of herself
as a secular saint that a good many interviewers had begun to
convey in articles, pamphlets, and books. She would happily have
traded away the reverence she increasingly encountered for the
bracing battles out on the hustings during the thirties and forties,
when she had championed causes that were then so controversial.
And yet people were responding to much more than the idealized
image that exhibitions or media coverage could convey—to a gift
for inspiring others that was far from new. After her death, many
of her students at the Seminar for Social Pedagogy wrote to
describe the spark or vitalization or sense of empowerment that
they had received from her in the thirties as something that
stamped them for the rest of their lives. And Elise Boulding, the
American economist, has described how she first met Alva in
Princeton in 1941:

> As I write, I can see her as if it were yesterday: a beautifully
> poised, centered woman with shining blond hair, sitting quietly
> opposite her husband in our apartment living room, deeply
> engrossed in a conversation about the state of the world. Her

presence vibrated for me. Here was a woman of intellect, participating in talk of a world I was just beginning to understand. The sense of a wider world, and ways to be present in it, which she left with me, have stayed with me all my life. Our contacts over the subsequent decades have been brief, but whenever we met there was connection. I am one of the many, many women for whom Alva Myrdal was an example, a way-shower.

By the seventies and eighties, this same ability of Alva's had developed into a form of radiance. I could see people responding to it wherever I went with her, even if only to buy fruit down the street from her apartment in the Old City. In newspaper polls, she was repeatedly voted Sweden's most admired woman. Posters began cropping up in more and more places carrying her saying "It is not worthy of human beings to give up." Even during her last months, when the power of speech was no longer in her control, the nurses who took care of her spoke of feeling that same radiance whenever they went to her bedside. And at her memorial service, Olof Palme spoke of "the radiance and cheerfulness of her personality" as contributing to the remarkable fact that someone "who was so far ahead of her time was nonetheless so beloved by her contemporaries."

What was it that provoked such an immediate response on the part of so many people? To my eyes, it seemed to be a spark of mutual and nearly tangible recognition of human dignity or worth—the very opposite of the icy, dehumanizing abstractions to which Lagercrantz referred in the passage quoted earlier. It was clear, from Alva's face and her eyes alone, that she had lived her life in utter confidence that life matters, and consequently that it matters how one lives and how one treats others. If one tramples on their dignity, she seemed to say, one degrades one's own; and if one has little regard for one's own dignity, one is unlikely to stand up for it in others.

Like so many others, Alva had been deeply committed to such a perception of common humanity in her youth; but unlike most, she had held to it all her life. Throughout, she could draw on her father's ideals of all that went into shaping "the good" and her mother's reverence for beauty and art as equally necessary to human existence; and to implement these ideals, she combined her father's "builder's spirit," stressing stepwise practical improvements, no matter how small at first, with her mother's gift for dramatizing and storytelling, while making use of her life experience in order to illuminate far greater human needs.

Alva, like most who hold such ideals, knew how painfully vast was the gulf between perceiving them and bringing about even their partial realization. Yet it was through attending so passionately both to her ideals and to the daily details of living, however unmanageable at times, that she gave her life meaning and in turn conveyed it to those around her. But because there was so much that she felt she had not accomplished and would now be leaving unfinished, the honors and the respect she received seemed to her undeserved.

Alva's discomfort with this attention to her was increased by her concern that Gunnar might feel overshadowed. He was respected as a scholar and was offered honorary degrees and honors every year, but since his primary interests were international, he knew that he no longer played the large public role in Sweden that he had once taken for granted. This may be one reason why Alva muted her skepticism about the honors that were increasingly bestowed on them abroad as man and wife. As early as 1970, when they received the German Publishers' Peace Prize together, they had been eulogized as a couple working jointly for peace. Likewise, the Ralph Bunche Institute at the City University of New York honored them jointly in 1975. And in 1977 they held a joint professorship at the Lyndon B. Johnson School of Public Affairs at the University of Texas in Austin. Not a month passed without their being invited—mostly in vain—to teach joint courses, address audiences, or receive honorary degrees together.

Photographed side by side, with their white hair and their clear blue eyes looking out of faces grown more alike over the years, their expressions hinted at creative possibilities for old age. In some mysterious sense they seemed to defy the ordinary life patterns associated with growing old. Both passed the traditional retirement age without stepping down from their posts. Both continued their passionate engagement with world affairs. On the world stage they came to be known by the epithet applied to them in Sweden since the 1930's, "the Myrdal couple."

Articles about them always stressed their joy in talking with one another and exchanging ideas over a lifetime. Alva used to say that she had never met another man with whom she could imagine a long life of conversation without growing bored early on. And their undertaking so many projects together was also unusual; their projects, over the decades, had meshed and grown to incorporate what each had done until now their concerns spanned the entire world, past, present, and future.

Although Alva had no wish to deny this public focus on the lifelong companionship, collaboration and mutual stimulation that she shared with Gunnar, she cringed whenever articles held them forth as a uniquely happy couple. And yet she was not sure what she could do but remain silent when Gunnar expounded to interviewers about their lifelong love affair and about the bliss of being so much together in retirement. She could hardly seem to disagree with him or even to qualify his statements in front of visiting reporters; yet by not doing so, she contributed, however unwillingly, to the creation of a false image. By 1980, *People* magazine could entitle an article about them

ALVA AND GUNNAR MYRDAL KNOW "THE GREAT
HAPPINESS OF LIVING TO BE VERY OLD TOGETHER"

And other magazine headlines succeeded one another:

THE BEST THING ABOUT OUR NEW LIFE: THAT I
GET TO SPEND 24 HOURS A DAY WITH ALVA

ALVA AND GUNNAR MYRDAL 1980: TWO WHO LOVE
AND INSPIRE ONE ANOTHER

This false projection of bliss seemed to Alva remote from the day-to-day reality of their lives and from the writing and disarmament activities that took most of her time after she had left public office. But she was also wary of the imbalance when all the attention went to her. "Even I am calmer and kinder when all goes well for Gunnar than when the tributes are only for me."

In 1982, the public attention was to escalate and grow double-edged in a way no one could have anticipated. Since the mid-1970s, many had called on the Norwegian Nobel Committee to award Alva the Nobel Peace Prize. Each year she was passed over—even in 1981, when many in the Norwegian Parliament came out publicly in support of her receiving the prize. When the news broke, that fall, that the Office of the UN High Commissioner for Refugees had been selected, for the second time, to receive the prize, a storm of public criticism broke out in Norway. Groups met all over the country to raise $60,000 for Alva as an unprecedented Norwegian People's Peace Prize. The award touched her more than any other honor. She traveled to Oslo to receive it in February 1982, shortly after her eightieth birthday, and donated the money to Peace Forum, the Swedish Labor Movement's peace organization she had helped to found.

That summer, only months after the press had summed up her life's work on the occasion of her eightieth birthday and the prize ceremonies, a new flurry of headlines burst on the scene, casting "the Myrdal couple" and especially Alva in entirely different light. Jan had written a book based on his childhood, entitled *Barndom* (*Childhood*) which was to be published later in the fall. As early as July, however, the newspapers carried interviews and excerpts from the book with such headlines as

JAN MYRDAL GETS EVEN WITH HIS PARENTS

ALVA AND GUNNAR NAUSEATED ME

ALVA IS BLOND AND SO COLD THAT I SHUDDER

I DETEST MY MOTHER AND FATHER BECAUSE THEY
NEVER GAVE ME LOVE

To gossip-hungry Swedes, this controversy created the sensation of the fall season. Few guessed at the depth of the pain this public repudiation caused Alva and Gunnar, and the media coverage gave no inkling of their extreme physical frailty. In the public's eye, "the Myrdal couple" were known as articulate and combative fighters in many a past cause. It was not the first time that their views on education, children, and families had focused attention on their personal lives. Why not indulge the taste for speculation about this couple once again through the son who spoke so freely, in interviews and letters, of his hatred for them and his certainty that they had never loved him?

Inevitably, much of the speculation centered on Alva, precisely because the book's portrait of her jarred so sharply with her public persona. Who was she truly? The beloved, brilliant, caring individual the world saw, or the shrill-voiced, rejecting, calculating mother conveyed by Jan, so cold that children shuddered when she touched them?

When the news first hit her, Alva wrote me that she had spent six days in sheerest horror, with the nights even more unendurable than the days: "Of course I realize that he is unhappy. But I have now persuaded myself that it is *too late* to do anything about that." Whatever her failures may have been in reaching Jan and helping him when he was small, she added, he had now wounded her so deeply in return that she could cease all guilt: the two of them could at last be quits.

Her poor health, kept to herself like so much else, contributed to her continual anguish at seeing one new headline after another and reading excerpts from Jan's book. Shortly after she first wrote me about it she was in the hospital with a concussion and an injured ear, having taken a bad fall. During the summer her sense of balance had deteriorated, possibly as a result of the medication given to her to help control her high blood pressure, and she had suffered several injurious falls. Because of her weakened condition, her physicians advised her not to pay any more attention to the book.

Try as she might, however, she could not put it out of her mind. She felt thrust back into the role of active mothering that she thought she had left behind so long ago, for the book spoke of a small child's feeling of having been not only displaced, set aside for more important activities, but so utterly rejected by his parents from the time he was born that the only response possible for that child, once grown, was to reject them in turn.

The book's portrayal of Alva brought a flood of affectionate letters from friends and strangers alike. The compassion generated by her age and vulnerability seemed merely to add to the love and respect that people showed her. There seemed no need for her to be "perfect" or right on every issue for her to inspirit and empower people and for her voice on issues of war and peace to continue to be heard.

In October 1982, Alva received a telephone call announcing that she had won the Nobel Peace Prize after all. She shared the award with her old friend and longtime UN colleague, the Mexican diplomat Alfonso García Robles. According to the Nobel Committee, the two had been chosen for their work, carried out in the face of ample grounds for pessimism about the prospects for disarmament, to further the struggle for disarmament and peace; and for having contributed, not only to "the patient and meticulous work undertaken in international organizations on mutual disarmament" but also to "the work of numerous peace movements with their greater emphasis on influencing the climate of public opinion and appeal to the emotions." Pointedly left out of this account was any mention of the superpowers, so glaringly unproductive during the past summer's special UN session on disarmament, when not a single substantial agreement had been reached.

Alva and Gunnar were now the only man and wife in the world who had ever received Nobel Prizes in entirely different fields. (Three other couples had been honored for joint work in the sciences: Pierre and Marie Curie shared the prize in physics in 1903 with Henri Becquerel; Marie Curie received a second Nobel Prize in 1911 for related work; Irène and Frédéric Joliot-Curie shared one in chemistry in 1935; and Carl and Gerty Cori shared the prize in medicine in 1947 with Bernardo Houssay.) Once again attention focused on Alva and Gunnar as a couple.

To outsiders, their combination of individuality and collaboration, which now stretched over a lifetime, aroused a sense of wonder. But those of us who knew of their frailty at the time wondered how they would cope with being in the spotlight once again. And we could not help finding a *New Yorker* cartoon about them, coming when it did, more poignant than the artist could have intended. The cartoon shows a suburban matron at breakfast, coffee cup in midair, trying to get her paunchy husband's attention away from his newspaper. Its caption reads:

"I said 'I wonder what Gunnar and Alva Myrdal kick around at breakfast.'"

17

Legacies

❖ ❖ ❖ ❖

*L*ight *snow was falling in Oslo* on the afternoon of December 9, 1982, as the Nobel festivities were about to begin. Earlier that day, Kaj's son Stefan had gone to help Alva and Gunnar pack and get ready for the train trip from Stockholm to Oslo. On the train, he had looked after their needs as gently as if he had "wrapped them in cotton," he reported to Kaj. Meanwhile she flew in from Germany and Derek and I from America. Our daughter Hilary had already come in along with other relatives and friends from different directions.

In Oslo's Grand Hotel, where Nobel Peace Prize winners are traditionally lodged, we were all shown to adjoining rooms on the floor that had been given over to the families of the two laureates. We had an odd sense of being thrust into an unfolding Ibsen play as we passed one another in the dark-paneled corridors, talking in whispers while Alva rested. Flashes of worry kept cutting across our joy at being together for this event. Alva had arrived pale and exhausted, her heart pain exacerbated by the strain of the trip—how would she get through the next two days? And Gunnar, increasingly incapacitated by Parkinson's disease, deaf and nearly blind, seemed querulously unable to focus on Alva's prize or on her pleas to be allowed to rest—why then, we wondered, was he so anxious to meet with the press?

As the sun set, we watched as Alva and Gunnar stood on the balcony outside their room, along with Ambassador García

Robles and his family, shivering in the chill air. A torchlight parade, looking from afar like an immensely elongated glow-worm, wound its way toward us along the tree-lined avenue below. We could see the faces of children, students, men and women all bundled up against the cold and singing softly, calling out to Alva and Ambassador García Robles and raising their torches as they passed beneath them. Alva waved back—rather like the pope, Hilary noted, as press photographers hanging over the railings of neighboring balconies recorded the scene.

Two days later, Kaj and I sat tensely in the crowded university auditorium, watching as Alva took the few steps up to the podium, cane in hand, to deliver her acceptance address for The Nobel Peace Prize. As a precaution against being struck with one of her attacks of aphasia, she had given us copies of her speech the day before and asked us to be prepared to read half of it each if she should indicate that she needed help.

Now she stood at the lectern, elegant in a tailored black wool suit, her white hair drawn back and fastened with a silver brooch, her expression both drained and determined. Her first words, as she looked out over the audience, were muted. Everyone hushed, leaning forward to listen. But with each new sentence, her strength seemed to come flooding back—she felt airborne, she later said. Kaj and I exchanged glances of relief. The words were hers, the moment hers.

Alva came quickly to the central topic in her speech—how the arms race, with its needless excesses of armaments and its aggressive rhetoric, had contributed to an ominous cult of violence in contemporary societies. Our civilization, she suggested, was in the process of being both militarized and brutalized. Because of the tremendous and needless proliferation of arms through production and export, sophisticated weapons were now freely available on the domestic market as well, right down to handguns and stilettoes. She pointed to the growth of terrorism, to the threat of assassination with which politicians were now forced to live, and to the many governments disposing of new means to persecute their own citizens and to intern them in prisons and concentration camps. And she singled out the powerful role of the mass media in promoting violence, most of all among the young, who were less able to filter out or select the impressions made on them by what they viewed. In turn, Western exporting of films and TV programs worked in tandem with the arms trade to satiate the Third World in patterns of brutality.

As a counterbalance to this climate of violence, Alva emphasized the crucial role of the new popular movements of protest that had recently arisen in opposition to the armaments race and to the growing militarization of the world. She applauded the writers and journalists who dared to speak out against war even in nations where doing so could mean imprisonment, and the physicians and other professionals who had formed international organizations to counter official evasions and falsehoods regarding the nuclear threat. She was convinced, she said, that "those who possess political power will be forced some day, sooner or later, to give way to common sense and the will of the people."

Technology could offer another counterbalance: even though it had contributed so immensely to the militarization of the world, it had also been harnessed for vast peaceful purposes. The work of Alfred Nobel symbolized to her both the destructive and the creative sides of technology. He had believed, wrongly, that dynamite would make war so senseless as to be impossible. But its constructive uses were legion; in the form of nitroglycerin, it could even soothe the cardiac pain that both she and Nobel had learned to live with.

Alva concluded by quoting a passage from Nobel's testament, calling for the Peace Prize fund to support "the holding and promoting of peace congresses." None had ever been held. Now it was high time to do so in order to subject questions of war and peace to a dynamic, thorough, and factual debate. Such a congress could both draw on and energize the popular movement against the arms race that was gaining such momentum.

In Alva's voice I could hear her old blend of clarity and emotion without an ounce of cloying "peace" rhetoric and her passionate concern that nations turn away from the precipice toward which she saw them moving, not for her own sake, since she was now near the end of her life, but for all who would live after her.

As she spoke, I wondered how she had summoned such strength—had even been able to prepare the address, given the poor state of her health during the preceding months. In addition to the ever-threatening aphasia, her recurring angina pains, and her sporadic difficulty in keeping her balance, she had developed a severe case of heart arrhythmia that no medical intervention seemed capable of controlling. Some of the medications that she was given for these various problems were at times so debilitating that she felt they were worse than the diseases themselves.

It was in part because she was so weak that the news earlier that summer of the impending publication of Jan's book *Childhood* had affected her so strongly. And Gunnar had made matters worse by deciding, much against Derek's advice and mine, to take up the battle with Jan in public. Dismissing Jan's claim that his book had been meant as fiction, not as factual autobiography, Gunnar issued a press release exposing what he felt were falsehoods in the portions of Jan's book that had already been excerpted in the press. When Gunnar went so far as to take legal recourse against the media for publicizing what he saw as Jan's attacks on himself and Alva, he was turned down on grounds of freedom of speech.

Jan counted the gesture as one more attempt on Gunnar's part to silence him and destroy his chances as a writer. He had not spent time with Alva and Gunnar since they were in their sixties and still robust. Now he knew them primarily through the media and may have thought even Alva strong enough still. Hadn't she been eulogized in the press on her eightieth birthday, the previous January, even as his book was being readied for the press? Hadn't there been glowing photos of her in Oslo, receiving the Norwegian People's Peace Prize, as late as February? She hardly seemed a figure likely to be dented by a book, no matter how hard-hitting.

But as the debate over Alva's role as a mother took on a life of its own in the media, as Gunnar continued pressing the issue of all that he saw as false in the book, and as friends from every walk of life sent letters of near-condolence to them both, Alva found it increasingly difficult to put the matter out of her mind. Why had Jan aimed his attacks so harshly at her this time? She had seen the periodic storminess of his relationship with Gunnar. But as she searched her memory, she could perceive no signals that he "had hated me throughout his childhood and all the years." And she wondered as much about her own reaction. Why, she wrote, had she ended up being so obsessed with the book?

> It is as if I, too, were forced into a regression—a compulsion to go through the whole experience of expecting his arrival, giving birth to him, seeing him develop. . . . That all this is connected with the physical changes brought on by old age does not make matters easier. Now it is so difficult to live with thoughts of what it is to have been a mother. And to have lost a son to whom I gave birth in such great love.

In October, Alva wrote me the only letter of reproach I have ever received from her, from the hospital where she had been taken in for heart tests and a brain scan. She wanted me to know that Kaj's and my urging her to think no longer about the book showed that we belonged to the many wonderful friends she had "who have nevertheless *not understood*."

What had we not understood? She explained that it had to do with how deeply crushed she was. She was trying to express her feelings in a "rhapsodic series of writings I am working on: *Elegy for a Lost Son*." It was not going to be an accusatory document in answer to Jan's. Rather, it would be a book of mourning and, perhaps, an effort at psychological interpretation. She intended it for her great-grandchildren—her grandchildren already knew her too well to need any such explanations, but their children would have so much less to go on if she did not reach out to them in this personal way.

I grieved over this letter, realizing the pain she must have experienced when writing it. It arrived a few days after we had learned that she had won the Nobel Prize. We had called to congratulate her and then called again a number of times to make plans and to hear how she and Gunnar were doing. Olof Palme, she reported, had been the first to arrive with roses to bring the news to them in their apartment, and had left behind a press attaché to help Alva deal with the flood of media inquiries. Friends and relatives had come as soon as they heard the news. Part of me hoped that these visits and all that would flow in the wake of the prize—the flowers, the letters, the requests for interviews— might allow her to set aside her anguish. But another part of me knew, from her voice over the telephone, that the moments of celebration and applause simply intensified the contrast with the underlying pain.

Should I touch on that possibility in writing back? I began doing so in a letter in which I spoke of sharing her anguish and of the cruelty I saw in her having to undergo the double ordeal of coping with the book's appearance and receiving the prize at a time when she was so ill and exhausted. But I knew no one who could overcome such dangers as she could, I added; and as for what the great-grandchildren would think, her courage in doing so could mean as much to them as her struggle for peace. I could not bring myself to mail this letter, however, so uncertain was I that it came even close to addressing the full depth of her feelings. I decided, rather, to discuss these concerns over the telephone and when we saw her a month later in Oslo.

It was doubtless sheer coincidence that the book finally appeared in the bookstores, after all the press notices and published excerpts and radio broadcasts, just around the time when the Nobel Prize was announced. Yet for Alva, the nearness in time of the two events represented a closing as of a vise, a coming together of the conflict between the two endeavors—family and work—in which she had aimed so high. Now, in what many saw as the culminating moment of her life's work, she was confronted with a public shaming of her role as a mother.

Who, then, was she truly? She knew how close Kaj and I and everyone in our two families were to her; and she cherished the affection showed her by Jan's son Janken and his family, who had lived one floor beneath her and Gunnar in the Old City. But none of this mattered in comparison to her grief. However certain she could be of all our love, it was her failure with Jan, the loss of her son, that consumed her.

I felt this without bitterness, having witnessed the same grief on the part of friends mourning the loss of a child or a spouse. To me, what mattered most was for Alva somehow to overcome the psychological blow even as she struggled with her several forms of physical debilitation and Gunnar's increasing gloom and irritability. We had been with them earlier that summer, helping them to move from the Stockholm apartment to a smaller one for old-age residents in the suburb of Djursholm, and before that in January to celebrate her eightieth birthday. Now she insisted that we must not fly to see her in Sweden; before long we would all be together in Oslo.

All these events and emotions were in the back of my mind as I listened to Alva give her Nobel address. And I could feel the brittle edge of her courage. So long as she had words at her command she would continue to speak out in public against aggression and enmity in every sphere of life. To be sure, as she said in the speech, she had no illusion that the day would come when human beings would live in a lasting state of harmony. Reason the more for struggling to restrain violence wherever one could—and to restrain, above all, those practices that contributed to the risk of nuclear war.

That very morning, she had awoken to find that Gunnar had seized the occasion of her prize to launch yet another media broadside at Jan. The Norwegian papers carried double head-lines—on the one hand, about Alva's winning the prize, and on the other, about Gunnar's reports that she had thought of suicide after Jan's book came out.

Our initial disbelief was followed first by uncomprehending dismay, then by pure anger at his exploiting, to pursue his ven-detta, what should have been a day of undiluted celebration. And

then again, we reminded ourselves of how his illness had, for
months already, distorted his understanding and his judgment. I
felt, however, that I had to confront him on this score, if only to
prevent further injury to Alva. I could no longer simply tune him
out as in the past. But he refused to listen. To him, the issue was
clear: Alva was in danger and this was the moment to gain the
greatest possible audience for saying so. Chivalry called for engineering such double-edged publicity about her. He had always
come to her aid whenever he felt her threatened, whether by illness
or by outside attacks. Most often, she had been grateful for his
help, pugnacious though it had been at times. But when he deployed that same pugnacity to protect her against her own son,
she felt torn in two. In her weak condition, she felt like the quarry
over which the battle was being fought, but also as though she
were the battlefield itself, across which the two rival armies
tramped back and forth at will.

On the way back to Sweden, Alva spoke to me about having
to guard against a further plan of Gunnar's. He wanted her to
deposit the prize money in their joint account, fearing that they
had given away so much during recent years that they might have
too little left for their personal needs. Arguing that the two of
them were one and the same person after such a long life together,
he wanted to be able to decide where the money should go. She,
however, wanted to dispose of it herself and asked my help, after
we arrived, to open a separate bank account for that purpose.
Then she could use the money to further the related struggles
against weapons and violence that she had discussed in her speech.

She was going to divide her share of the Peace prize, amount-
ing to $78,000, into two halves, after retaining a small amount
to pay for secretarial help. One half would go to subsidize a study
of nuclear weapons deployments at sea—current and future. As
early as 1970, she had given a talk in Malta, entitled "No Arms
on the ocean floor," to help inaugurate the organization *Pacem
in Maribus* started by her old friend Elizabeth Mann Borgese. But
while she looked forward to collaborating with Dr. Mann Borgese,
now a professor at the University of Dalhousie in Halifax, Can-

ada, on this project, by the time it got under way she was no longer well enough to do so. She was nevertheless pleased to see it result in a provocative conference, "The Denuclearization of the Oceans," on the legal and strategic issues involved, and then in a collection of essays with that title edited by R. B. Byers.

Alva had designated the second half of the money for a study of the ethical aspects of the "culture of violence" that she had discussed in her Nobel speech. This project began taking shape during the spring and summer of 1983. Alva wanted to focus it on what she called "antiviolence." Just as the antislavery movement in preceding centuries had gone far beyond merely refusing to take part in institutionalized slavery, so she wanted to consider, not just the nonviolent alternatives to practices of violence, but also methods of taking up active resistance to these practices. To be sure, the resistance would itself have to be nonviolent in order not to be self-contradictory, but that did not mean it could not exert force by lawful means.

Above all, the project had to carry out concrete actions rather than merely discuss and interpret forms of violence. For this purpose, Alva urged that greater attention be given to identifying "the instruments for exerting or promoting violence." She had in mind the ways in which violence is used, relied on, often exploited for power or monetary gain thoughout society, in families no less than in politics or in professions such as science, journalism, sports, and entertainment—and the absence, on the part of all who trade in violence, terror, and weaponry, of personal responsibility for what she saw as the resulting social damage.

By active resistance she had in mind, in the first place, singling out and calling to task those institutions and individuals most centrally involved as "propagandizers and profiteers of violence." What responsibility should scientists, technicians, and industrial workers bear for the production of weapons in the context of the arms race? What role did participants in the mass media's cult of violence, blood, and sensationalizing play? And what about many in the public, feeding on a steady diet of sensationalized brutality and growing inured to the crimes of violence perpetrated by governments or by street criminals? In so many walks of life, even in a relatively humane society like that of Sweden, she saw the result of countless individual and institutional failures to take responsibility as contagious: "brutality, even in human relations, is becoming characteristic of our time."

Alva asked me to be part of a small group that began studying these issues, concentrating, to begin with, on Swedish society. I was eager to work on this project with her, especially since I could feel her channeling all her remaining strength in this direction. Antiviolence as a concept encompassed all her past resistance to injustice and all her concern for human beings. It seemed to me to represent her ultimate resistance on the part of all victims, the more deeply felt because of her own struggle against being overwhelmed by illness and suffering.

If I could help carry the project forward even as her strength ebbed, I would feel that I had shared with her a task that I also cared for profoundly in its own right. Her concern for these issues was so much more of a legacy, to my mind, than the property at stake in her and Gunnar's wretched will, likely to leave behind only needless disputes. Alva had often spoken to us all, and especially to her grandchildren, of wanting to hand over certain passionate interests of hers, much as someone running a relay race hands the baton over to a partner who will carry it forward. As illness gradually forced her to curtail her own activities, she would return again and again to this image of handing over the baton and consider what interests and talents grandchildren and great grandchildren, even those not yet born, might in the end share with her and Gunnar.

Kaj and I alternated visits to them as often as we could and tried to persuade Alva to come to stay with us for a longer period. But she demurred, feeling that she could not leave Gunnar. And he, now almost completely blind, could not envisage such a journey, especially since he still persevered each day in dictating additions and changes to *An American Dilemma Revisited,* begun in 1973. He would finally decide not to publish it, on the ground that he could not in good conscience envisage signing his name to a book once he knew that he would not be able to go over the proofs in person. We grieved to think of all that he had sacrificed in his life for the sake of carrying forward this work; but at the same time we had to admire his rigorous, probing, workmanlike devotion to research and writing. That example, too, we would regard as his legacy, once again of far greater importance than what was or was not in his and Alva's will.

In April 1983, even though it was already excruciatingly hard for her to write, Alva gathered her strength to compose a long letter about her life to Kaj and me:

My dear daughters,
Here I sit down by the typewriter to write something quite impromptu, though I WANT TO WRITE ABOUT SOME-THING VERY SERIOUS!

It is something I have come to ponder more and more: How is one an individual and how is one's fate shaped in interaction with other people? How does one in turn contribute to form-ing these other people? How close can one really BE to other people? How *is* an individual vis-à-vis another individual? How do I become myself? How have I really been with you? How have I come to displace my own self in order to fit in with other selves? Where does one self merge with another?

This has become a problem now that I have lived so long. I can see, as if in a 50- or 60-year rearview mirror, the com-pletely preposterous displacements that have taken place be-tween what I have become, and done, and what I should have been able to, perhaps ought to, have planned. But I did not plan it. To a large extent, life just became.

Of course this is especially clear in a historical-sociological perspective now, when living conditions have become so dif-ferent. If *then* had been *now* I would of course never have taken the name Myrdal. Even now, after the passage of the new laws concerning names, I am tempted to call myself Alva Reimer Myrdal. Why should the genes from the female side be denied?

But as things were then, it seemed to me self-evident to give up so much of my own. This [was so] ever since I met Gunnar, to whom I now see that I was so ludicrously obedient. . . . And I, who was called an advocate of women's rights early on, never insisted on a profession of my own, going along quite naturally with being an "appendix." Of course I could not keep from undertaking certain things, but it was Gunnar's path, his "career," his interests that had to have first claim and even decide where we—the family—should live.

I never objected to the idea that I should be the one who got up at night to take care of the children. Gunnar has, as a typical father of that period, never even learned what a diaper is. Note well that I say "typical"—there were so incredibly many choices to make in which the division of roles was never questioned.

Hear now that I am not complaining. I have not begun to question "the natural order" until later, gradually. Outwardly seen, one was even a "professorska" [professor's wife]; that was supposed to suffice as occupation.

While Gunnar's path can be described as a straightforward *career*—which, however sometimes moved off into a new direction—I have never had a "career"; my path was more like a pleated ribbon where I myself nevertheless managed to insert one self-created activity after another.

A director of studies was what I became, with 3000 [crowns] a year, at a Seminar that I had conceived, planned, led entirely by myself. And the successes that I have undoubtedly achieved have not been called forth or even expected by anyone.

One thing has to be drummed into my children: mine was not a "career." My life has, rather, been filled with *campaigns,* both before and after the time of my professional work—that first began when I was exactly 47 years and one day old. That this offer came (after I had declined two others, one position as significant as that of vice director for UNESCO, out of consideration for the family—that is, so long as the positions would have required that I be the one causing the family to move) was something of such dreamlike satisfaction that I could not resist it. But by then Gunnar had already relocated the family—a departure that tore away the ground for all my meaningful work. Would there remain only hostessing duties? For no job was foreseen.

One sign that I had insight into the true nature of the situation is that when I was asked to speak in the UN lecture

series, I entitled my talk "The [Surplus Energy] of Married
Women."

Why do I now speak of this as a problem?

Yes, as the problem of twosomeness. Perhaps it is a problem
that is eternal and ever-present, always "solved" at best
through compromises. In my case it was, of course, especially
problematic.

But shouldn't I in that case have changed my way of life
radically at some point? If I now look backward as if in a
rearview mirror, I have to pose that question concerning two
particular occasions. Both times it would of course have meant
divorce. But why not? That is the question I have to pose to
myself.

Alva went on to describe two of the three searing departures
that she always later regarded as mistakes. (The first, in 1929,
when she left Jan in Sweden, did not give rise to such thoughts
of divorce, since she and Gunnar were not in conflict then: both
wanted to go to America and both were convinced that it was
better for Jan to stay in Sweden.) But when she left us all to go
once again to America in 1941 to join Gunnar, the situation was
different: she did not want to leave and he did everything to make
her go. "Then my sense of obedience to Gunnar was decisive—
as usual." Another "occasion was in 1947":

Gunnar had what he now calls a defeat in the government
and the whole family moved to Geneva. I believe that we never
made it clear to ourselves what it meant for all of us with this
shifting around, the bonds of friendship that burst, the sense
of alienation in a new language to begin with. A comfort in
whom we had faith for a long time was Karin Anger.

But only after a year did it become clear to me that I did
not have the marriage to rely on this time. On February 1
1949 I took the more than tempting job at the UN "on trial."
Jan had then left home, but Sissela was 15 years old (half a
year with me in New York) and Kaj 13. That time, I probably

made the wrong choice again. But only *today* have I thought
through what it would have been like to 1) divorce and 2)
take the girls with me, first to New York and then to Paris.
Of course, it gradually did turn out to be Paris for the three
of us. I let myself drift along with the dream that all would
"turn out well." But now I see clearly that I first became a
free person in 1949. And so *happy* in New York, in Paris, in
New Delhi.

And now, here I sit. When everything has become so difficult
for Gunnar. And with Jan as my almost constantly bleeding
cross. The price that you had to pay, I may never have acknowledged clearly, not even in letters. Or during our living
together—with Kaj as late as in India. And we have of course
also had so much in common. Even intellectually. A common
ground of values, a heartfelt understanding and deep affection—at least I feel that for you.

Here I could end. Don't know whether I will choose to
analyze further.

Perhaps another time.

Alva

Kaj and I wrote back and telephoned to convey our love and
to say once again that we did not blame her or carry any grudges
in connection with the departures over which she agonized in her
letter. She had meant so much more to us than that, in childhood
and throughout our lives. I understood, I wrote, what she meant
in speaking about her path; and thought that it was astounding
that she, in spite of the "obedience" to which she referred, had
arrived at what *she* wanted and could do. Given all that she had
longed to accomplish, her achievement lay in pursuing those goals
with such creativity and strength in spite of the obstacles that she
had encountered from childhood on, and in helping, thereby, to
motivate and show the way to so many others. Least of all should
she worry, I wrote, about whether the move to Geneva had hurt
me. It had, on the contrary, been the answer to all my longing
for adventure at the time.

I enclosed with my letter to Alva one from Derek, which,

coming from someone who knew us both so well, we hoped she also would take into account as she focused her rearview mirror on the past:

Dear Alva,

Sissela talked to me last night about the letter she had just received from you. I couldn't resist writing simply to add my perceptions, for whatever they may be worth. First of all, I feel absolutely sure that leaving Sweden for Geneva was not for Sissela the painful uprooting that it might have been for a girl of twelve. Instead, it was much closer to a liberation. . . .

Even more important has been her lively affection and admiration throughout our married life for you. When we first met, I saw some signs of the minor misunderstandings, strains and awkwardness that girls in their teens seem so often to have toward their mothers. Almost immediately after our marriage, these slight tensions disappeared, to be replaced by a wonderful kinship and warmth of feeling that have persisted without interruption through these many years.

Surely what matters most is the lasting impact of a mother on her child. In Sissela's case, that mark has been a personal example of what an individual and a woman, wife, and mother can achieve. For her, your example has provided a sense of liberation and a source of unlimited aspirations and higher standards totally devoid of any feelings of envy, resentment, competition, or inferiority. That is a wonderful effect to have had upon another human being. . . .

Much love—Derek

On July 18, Alva wrote more briefly to continue what she called her "confessions." This time she reminisced about the period between 1934 and 1938, when she felt so pressed by the many requests to campaign for the reforms that she and Gunnar advocated that she was eager for us all to move to America. The same impulse to get away from incessant speech making and other scattered activities was a reason for her joining Gunnar in the United States in 1941:

When I didn't have a real job, I came to experience this substitute existence as one of duty that was, once again, interrupted. Not until 1948 was this splintered pattern, very interesting but also very strenuous, broken off. To become something *myself*—at the age of forty-six—was therefore a temptation that I could not resist. And cannot regret—in spite of everything.

In subsequent letters, Alva conveyed her increasing difficulties in writing and speaking and her conflicted feelings about whether or not to stop taking part in public life. She feared taking on responsibilities she would not be able to carry out; yet she refused, at the same time, simply to give up and subside into silence. And she cherished the links with those with whom she had worked for so many years in different campaigns. In October 1983, she wrote of having attended a symposium for former students of the Seminar for Social Pedagogy that she had helped start almost half a century earlier, and of the wonderful spirit she felt among the "four or five hundred 'heirs' working, by then, on behalf of the new and still far from fully implemented pedagogy."

I was happy yesterday. But I realized, when it was my turn to lecture, how handicapped I have become. This was the last time, I decided. But for December 10, Human Rights Day, I have initiated a great public gathering to mark the ending of the "fiery fall" of mass resistance against nuclear weapons. Still, [I won't] stop writing and agitating. Agitating for common sense and reason.

Early in 1984, however, a stroke forced Alva to retire from public life altogether. Thereafter, her brain tumor combined with heart problems to incapacitate her more and more. Even as the walls of her aphasia were closing in, however, she cast about for ways in which to communicate with us all and struggled to provide clues whereby we might come closer, help her to achieve an accounting, an explanation for her life. It was her question, in July 1984, "What happens if I can no longer explain anything?"

that led me to wonder whether I might be able to help with the explaining. Each time I came to Sweden after that, I tried to learn more about her life, beginning with her childhood and her youth. Late in January 1985, one year before her death, my diary notes that

> I dreamed about Alva. And she spoke! I could ask her about her youth—about Andreas and Märta and more about Gunnar. And she pointed to passages she had written out for me—the wonder of hearing her voice, seeing words written in her own hand.
>
> And then the reality. That she is not through with life and feels that she must *explain*: in that situation the aphasia has to be like being walled up in a tower, buried alive.

Alva's last months were serene by comparison. In January 1986, she slipped into a state of unconsciousness from which she never awoke. She died on February 1, the day after her eighty-fourth birthday.

After a family funeral ceremony, a memorial service was held for Alva in Storkyrkan, the cathedral in the Old City only blocks away from where she and Gunnar had lived for twenty years. It began with a massive torchlight parade winding in the winter night through the streets of Stockholm and over the bridge into the Old City. Kaj, Derek, and many in the family walked in front, along with Olof Palme and his wife Lisbet. Gunnar, who was not strong enough to take part, went directly with me to the cathedral. He sat surrounded by family, and though he could not see far, he knew that the aisles were filled with so many of his and Alva's friends and former colleagues in the government and the diplomatic corps. Many others stood with candles outside, listening to the bells ringing and to the outdoor broadcast of the service.

Alva's old friend Krister Stendahl, then bishop of Stockholm, conducted the secular service. The church choir was followed by a children's choir and then by a tribute from Olof Palme, speaking, though no one could have known it then, for the last time in public before being felled by an assassin's bullet two weeks later:

a victim of the violence against which he and Alva had taken such a forceful stand. In part, his tribute reads:

> Alva Myrdal had very clear eyes. They reflected the clarity of her thinking, the orderly and methodical way she handled every project, the happy faith in reason that carried her through life.
>
> In her eyes, you also encountered warmth, thoughtfulness, her ability to understand the situation of others. You felt encompassed not only by her thoughts but also by her heart.
>
> . . . When you talk about Alva Myrdal, people become inspired. To them, she signifies happiness about life's potential, a bright faith in the future. A person can hardly hope for a better monument.

At the end of the service, the congregation joined in singing "We Shall Overcome," a hymn that Alva especially loved and that stood for so much that she and Gunnar had worked toward, separately and together.

Gunnar lived on, achingly alone, unwilling to move away, his memory too weak to remember from one visit to the next the family members and friends who came to see him. Like Alva's, his last months were peaceful. He died on May 17, 1987, in his eighty-ninth year. As we gathered, with those closest to him, around his bier, Kaj placed upon it the portrait of Alva at fifteen in her white confirmation dress that he had carried with him since their first meeting wherever he traveled in the world.

And Alva's question about what happens when one can no longer explain anything—what has become of it? Memories, unanswered questions, traces I have followed, a dialogue I have sought to keep up. For me they have led beyond words and beyond explanations. To Alva's life itself and what she did with it. To the ways in which she marked my life and the lives of others. To her intrepid spirit.

Acknowledgments

❖ ❖ ❖

It would not have been possible for me to write this book without the kindness of a great many relatives and friends of my parents in putting materials at my disposal. I wish to thank them all, as well as Sara Lightfoot, André Schiffrin, and Deane Lord for their interest and support from the beginning.

I wish to give special thanks, also, to Stellan Andersson at the Arbetarrörelsens Arkiv—the Archives of the Swedish Labor Movement—in Stockholm for his patient and most knowledgeable assistance in making available the materials given to the Archives by my parents. Apart from published works or private diaries, notes, and letters in my possession, most of the documents by and about my parents quoted in this book are on deposit there. The photographs I have used also come from the Archives, except as otherwise noted or when they belong to private family collections.

This book represents a substantially revised translation, as well as a continuation of *Alva: ett kvinnoliv*, written in Swedish and published in 1987 by Bonniers Förlag in Stockholm. The earlier book ended with the chapter entitled "Career," just before my mother left, in 1955, to begin her assignment as Swedish Ambassador to India. In preparing the additional chapters about the last three decades of my mother's life for the present book and in revising the earlier chapters, I have been fortunate to be able to draw on much material not previously available to me.

Even as this book goes to press, hardly a week passes without

363

my receiving a new article, dissertation, or book concerning one or both of my parents. I am most grateful to all those who have been kind enough to send me their works, many of which bring fresh perspectives on my parents' lives. Given the volume of such work now under way, however, I recognize that I would have still more to go on, were I to revise this book in four or five years. The same would be true in the year 2000, when a body of personal letters, sealed at my parents' request, will be made available.

In working first with the Swedish text and then with the present one, I have had the benefit of receiving advice from three superb editors: Karin Jacobsson of Bonniers Förlag, Susan Rabiner, then at Pantheon Books, and Merloyd Lawrence, who has seen the book through to completion at Addison-Wesley. To all of them go my warmest thanks.

I am grateful, above all, to Kaj Fölster, Derek Bok, Hilary Bok, Victoria Bok, and Tomas Bok, all of whom provided warm encouragement, their own insights concerning the events and persons figuring in the book, and challenging critiques as I worked on successive drafts.

Cambridge, Massachusetts
January 1991

Published Works of
Alva and Gunnar Myrdal

❖ ❖ ❖ ❖

Alva Myrdal's works are listed and commented upon in a bibliography by Barbro Terling: *Alva Myrdal, Kommenterad bibliografi, 1932–1961* (Stockholm: Alva och Gunnar Myrdals Stiftelse, 1987). A second volume, dealing with the writings after 1961, is under way. Gunnar Myrdal's works are presented in Kerstin Assarsson-Rizzi and Harald Bohrn, eds., *Gunnar Myrdal: A Bibliography, 1919–1981* (New York: Garland Publishing, Inc., 1984).

The following works by Alva and Gunnar Myrdal, noted in this book, are available in English.

By Alva Myrdal

Nation and Family. New York: Harper & Brothers, 1941; Cambridge, Mass: MIT Press, 1968 (paperback edition).

Women's Two Roles. (With Viola Klein.) London: Routledge & Kegan Paul, 1956. Revised edition, 1968.

The Game of Disarmament. New York: Pantheon Books, 1976. Revised and enlarged edition, 1981.

By Gunnar Myrdal

An American Dilemma: The Negro Problem and Modern Democracy. New York: Harper & Row, 1944; New York: Pantheon Books, 1975 (reissued).

The Political Element in the Development of Economic Theory,
trans. Paul Streeten. London: Routledge & Kegan Paul, 1953.
Translated from the original Swedish edition, published 1930.
Asian Drama: An Inquiry into the Poverty of Nations. New York:
Pantheon Books, 1968.

Index of Names
and Places

❖ ❖ ❖ ❖

G

H

I

J

K

L

M

About the Author

❖ ❖ ❖ ❖

Sissela Bok was born in Sweden and educated in Switzerland, France, and the United States. She received a Ph.D. in philosophy from Harvard University in 1970. Since 1985 she has taught philosophy at Brandeis University and earlier has taught courses in ethics and decision making at Harvard Medical School and the John F. Kennedy School of Government. She is the author of numerous articles on ethics, literature, and biography, and of: *Lying: Moral Choice in Public and Private Life* (1978), *Secrets: On the Ethics of Concealment and Revelation* (1982), and *A Strategy for Peace* (1989).